Romantic Women's Writing and Sexual Transgression

Edinburgh Critical Studies in Romanticism
Series Editors: Ian Duncan and Penny Fielding

Available Titles

A Feminine Enlightenment: British Women Writers and the Philosophy of Progress, 1759–1820
JoEllen DeLucia

Reinventing Liberty: Nation, Commerce and the Historical Novel from Walpole to Scott
Fiona Price

The Politics of Romanticism: The Social Contract and Literature
Zoe Beenstock

Radical Romantics: Prophets, Pirates, and the Space beyond Nation
Talissa J. Ford

Literature and Medicine in the Nineteenth-century Periodical Press: Blackwood's Edinburgh Magazine, *1817–1858*
Megan Coyer

Discovering the Footsteps of Time: Geological Travel Writing in Scotland, 1700–1820
Tom Furniss

The Dissolution of Character in Late Romanticism
Jonas Cope

Commemorating Peterloo: Violence, Resilience and Claim-making during the Romantic Era
Edited by Michael Demson and Regina Hewitt

Dialectics of Improvement: Scottish Romanticism, 1786–1831
Gerard Lee McKeever

Literary Manuscript Culture in Romantic Britain
Michelle Levy

Scottish Romanticism and Collective Memory in the British Atlantic
Kenneth McNeil

Romantic Periodicals in the Twenty-first Century: Eleven Case Studies from Blackwood's Edinburgh Magazine
Edited by Nicholas Mason and Tom Mole

Godwin and the Book: Imagining Media, 1783–1836
J. Louise McCray

Thomas De Quincey: Romanticism in Translation
Brecht de Groote

Romantic Environmental Sensibility: Nature, Class and Empire
Edited by Ve-Yin Tee

Romantic Pasts: History, Fiction and Feeling in Britain, 1790–1850
Porscha Fermanis

British Romanticism and Denmark
Cian Duffy

The Lady's Magazine (1770–1832) and the Making of Literary History
Jennie Batchelor

Mary Wollstonecraft: Cosmopolitan
Laura Kirkley

Romanticism and Consciousness, Revisited
Edited by Richard Sha and Joel Faflak

Remediating the 1820s
Edited by Jon Mee and Matthew Sangster

Romanticism and the Poetics of Orientation
Joey S. Kim

Romantic Women's Writing and Sexual Transgression
Edited by Kathryn Ready and David Sigler

edinburghuniversitypress.com/series/ecsr

Romantic Women's Writing and Sexual Transgression

Edited by Kathryn Ready and David Sigler

EDINBURGH
University Press

Edinburgh University Press is one of the leading university presses in the UK. We publish academic books and journals in our selected subject areas across the humanities and social sciences, combining cutting-edge scholarship with high editorial and production values to produce academic works of lasting importance. For more information visit our website: edinburghuniversitypress.com

© editorial matter and organisation Kathryn Ready and David Sigler, 2024, 2025
© the chapters their several authors, 2024, 2025

Edinburgh University Press Ltd
13 Infirmary Street
Edinburgh EH1 1LT

First published in hardback by Edinburgh University Press 2024

Typeset in 10.5/13pt Sabon LT Pro
by Cheshire Typesetting Ltd, Cuddington, Cheshire

A CIP record for this book is available from the British Library

ISBN 978 1 3995 0762 2 (hardback)
ISBN 978 1 3995 0763 9 (paperback)
ISBN 978 1 3995 0764 6 (webready PDF)
ISBN 978 1 3995 0765 3 (epub)

The right of Kathryn Ready and David Sigler to be identified as editors of this work has been asserted in accordance with the Copyright, Designs and Patents Act 1988 and the Copyright and Related Rights Regulations 2003 (SI No. 2498).

Contents

Notes on Contributors	vii
Editors' Acknowledgements	x
1. Introduction *David Sigler*	1
2. Feminising Romantic Sexuality, Perverting Feminine Romanticism *Kathryn Ready*	14
3. Reorienting Multi-dimensional Sex with Objects in *Millenium Hall* *Kate Singer*	30
4. The Necrophilia of Wollstonecraft's 'The Cave of Fancy' *David Sigler*	52
5. Sexual Violence, Sexual Transgression and the Law in Mary Hays's *The Victim of Prejudice* *Kathleen Emily Hurlock*	72
6. 'Thoughts that Breathe and Words that Burn': Barbauld, Masturbation and the Novel *Kathryn Ready*	86
7. Resistive Embodiment and Incestuous Desire in Mary Shelley's *Mathilda* *Crystal Veronie*	106
8. 'Our Dire Transgression': Mary Diana Dods in the Biblical Sense *Colin Carman*	126

9. George Sand, *Indiana* and the Transgressive Work of
   Idealism   139
   Richard C. Sha

10. Emily Brontë's Shelleyan Poetics of Sexual Ambivalence   158
    Amanda Blake Davis

11. Primroses in the Porridge: Hareton Earnshaw's Transgression
    against his Homosocial Family in *Wuthering Heights*   174
    Chantel Lavoie

Index   191

Notes on Contributors

Colin Carman is the author of *The Radical Ecology of the Shelleys: Eros and Environment* (2018) and Assistant Professor of English at Colorado Mesa University in Grand Junction, Colorado. A former fellow at the Huntington Library in California and a residential fellow at the Jane Austen House in England, he has contributed to five book collections, including *Lacan and Romanticism* (2019), *Romantic Ecocriticism* (2016) and *The Brokeback Book* (2011). His articles have appeared in such journals as *ISLE, European Romantic Review, GLQ, Studies in Scottish Literature* and *Horror Studies.*

Amanda Blake Davis is Lecturer in English Literature at the University of Derby and Honorary Research Fellow in the School of English at the University of Sheffield. Amanda began her current project, *Shelley's Trees: Intermedial Ecologies*, as a Postdoctoral Research Fellow at the University of Derby in 2021, exploring drawings of trees and other botanical figures in the poet's manuscripts through what she terms Shelley's 'intermedial ecology'. Alongside this project, Amanda is preparing her first monograph, *Shelley and Androgyny.* Amanda's primary research interests are in Romantic and post-Romantic poetry, and she has published articles in the *Keats-Shelley Review, English: Journal of the English Association* and *Romanticism on the Net.* Her article, '"Ephemeral are gay gulps of laughter": P. B. Shelley, Louis MacNeice, and the Ambivalence of Laughter', won the 2020 English Association Essay Prize.

Kathleen Emily Hurlock is a PhD student in English and Women's Studies at the University of Georgia. Her work focuses on various intersections between transhistorical, transnational women's writings and feminist theory, particularly with regard to feminist education and reproductive labour. Previously, she has contributed two entries to the *Encyclopedia* of *Queer Studies in Education* (2021) on the matrix of intelligibility and queer psychoanalytic theories. She has also presented papers at the British Women's Writing Conference and the National Women's Studies Association.

Chantel Lavoie is Professor in the Department of English, Culture, and Communication at the Royal Military College of Canada. Her monograph *Collecting Women: Poetry and Lives, 1700–1780* came out in 2009, and a second, titled *Writing through Boyhood in the Long Eighteenth Century: Age, Gender, and Work*, came out in 2023. A poet as well, her collections of verse are *Where the Terror Lies* (2012) and *This is About Angels, Women, and Men* (2022). She lives in Kingston, Ontario.

Kathryn Ready is Professor of English at the University of Winnipeg. Her general field is eighteenth-century British literature and culture, with publications and ongoing projects related to women's writing, genders and sexualities, literature and science, and religion, politics, and sociability in the period. She is co-editor of *L'Art de l'échange: Modèles, formes et pratiques de la sociabilité entre la France et la Grande-Bretagne au XVIIIe siècle / The Art of Exchange: Models, Forms and Practices of Sociability between Great Britain and France in the Eighteenth Century* (2015).

Richard C. Sha is Professor of Literature at American University in Washington, DC. He is also an affiliate of the Department of Philosophy and the Center for Behavioral Neuroscience. He has written three monographs: *The Visual and Verbal Sketch in British Romanticism* (1998), *Perverse Romanticism: Aesthetics and Sexuality in Britain 1750–1850* (2009), and *Imagination and Science in Romanticism* (2018, 2021). His last book won the Jean-Pierre Barricelli Prize in 2018. Together with Joel Faflak, he has co-edited *Romanticism and the Emotions* (2014) and *Romanticism and Consciousness, Revisited* (Edinburgh University Press, 2022). He is the author of forty-two articles, the most recent of which have been on Voltaire, Sand, Wing-Tek Lum, and on the Romantic Sublime.

David Sigler is Professor of English at the University of Calgary. He is the author of *Sexual Enjoyment in British Romanticism: Gender and Psychoanalysis, 1753–1835* (2015) and *Fracture Feminism: The Politics of Impossible Time in British Romanticism* (2021), and co-editor of the journal *Romanticism on the Net*.

Kate Singer is Professor in the English Department and Critical Social Thought program at Mount Holyoke College. She is the author of *Romantic Vacancy: The Poetics of Gender, Affect, and Radical Speculation* (2019) and co-editor, with Ashley Cross and Suzanne L. Barnett, of *Material Transgressions: Beyond Romantic Bodies, Genders, Things* (2020). She has published essays on Percy Shelley, Mary Shelley, Maria Jane Jewsbury, Letitia Elizabeth Landon, Mary Robinson, Jane Austen, and Mary Wollstonecraft. She is currently co-editing a volume with Omar F. Miranda on Percy Shelley entitled *Percy Shelley for Our Times* as well as a Routledge handbook on global Romanticism. She is also working on a project exploring Romanticism, critical theory, tropes of shapeshifting and notions of ontological change.

Crystal Veronie is Instructor of English at the University of Alabama. She completed her doctorate from the University of Southern Mississippi in 2022 with a dissertation focusing on the writing of Mary Shelley, Sara Coleridge, Charlotte and Emily Brontë, and Elizabeth Barrett Browning. Crystal was a 2020–1 recipient of a Harry Ransom Center fellowship for her project, 'Resisting Medical Authority: Sara Coleridge's Writing and the Evolution of Resistive Embodiment'. Her article, '"When my hands are empty / I will be full": Visualizing Two-Spirit Bodies in Chrystos's *Not Vanishing*', was published in *Studies in American Indian Literatures*.

Editors' Acknowledgements

We thank the contributors to this volume for entrusting us with their work.

It has been an honour to work with EUP and the series editors Ian Duncan and Penny Fielding. We thank them for their openness to our project and support of it, and for their expertise as readers. We have appreciated the chance to work with Michelle Houston, Susannah Butler, Emily Sharp, and Elizabeth Fraser, in their roles as EUP editors.

Further thanks go to Janelle Grue, who has very skilfully helped us prepare the manuscript for submission. Ms Grue's assistance was made possible by funding provided by the Department of English at the University of Calgary, under the leadership of Jacqueline Jenkins. Support for indexing was provided by an Insight Grant from the Social Science and Humanities Research Council of Canada (Agency Reference Number 435-2017-0037), which enabled Cameron Duder to compile the index most expertly. Further funding was provided by a Discretionary Grant from the University of Winnipeg.

We thank our colleagues at the University of Winnipeg and University of Calgary for their continued support.

The idea for this collection came to us in Chicago at the 2019 North American Society for the Study of Romanticism conference, where we first realised a happy confluence of interests and identified the gap in scholarship that we might address through our combined efforts. We thank NASSR for enabling this productive encounter and connecting us with many of our contributors. We also thank the Canadian Society for Eighteenth-Century Studies for the inspiration it has given us, and in particular we would like to thank one of its members, Nour Afara.

We acknowledge that we have been doing the editorial work of the collection from Treaty One and Treaty Seven Territories, being respectively the territories of the Anishinaabeg, Cree, Dakota, Dene, Métis, and Oji-Cree Nations, and the territories of the Blackfoot Confederacy

(Kainai, Piikani and Siksika) as well as the Tsuu T'ina Nation and Stoney Nakoda First Nation, consisting of the Chiniki, Bearspaw, and Goodstoney First Nations. The city of Winnipeg is the heartland of the Métis people, and the city of Calgary is home to the Métis Nation of Alberta, Region 3. As settler scholars, we recognise our own complicity in the colonisation of these lands and the part that eighteenth- and nineteenth-century British literature has played, and continues to play, in that colonising process.

We thank the Fralin Museum of Art at the University of Virginia for permitting us to reproduce a painting from its collection, Angelica Kauffmann's *Ulysses and Circe*, for the book cover (Angelica Kauffmann, Swiss [1741–1807], *Ulysses and Circe*, 1786, oil on canvas, 55 × 41¼ in. [139.7 × 104.8 cm], courtesy of The Fralin Museum of Art at the University of Virginia. Museum purchase with Membership Acquisition Fund, 1976.24). We thank the Brontë Society for permission to reproduce the image *The North Wind*, Emily Brontë, watercolour, 1842. The original painting was once in possession of the Heger family; its present location is unknown. It was reproduced as a frontispiece to *Brontë Society Transactions* 11 (1949) and is reproduced in this volume by courtesy of the Brontë Society.

Chapter 1

Introduction

David Sigler

'It was the Romantics', wrote Mario Praz in 1933, 'who gave a psychological turn to the refinements of perversity'.[1] A word like 'refinements' mines perversity, even perversion, for its aesthetic qualities. With Praz's *The Romantic Agony*, Romantic literature began to be appreciated as a wellspring of transgressive sexual fantasies; such fantasies became central to 'Romanticism' as a literary movement. In the decades since, Praz's insights, if not his methodologies, have been durable. For instance, our own era's most meticulous historicist study of Romantic-era sexuality, Richard C. Sha's *Perverse Romanticism* (2009), finds that 'Perversion enables us to reimagine Romanticism from the ground up', a claim that distinctly echoes Praz's findings, despite their very different methods and archives. Sha shows, as Praz had, how sex became slowly separated from function during the Romantic period to become something aesthetic, and thus purposeless, and thus perverse. Like Praz, Sha endeavours to trace 'lost histories of subversion within perversion';[2] also like Praz, he focuses primarily, though not exclusively, on male writers.

The contributors to *Romantic Women's Writing and Sexual Transgression*, Sha included, are bent on recovering such lost histories from within the universe of Romantic-era women's writing. This is necessary not just for inclusion's sake but also because, as James Penney argues, the encounter with sexual difference is crucial if we are to ascertain 'the inherently antinormative quality of sexual desire'.[3] But therein lies the rub. Women writers have seldom figured centrally in the study of transgressive sexuality in the Romantic period, as the next chapter of this book, Kathryn Ready's overview of the field, will reveal. The influential scholarly paradigm of distinctly gendered traditions of Romanticism, 'masculine' and 'feminine', has encouraged the perception that Romantic-era women writers tended to stay within narrow sexual bounds in their lives and writing, or that they transgressed mainly in secret, or that they concerned themselves with other things. It has even been suggested that the women writers of this period were not actually 'Romantics' at all (to their credit), given the extent to which 'Romantic' writing was preoccupied with the theme of sexual transgression.[4] Male poets of genius were supposedly afflicted with aberrant desires, which tended to render them effeminate, even though women writers would not qualify as perverse geniuses in the same way.[5] Praz, for whom Romanticism was a pan-European affair spanning the whole nineteenth century, only found space in *The Romantic Agony* to discuss two women writers in passing, Ann Radcliffe and Mary Shelley, and only one or two of their works apiece. Yet, Praz insists that such inattention to women's writing represents no loss to the scholarly field, for when it comes to the works of Radcliffe and Shelley,

> there may be nothing more in this than another of the many manifestations of feminine imitativeness. As the literary tradition has been the monopoly of man, ... it is natural that women writers should slavishly adopt in their works the masculine point of view.[6]

And thus, the subfield of Romantic sexuality studies was born. Obviously, no respected scholar today would share Praz's wildly sexist assessment – everyone now recognises Radcliffe and Shelley to be among the era's most innovative writers and would deem dozens of other female writers to be essential reading from the period. Yet, the study of Romantic-era sexuality remains in many ways trapped in Praz's world. Scholarship for several decades now has tended to highlight how women mainly 'wrote in the non-romantic tradition in celebration of the private sphere of home, family, and local neighborhood'.[7] We have learned how to read women authors as powerful contributors to the literary era, but only by learning to appreciate work that is less than transgressive, sexually speaking – that is, by broadening our sense of which themes may count as 'Romantic'.

The situation is complicated. British Romantic writing helped to establish the home, family and neighbourhood as 'private', desexualised institutions, an ideological shift that brought 'sexuality' into the public sphere at the cost of cutting people off from each other, as Adam Komisaruk has shown.[8] Nevertheless, as Roxanne Eberle suggests, the ideological development of separate spheres brought with it a literary backlash, featuring a 'new sexually transgressive heroine' found in women's writing across the nineteenth century, who could serve as the engine for 'social critique'.[9] Other important books have placed women's writing within conversations about perversion, female domination, sexual aggressivity and nymphomania.[10] Though these works have been too few and far between, it is becoming apparent that, 'far from being meek inhabitants of an ideological straitjacket of gendered roles' during the eighteenth century, 'women also took responsibility for their sexual domain even at the expense of their reputation', as Julie Peakman indicates. Peakman considers women's writerly acts of sexual transgression as forms of 'practical feminism' in the absence of a fully developed feminist political discourse,[11] while Jillian Heydt-Stevenson notes that 'the stereotypical sexual repression associated with the Victorians ... was not the standard in Romantic-era women's writings'.[12] We are inspired by such findings. Today, as the narrative of separate male and female Romanticisms is increasingly called into question and as our understanding of Romantic-era sexual culture has deepened, there is an opportunity to explore more fully the wealth of material produced by Romantic women writers, many of whom were theorising various perversions in their literary writings and/or leading transgressive sexual lives. Women need no longer be considered merely the objects of an ascendant medicalising discourse of sex and sexual difference in the Romantic period, nor merely adjunct contributors to the literary theorisation of sex. Women's writing, this volume will endeavour to show, contributed meaningfully to the ascendant regime of 'sexuality' and also, in doing so, paradoxically resisted that regime, and the ambivalence that arose from that cultural and literary negotiation called into imaginative being new frameworks for thinking about sex.

We hazard to call these frameworks 'sexual transgression', a suitably capacious term for a wide range of sexual commitments. It is a broader term than the sexological-psychoanalytic word 'perversion', which can be individualising even when stripped of its moral connotations, as Jacques Lacan, like Sha, was always careful to do. 'Sexual transgression' is a narrower term than the Foucauldian term 'sexuality', in the sense that it places itself specifically and only at the boundary between acceptability and perversity – so, neither within the charmed circle nor quite beyond it.[13] As Néstor A. Braunstein suggests, the academic study of non-normative sexuality, just in general, has been basically at a crossroads between Lacanian approaches to perversion and Foucauldian-inspired histories of sexuality; Braunstein reveals how this dichotomy has shaped the fields of sexuality studies and queer theory.[14] Both prevailing approaches have been important for scholarship on sexuality in British Romantic studies; yet, neither approach has much enabled us to analyse women's writing as a productive or primary site of transgressive sexual thought.

For scholars today, 'perversion is indeed commonly associated with transgression, especially in the realm of sexuality'.[15] A Lacanian account of perversion, while admirably non-pathologising, tends not to work socially and instead considers how the subject fills in for the lack found in the Other. This may have political consequences but is seldom understood as a feminist act in the way that Peakman or Eberle have made thinkable. Because the Other is an internalised structure, a psychic creation brought to bear specifically on an individual, the actual transgressiveness of sex tends to get lost in such a model. Lacan even specifically warns that 'we don't ever transgress. Sneaking around is not transgressing ... There is no transgression here, but rather an irruption, ... a surplus'.[16] A year later, he calls the verb 'to transgress' a 'grotesque word', irrelevant to concerns about the real; he cautions that the concept of transgression helps to sustain religious cultural norms.[17] Recent Lacanian studies of sex have taken that warning to heart and specifically ask us not to think about sex in terms of transgression.[18] Within Romantic literary studies, psychoanalytic scholars have struggled to place the political dimensions of women's writing within discussions of non-normative enjoyments. (Though there have been some exceptions, such as D. A. Miller's and Daniela Garofalo's work on Jane Austen.[19]) Meanwhile, Michel Foucault, for all of his insight into large-scale discursive and institutional structures, is notoriously oblivious to women's sexual feelings: 'No one finds anything regarding a woman's relation to "pleasure" here [that is, in Foucault], even less *jouissance*', notes Braunstein.[20] It happens that Foucault's favoured archive is largely medical, psychiatric, governmental, regulatory – that is, sites of power-knowledge that, in the eighteenth and nineteenth centuries, were especially controlled by men and built to serve their interests. Women were the objects of such knowledge but not often its creators. But in the literary arts, women could find new ways to transgress.

The term 'transgression' is often used to indicate a crossing of boundaries. That assumption makes sense given the dictionary definition of the word but is nonetheless something that our collection will endeavour to reconsider. The Lacanian scholar Astrid Gessert, typifying the standard approach, maintains that

> the word 'transgression' implies 'stepping over'. For something to be transgressed there must be a line, a division. It also often has a negative connotation, with the idea that this stepping over a line is illegitimate, that there is a homebase where one should rightfully be and another realm that is out of bounds.[21]

In a second and more fluid example, the editors of a recent collection on Romantic-era literature, *Material Transgressions* (2020), see a general resistance to fixity and categorisation in the term 'transgression', one carried out through the literary crossing of cultural boundaries.[22]

But, upon closer inspection, the boundaries in question tend to have a paradoxical, M. C. Escher-like structure, rendering any thought of a 'beyond' meaningless. This present collection represents our collective endeavour to rethink the meaning of transgression.

Our term 'sexual transgression', despite being more specific than 'transgression' per se, can strangely seem euphemistic in comparison, in part because it covers a wide range of sex acts at very disparate levels of severity, and in part because the term itself is redundant. If, as Freud suggests, human society basically exists to constrain, guide, and reroute the libido, then anything that has avoided desexualisation carries on transgressively.[23] Why speak of 'sexual transgression' when the sexual is in itself transgressive, when things are 'sexual' only by virtue of their bearing an excess that cannot be synthesised into existing structures of meaning? In this sense, 'sexual transgression' can seem to be a non-concept, a term that, instead of clarifying matters, seeks to make (through a conspicuous lack of specificity) a secret of something that had already long been treated as one. But while the term lacks any specific parameters, it precisely, for this reason, can become a meaningful way to think about the procedures of resistance: rather than classifying types of urges or recording in detail eyewitness accounts of specific non-normative sex acts, 'sexual transgression' asks us to think about sex as an ill-fitting social function, making it unavoidable to think about sex acts in relation to laws and/or mores instead of just a figment like the Other. The term grapples with the paradox of how something supposedly secret can also be scandalous: 'Sexuality has always had a link with scandal', explains Jeremiah L. Alberg, because sexual matters are by their nature transgressive.[24] In this sense, we are offering a different model of thinking transgression than was featured in *Material Transgressions*, in which Romantic-era writing is said to 'move beyond prescribed limits' in a New Materialist manner.[25] Our work also departs from the *Material Transgressions* model in focusing specifically on sexual transgression as a special province of writerly transgression, one involving but not exactly coterminous with 'bodies, genders, things', and bringing with it its own paradoxical logics and taxonomies. The 'sexual' part ensures that any 'beyond' is only to be found 'within', such that no fantasy of escape from cultural prescription can be much entertained. We will find that sexual transgression is not so cut and dried as moving beyond the confines of the charmed circle or of exploring a realm of sexual activity beyond and in breach of those privileged cultural codes. As Georges Bataille stresses, 'often the transgression of a taboo is no less subject to rules than the taboo itself', which is why 'organized transgression together with the taboo make social life what it is'.²⁶ Sexual transgression is part of the taboo and works in parallel with it to organise violence; it is never outside or beyond any boundary, and does not aspire to be.²⁷

In literary studies, the capaciousness of a term like 'sexual transgression' can help us identify formal affinities between a wide range of writings, and to think about those writings in relation to ideological systems of social control. The term seeks out unexpected coalitions as a response to the taxonomising impulses of nineteenth-century sexology or the modern *DSM*; the formalism implied by the term has a way of taking the study of sexuality out of the moral register while still recognising sex as a moral problem. As a result, desire becomes a disruptive force in and as part of the social relation rather than as an individual's proclivity, and a force that accrues meaning in relation to the prevailing ideological demands of a particular historical moment. In this way, the term 'sexual transgression' may activate broad, unfamiliar forms of historical-literary analysis precisely because of its anodyne blankness. Or so is our hope!

I present Elizabeth Moody's comic poem 'To Dr. Darwin, On Reading His Loves of the Plants' (1798) as a case in point because 'women's pursuit of natural philosophy was linked to sexual transgression' in the cultural imagination.²⁸ Moody's poem responds directly to Erasmus Darwin's titillating scientific poem of 1791, *The Botanic Garden*. Darwin's poem was very popular with female readers, including many with reputations for great propriety, and perhaps for that reason became a flashpoint in a culture war around the appropriate scope of women's curiosity in sexual matters.²⁹ While male critics such as Richard Polwhele saw the situation as an opportunity to chastise women readers for their sexual curiosity, women writers – such as Moody, the wife of a clergyman and someone celebrated for her authorial modesty and taste – found, even within those bounds, a more complicated and generative way to respond to Darwin, one that perhaps can illustrate the stakes of 'sexual transgression' as an interpretive framework. In my brief analysis of the poem to follow, I want to show how Moody's thoroughly transgressive writing can be said to find its footing in the Romantic era's prevailing moral codes, helping to enforce them, announcing itself subject to them, but also flouting them through the rigour of the observance, such that it arrives at a complex feminist response to a repressive sexual culture.

In his botanical research, Darwin uncovered a world of plants in which taxonomic categories collapse, gender roles reverse, polyamory reigns, and immodest sexual arrangements (for pollination and the like) are revealed to be natural. In addition to the scandal of these scientific findings, Darwin's text seems bent on giving pleasure to female readers and was 'criticized for its porn-like characteristic[s]'.[30] Moody, like many women of her time, sees in Darwin and botany a pathway into indulgence:

> Darwin sung his gossip tales,
> Of females woo'd by *twenty* males.
> Of *Plants* so given to amorous pleasure;
> Incontinent beyond all measure.[31]

These lines show a fascination not with botany per se but with women and their immeasurable, excessive capacity for pleasure, a capacity which seems poised to remake the world in a feminine way – with even Darwin's text discursively feminised as 'gossip'. The phrase 'beyond all measure' puts female pleasure in relation to, and yet 'beyond', the repressive systems metonymised by botany and sexology as scientific discourses. This is the core paradox – we have a beyond that is not, and cannot be, beyond. In that sense, it is a vision of 'sexual transgression'. In response to the paradox, the text registers the speaker's titillation by performing, with all irony, the enforcement of social norms. The speaker winkingly castigates Darwin for his immorality in revealing how trees routinely betray their 'wives': 'were it not for thee, / I sure must venerate this tree' ('TDD' 76–7). Darwin is now the killjoy. Moody's irony is complex and various: in expressing displeasure not in the tree's behaviour but in Darwin for bringing the situation to light, the speaker seems to side with a world of licentiousness, even while expressing what seems to be moral disapproval. She does not seek to resist sexual regulation but is instead backhandedly grateful to Darwin for inaugurating, basically, new ways to monitor sexual pleasure: now, thanks to science, we can detect transgression even in nature and disavow it, zealously if fascinatedly. Yet, the end of the poem mocks Darwin for 'libel[ling]' innocent plants and flowers, as if Darwin's exposé, in its commitment to telling the truth about plants, were itself misguided, obsessional, perverted. The (mock) outrage seems to lie in Darwin's decision to publish such findings, rather than in his botanical research itself ('TDD' 86). And yet, the scandal cannot be contained by an encounter with the text, as 'beyond all measure' indicates an excess to metrical composition. In proto-Freudian style, Moody extols a botanical monograph for its capacity to provoke wish-fulfilling dreams, and thus generate a *jouissance* both absent from the text and caused by it.[32] An illicit secret has been laid bare, and the speaker is ashamed and overjoyed by her desire in hearing it expressed. The imputed perversion moves easily between the promiscuous plants, to Darwin as a discoverer of their wayward pleasures, to Darwin as a poet, to the speaker's 'rich fancy' as a reader of Darwin, to Moody as an author, given the ways that her poem, in analysing Darwin's, announces the same scandalous situation found libellous already, and presumably from there to the reader of Moody's poem ('TDD' 48). This ambiguity – namely, the capacity to jump between analytical levels in pursuit of illicit *jouissance* – is the central joke of the poem. Moody suggests that the moral system regulating sex produces illicit, exquisite sexual pleasure precisely because the subject internalises ideology and sexual enjoyment clings to the signifier but opens space 'beyond' it. Given this situation, pleasure becomes transgressive simply by skipping across and in between these interpretive levels, confounding them.

Yet, 'To Dr. Darwin' is also a confessional poem. It depends upon a speaker who is said to be present, a real entity reading a real book on a real scientific subject; the speaker explains how that experience has stimulated and stamped out her illicit wishes. She is supposed to be more than just a textual effect – the speaker is a character here, and she speaks for the implied reader. And this aspect of the poem cuts against its tendency to highlight its many layers of narrative mediation. The speaker confesses that botanical *jouissance* has taken hold of her heart. She recognises it in herself as a suspicious and foreign affect, a perverse im-plant-ation. Sexual fantasy, for her, is understood as a kind of imagined relation to language, rather than something innate or imagined by poets or discovered in nature by scientists. The Darwinian fantasy has taken root in her mind for scientific reasons and because of the tree's promiscuity and because she has been reading a dirty sex poem. *Jouissance* is here both a literary and scientific experience, operating in between these levels and as an excess to them: It is 'Fiction's magic hand' that ensures that 'Enchantment breathes through every line' ('TDD' 40–2). The era's fascination with masturbatory reading, analysed by Kathryn Ready in her essay on Anna Letitia Barbauld in this volume, becomes apparent here. 'Enamour'd we the verse pursue, / And feel each fair delusion true', the speaker says, acknowledging that she has been seduced by a poem, by its materiality of language, which is part of any scientific knowledge it may disclose but also in excess of it ('TDD' 43–4). The perversion here is found not just in trees but in 'poetic brains', and this differentiates Darwin from Linnaeus ('TDD' 38). Darwin's scientific world is attached to the literary world and is inseparable from the speaker as a reader and as a psychological being. Any distinction between trees, verse, Darwin, and the speaker becomes impossible, 'Since thus thy fascinating art, / So takes possession of the heart' ('TDD' 81–2).

That crossing and indeterminacy is itself a kind of sexual transgression. Consequently,

Warm to my sight the visions rise,
And thy rich fancy mine supplies.
Thy themes rehearsing in my bower;
From those I picture ev'ry flower[.] ('TDD' 47–50)

The tone registers delight and titillation with the impossible, synesthetic pleasures ('warm to my sight') that arise from this sort of crossing. The speaker is neither the subject ('to my sight') nor object ('mine supplies') of this discourse; the fancy that is 'mine', consequently, is recognised specifically as 'th[ine]'. There are no boundaries, psychic or discursive, to transgress; there is no inside or outside of 'me' or of sexual propriety. The speaker makes a point to locate these disorienting pleasures within the prevailing moral universe, and so playfully chides Darwin for being the bearer of good news. The admonishment is itself a sexual act because sex, in Moody's universe, is a form of writing; it is at the same time a modern scientific discovery, yet natural and pre-discursive, yet rhetorical; it is internal, alien, authentic, and fabricated. Its very constructedness and conventionality produce something unrecognisable within the speaker's own innermost 'heart', and this is the secret object of the natural sciences. It would be impossible to say whether the poem is more invested in the violation of sexual rules of conduct or the maintenance of such rules because this very maintenance has been turned into an illicit sex game and a fetish. To speak of a charmed circle in this setting would not make sense.

Sam George, analysing this poem, highlights its ironic tone and Moody's refusal to condemn Darwin's discoveries in any sustained way. But to make this case, George swerves from the sexual content to focus instead on issues of genre. 'Reputation was extremely important to these women', she explains, which is why Moody's response was not the encomium to *jouissance* it may seem.[33] And so, even in a study of women's writing, botany and sexual boundaries, 'To Dr. Darwin' becomes a poem about poetry, not sexual pleasure after all. And, says George, this poem is said to be among the more sexually engaged of this type! Apart from the exceptional cases of Moody and Anna Seward, she explains, 'women poets simply remained silent on the issue of sexuality' in responding to Darwin's work.[34] 'Women's fascination with Darwin seemed not to be primarily about sexuality but with the space botany afforded them', says George, because 'botany was a means of gaining entrance into professional writing'.[35] Everything in the analysis works to desexualise the scene of writing, despite the obvious sexual language of the poem and the scandal of the wider cultural context. I would suggest that this happens because, as a field, we haven't developed an adequate way to see how a woman's public, professional presence as a writer could be linked to the private scene of *jouissance* as depicted in her verse and produced through her acts of writing.

This division between the sexual and professional is not the fault of George, whose work is pioneering for sexuality studies in Romanticism and endlessly worthwhile. Rather, we have as a field found no way to decide whether sexual pleasure is discursive (per Foucault), deathly (per Lacan) or textual. The problem is not limited to studies of the period's women's writing and botanical sciences. For George, the materiality of poetry deactivates the sexual content of even a directly sexual poem. Analogously, for Andrea K. Henderson, the capitalist discourses of finance and speculation are the true meaning of the public fascination with sexually dominant women in the eighteenth century.[36] For Peakman, the booming eighteenth-century market for printed confessions and exposés was, yes, a search for salacious materials, but primarily 'a means to ensure errant people were kept in their place'.[37] Repeatedly, in the field's most important books about women's writing and sexual pleasure, the sexual transgression patently at hand gets treated as if it were a coded commentary standing in for some other desexualised discourse. What had seemed to be titillating is replaced, in the analysis, with more reasonable concerns about professional advancement, economic speculation or social control. It is as if our field assumes that the natural sciences, political economy and print culture were the truly depraved and unmentionable things, and so could only be indirectly discussed through coded imagery of women having explicit, fetishistic and illicit sex.

Hence, we still have trouble, as Praz did, accepting that women writers gave their own psychological turn to the refinements of perversity. To really engage with this would be to rethink the parameters of Romantic agony. This collection proposes that, if we are to locate sexual transgression in Romantic-era women's writing, we will have to learn how to confound the distinctions of inside and outside, vehicle and tenor, subject matter and genre. We will have to bring the history of sexuality to bear on psychoanalytic intimacies and show historians of sexuality how to reckon with *jouissance*. Instead of replacing one with another, we will have to read a text between and through its various levels until the striations of self, other, institution, society, genre and ideology are indistinguishable. Perversion, as a concept and construct, is well poised to activate such work, as a variety of sexual transgression. That is because 'perversion', as the psychoanalysts say, 'is both pervasive and singular. It is the engine of the fantasies of each singular subject ...; it is a constant if discomforting thread in cultural production; and it is a forbidden, secretive but somehow core facet of society as a whole'.³⁸ If taken seriously as a structural presence in women's writing, it will reveal sexual transgression to be strategic resistance to an emergent heteronormative, sexist and racist system of social control, but also as a construction within those ideological discourses, not one cancelled out by them³⁹ – it is an internal excess, not a going beyond. A writer's constant recourse to the limits of permissibility might indicate the constant breach of those limits, and vice versa, which would mean that we had learned to see women writers as actual participants in the cultural discourse surrounding perversion in the late eighteenth and early nineteenth centuries. Women were not simply the objects of the period's emergent medical or psychological discourses but were eager participants in the era's literary-theoretical exploration of sexual transgression – which is to say that they were Romantics in Praz's sense, even if Praz himself didn't think so.

Notes

1. Mario Praz, *The Romantic Agony*, trans. Angus Davidson (London: Oxford University Press, 1933), 106.
2. Richard C. Sha, *Perverse Romanticism: Aesthetics and Sexuality in Britain, 1750–1832* (Baltimore: Johns Hopkins University Press, 2009), 11, 81.
3. James Penney, *The World of Perversion: Psychoanalysis and the Impossible Absolute of Desire* (Albany: SUNY Press, 2006), 214.
4. Marlon B. Ross, *The Contours of Masculine Desire: Romanticism and the Rise of Women's Poetry* (New York: Oxford University Press, 1989); Anne K. Mellor, 'Were Women Writers "Romantics"?', *Modern Language Quarterly* 62, no. 4 (December 2001): 393–405.
5. Dino Franco Felluga, *The Perversity of Poetry: Romantic Ideology and the Popular Male Poet of Genius* (Albany: SUNY Press, 2005), 15–16.
6. Praz, *The Romantic Agony*, 113.
7. William St Clair, *The Reading Nation in the Romantic Period* (Cambridge: Cambridge University Press, 2004), 215.
8. Adam Komisaruk, *Sexual Privatism in British Romantic Writing: A Public of One* (New York: Routledge, 2019).
9. Roxanne Eberle, *Chastity and Transgression in Women's Writing, 1792–1897: Interrupting the Harlot's Progress* (Basingstoke: Palgrave Macmillan, 2002), 4.
10. Adriana Craciun, *Fatal Women of Romanticism* (Cambridge: Cambridge University Press, 2003); Andrea K. Henderson, *Romanticism and the Painful Pleasures of Modern Life* (Cambridge: Cambridge University Press, 2008).
11. Julie Peakman, *Amatory Pleasures: Explorations in Eighteenth-Century Sexual Culture* (New York: Bloomsbury, 2016), 51.
12. Jillian Heydt-Stevenson, 'Sexualities', in *The Cambridge Companion to Women's Writing in the Romantic Period*, ed. Devoney Looser (Cambridge: Cambridge University Press, 2015), 199.

13. Gayle S. Rubin, 'Thinking Sex: Notes for a Radical Theory of the Politics of Sexuality', in *Pleasure and Danger: Exploring Female Sexuality*, ed. Carole S. Vance (Boston: Routledge and Kegan Paul, 1984), 267–319.
14. Néstor A. Braunstein, *Jouissance: A Lacanian Concept*, trans. Silvia Rosman (Albany: SUNY Press, 2020), 131–43.
15. Astrid Gessert, 'Exploring Transgression from a Lacanian Perspective', in *Perversion Now!*, ed. Diana Caine and Colin Wright, Palgrave Lacan Series (Cham: Palgrave Macmillan, 2017), 35.
16. Jacques Lacan, *The Seminar of Jacques Lacan, Book XVII: The Other Side of Psychoanalysis*, ed. Jacques-Alain Miller, trans. Russell Grigg (New York: Norton, 2007), 19–20.
17. Jacques Lacan, *The Seminar of Jacques Lacan, Book XIX: ... Or Worse*, ed. Jacques-Alain Miller, trans. A. R. Price (Cambridge: Polity, 2018).
18. Alenka Zupančič, *What Is Sex?* (Cambridge, MA: MIT Press, 2017), 89–90.
19. D. A. Miller, *Jane Austen, or, The Secret of Style* (Princeton: Princeton University Press, 2003); Daniela Garofalo, 'Doating on Faults in Jane Austen's *Emma*', *European Romantic Review* 28, no. 2 (2017): 227–40; Daniela Garofalo, 'Abandoned by Providence: Loss in Jane Austen's *Persuasion*', in *Lacan and Romanticism*, ed. Daniela Garofalo and David Sigler (Albany: SUNY Press, 2019), 61–80.
20. Braunstein, *Jouissance*, 141.
21. Ibid., 35.
22. Kate Singer, Ashley Cross, and Suzanne L. Barnett, 'Introduction: Living in a New Material World', in *Material Transgressions: Beyond Romantic Bodies, Genders, Things*, ed. Kate Singer, Ashley Cross, and Suzanne L. Barnett, Romantic Reconfigurations: Studies in Literature and Culture 1780–1850 Series (Liverpool: Liverpool University Press, 2020).
23. Sigmund Freud, *The Standard Edition of the Complete Psychological Works of Sigmund Freud*, trans. James Strachey (London: Hogarth Press, 1964), 21: 108–16.
24. Jeremiah L. Alberg, 'Mimesis as Scandal: Rousseau and Derrida', *Contagion: Journal of Violence, Mimesis, and Culture* 22 (Spring 2015): 35, https://doi.org/10.14321/contagion.22.1.0031.
25. Singer, Cross and Barnett, 'Introduction', 3.
26. Georges Bataille, *Erotism: Death and Sensuality*, trans. Mary Dalwood (San Francisco: City Lights, 1986), 65.
27. Ibid., 79.
28. Adriana Craciun, *British Women Writers and the French Revolution: Citizens of the World* (Basingstoke: Palgrave Macmillan, 2005), 37.
29. Sam George, *Botany, Sexuality and Women's Writing, 1760–1830: From Modest Shoot to Forward Plant* (Manchester: Manchester University Press, 2007), 105–52.
30. Tristanne Connolly, 'Flowery Porn: Form and Desire in Erasmus Darwin's *The Loves of the Plants*', *Literature Compass* 13, no. 10 (2016): 606, https://doi.org/10.1111/lic3.12347.
31. Elizabeth Moody, 'To Dr. Darwin, On Reading His Loves of the Plants', in *British Women Poets of the Romantic Era: An Anthology*, ed. Paula R. Feldman (Baltimore: Johns Hopkins University Press, 1997), ll. 2–5. Further references to this text will be given parenthetically by line number, with 'TDD'.

32. Freud, *Psychological*, 4.169–76.
33. George, *Botany, Sexuality*, 139.
34. Ibid., 139.
35. Ibid., 138–9.
36. Henderson, *Romanticism and the Painful Pleasures of Modern Life*.
37. Peakman, *Amatory Pleasures*, 57.
38. Diana Caine et al., 'Introduction: Mapping Perversion in the Contemporary World', in *Perversion Now!*, ed. Diana Caine and Colin Wright, Palgrave Lacan Series (Cham: Palgrave Macmillan, 2017), 5.
39. Alison Moore, 'Rethinking Gendered Perversion and Degeneration in Visions of Sadism and Masochism, 1886–1930', *Journal of the History of Sexuality* 18, no. 1 (January 2009): 138–57.

Chapter 2

Feminising Romantic Sexuality, Perverting Feminine Romanticism

Kathryn Ready

There was a time when scholars of eighteenth-century studies lamented the relative unsexiness of their field in comparison with that of the risqué Romanticists, whose prominent writers, especially the Shelleys and George Gordon, Lord Byron, led far more flamboyantly unconventional lives and more openly flouted contemporary sexual mores than the apparently staid canonical writers of British Neoclassicism. Then came the eighteenth-century sexual turn, influenced by the establishment of the history of sexuality as a field, led by Michel Foucault, Thomas Laqueur, Tim Hitchcock and others. As a result, the eighteenth century sometimes seems as much the Age of the Body as that of Alexander Pope and Samuel Johnson.[1] Despite the stories of personal scandal spicing up the annals of Romantic literature, historians of sexuality have often treated the Romantic period as a footnote to the eighteenth century, regarding the Regency as a last hurrah for the libido before it was silenced under the frown of Victorian moralism. Many others have passed over the period altogether. Addressing this oversight, Richard C. Sha complains of a too common perception of the Romantic era as 'a seemingly asexual zone between eighteenth-century edenic "liberated" sexuality and guiltless pleasures, and the repressive sexology of the Victorians that enabled real sexuality to emerge', and Andrew O'Quinn bemoans the fact that despite the work of a notable few 'the question of sexuality has proved to be less pressing to the majority of Romantic scholars'.[2] Understood as synonymous with idealism and transcendence, Romanticism as a movement has been supposed not to be significantly engaged with bodies and sexualities.

One early intrepid adventurer into the realm of Romantic sexuality is Mario Praz. In *La carne, la morte e il diavolo nella letteratura romantica* (1930), translated into English by Angus Davidson under the title *The Romantic Agony* (1933) and reissued in this translated form in the 1950s and 1970s, Praz identifies a telltale Romantic preoccupation with illicit sexuality and the transgressive sexual types of the *homme fatal* and *femme fatale*.³ He offers a historical explanation, connecting this preoccupation to a longing for intensity and thrilling escape that marked an urban bourgeoisie living in the increasingly mundane and stultifying world of modern industrial capitalism. Yet, many first readers of *The Romantic Agony* disliked its sexual focus, and the impact of this text on Romantic studies has been belated.⁴

In recent years, Romanticism has finally begun to assume its own place within the study of the history of sexuality. This development is only fitting since, according to the *OED*, the use of the term 'sexuality' dates to the early nineteenth century, first employed in the context of plant biology and entomology. As it happens, the early nineteenth century has been recognised equally as giving rise to a modern conception of pornography. It was at this time that pornography came to be understood as material intended for popular consumption, with the main purpose of sexual arousal, in contrast to the curious hybridity of pre-pornographic texts, which promiscuously mix sexual titillation with other generic conventions and discourses, philosophic, religious, political and scientific. A key figure cited in the transition is Thomas Rowlandson, who, in addition to subordinating public affairs to sexual ones in his career as a political caricaturist, engaged in sideline projects such as illustrating Jean Barrin's 1683 *Venus in the Cloister*.⁵ Of course, the Romantic period witnessed the first anonymous publications by Donatien Alphonse François de Sade, otherwise known as the Marquis de Sade. Foucault considers Sade's publications, starting with *Justine, or The Misfortunes of Virtue* (1791) and *Juliette* (1797–1801), to reflect the 'discursive explosion' in materials related to sexuality that denotes the entry into our modern sexual moment.⁶

An important touchstone for all scholars, Romanticists included, interested in the history of sexuality has been the Foucauldian argument that the nineteenth century was marked by the process of medicalising and pathologising bodies and sexualities. As Foucault acknowledges, the nineteenth century saw the reduction or elimination of harsh physical punishments and capital offences against those found guilty of sexual crimes. Perhaps the most familiar example is the sentence for sodomy, which in 1861 went from execution to penal servitude of ten years to life in the United Kingdom of Great Britain and Ireland. At the same time, Foucault argues that 'peripheral sexualities' were increasingly subject to surveillance and control through other means, notably medicine and the emergent field of psychology.⁷ In the nineteenth century, 'marriage relation' or 'legitimate alliance' became an implicit norm. Interest in marriage diminished in favour of 'the sexuality of children, madmen and women, and criminals; the sensuality of those who did not like the opposite sex; reveries, obsessions, petty manias, or great transports of rage', with a marked expansion in 'the list of already condemned forms [of sexuality] such as adultery or rape', marriage with 'close relative[s]', 'sodomy', seduction of nuns, 'sadism', deceit of wives or violation of cadavers.[8] Moreover, the exercise of power, formerly exerted in terms of negation, became a source of pleasure in itself in the hunt and capture of those who threatened the implicit norm. Along with this process of medicalisation and pathologisation, the nineteenth century first established different kinds of sexuality as identity categories, including homosexual identity.[9]

In *Making Sex: Body and Gender from the Greeks to Freud* (1990), Laqueur has supplied another key framework for studying Romantic sexuality. Within the history of sexual anatomy and physiology, he posits a transition, beginning in the eighteenth century, from a one-sex model that regards male and female genitalia as inversions of one another to a two-sex model that considers them as essentially different. As he further explains, the one-sex model was associated with assumptions that female sexual pleasure was necessary for reproduction and that women were more easily sexually aroused than men. Such a conception of female sexuality was compatible with representations of women in Judeo-Christianity and ancient classical sources. The nascent sense of an essential sexual difference had significant consequences in eighteenth-century British society, as women were placed into an entirely separate anatomical category from men and their sexuality subjected to its own discipline. At the same time, the gradual ascendancy of the two-sex model has been linked to what Hitchcock characterises as an increasingly 'phallocentric' model in the eighteenth century that valorised heterosexual, penetrative sex over other kinds of sexual activity.

Interestingly, the now four-decades-old project of recuperating female Romantic writers has produced what amounts to a two-sex model of Romanticism: masculine and feminine. As a movement, British Romanticism was largely defined in reference to the six canonical male Romantic poets (and sometimes five, excluding William Blake) for well over a century. Many of the first Romanticists who gave serious consideration to women writers of the period found evidence for two distinct, and distinctly gendered, strains of British Romanticism. For example, Margaret Homans contrasts the male Romantics, who exalt the imagination of the male poet and assert the male subject at the expense of a female object, with the female Romantics, who exhibit ambivalent subjectivity and forge a poetic identity out of otherness.[10] Meena Alexander similarly distinguishes between the male Romantics, whose model of poetic identity claims the authority of self and is rooted in abstract mental activity, and the female Romantics, whose model of poetic activity grounds itself on a sense of connection with others and is rooted in literal, physical experience.[11] Marlon B. Ross posits a 'masculine' Romanticism based on self-possession, on the yearning for transcendence and escape from the life cycle, beginning in birth and ending in death, and prioritising the self over others.[12] He conceives a 'feminine' Romanticism 'based on the necessity of shared space (the womb), on the necessary limits of beginning (birth) and ending (death) in time and space, on the need to share knowledge without a hierarchy of words'.[13] Anne K. Mellor identifies a 'masculine' Romanticism celebrating the visionary, the imaginative, 'the spontaneous overflow of powerful feelings', and a 'feminine' Romanticism celebrating the workings of the rational mind and the equality of the sexes.[14]

Recently, Romanticists have called this narrative of separate Romanticisms into question. Susan Wolfson acknowledges that the 'poles' of 'masculine' and 'feminine' Romanticism, 'the first ... a nexus summed (variously) as egotistical, colonizing, appropriative, imperialistic, anti-domestic, sublime', and 'the other, a matrix summed (variously) as self-less, object-oriented, empathetic, sympathetic, communal, domestic', can 'feel too sheer, too schematic, slighting not only the aberrations, contradictions, or double-exposures across the divide, but also the instabilities and complexities of particular encounters'.[15] While recognising the efforts to theorise separate traditions of 'masculine' and 'feminine' Romanticism as a valuable exercise in conjunction with a project of recuperation, she and others have worried that such efforts might finally reinforce the marginalisation of women writers. From the beginning, theorists of 'masculine' and 'feminine' Romanticism were concerned to avoid totalising, oversimplifying and potentially essentialising pronouncements. For example, Homans, Mellor and Ross allow at least one of the canonical male Romantics, John Keats, strong affinities with 'feminine' Romanticism.[16] Indeed, Mellor indicates that she prefers to think of 'masculine' and 'feminine' Romanticism not as 'binary opposites but rather the endpoints on a continuum that ranges not only through ... Romanticism but also through the corpus of individual writers'.[17] However, it has been recognised that such caveats do not entirely neutralise the danger of essentialisation. As Adriana Craciun discerns, 'gender-complementary models' of Romanticism, 'while valuable for their gender specificity, often reinscribe the rigid gender boundaries which many women and men of the Romantic period defied' in the realm of sexuality and elsewhere.[18] In *Fatal Women of Romanticism* (2003), Craciun demonstrates how female Romantic writers variously enacted this defiance, including in literary representations of the *femme fatale*. This work places her in the vanguard of Romanticists engaging directly with Laqueur's two-sex model. Craciun further underscores significant divergences in male and female literary representations of the *femme fatale* and the limitations of analyses based exclusively on male writers, challenging Praz's association of the *femme fatale* straightforwardly with masochism and the Byronic *homme fatal* with sadism, and his assumption that the *homme fatal* reigned supreme in the early part and the *femme fatale* in the latter part of the century.

At this point, many questions linger about how women writers fit into a tradition of Romanticism in which transgressive sexuality is taken as a defining feature: the Romanticism of 'the defiant Byronic poet of worldliness and weltschmerz', who has been seen as anticipated in Sade, as opposed to 'the contemplative Wordsworthian poet of nature and nation' (to borrow a formulation from Stephen C. Behrendt).[19] While significant attention has been paid to the sexual transgressions of male writers such as Sade, William Beckford, Matthew Lewis, Byron and Percy Bysshe Shelley, women writers have not figured centrally within the study of Romantic-era sexuality. With some noteworthy exceptions, sexual transgressions and perverse sexualities in female Romantic writing are even more strikingly understudied than sexuality at large.

The reasons for this state of affairs are no doubt many and varied. Male writers have historically dominated the general scholarship in Romantic studies and continue to enjoy at least some pre-eminence over women writers. Another explanation may be found, as the work of Craciun suggests, in Laqueur's documented shift from the one-sex to the two-sex model, culminating in the celebration of a sexless, spiritual and domestic womanhood in the Victorian Angel in the House. Whether socially sanctioned or not, women's expression of sexual desire appears to have become increasingly controversial throughout the century, as witnessed in the downgraded reputation of sexually outspoken female writers from the beginning of the long eighteenth century such as Aphra Behn. Indeed, more and more women were advised to hide all proofs of sexual worldliness, Johnson (in an oft-repeated anecdote) rebuking Hannah More for disclosing that she had read Henry Fielding's *Tom Jones* (1749) and Maria Edgeworth receiving harsh treatment at the hands of reviewers for purportedly too frank fictional treatments of male libertinism.[20] Indeed, as David Sigler attests, sexual enjoyment itself threatened to efface womanhood in the Romantic era, making it necessary for women to be circumspect in addressing sex.[21] A number of the male Romantics can be seen positioning themselves in sexual rebellion against female writers (including former mentors), whom they recast as humourless and sexually repressed, even asexual mother-teachers. This desexualising move is evident in Robert Southey and Samuel Taylor Coleridge's nicknames for Anna Letitia Barbauld: 'Mrs. Barebald' and 'Mistress Bare and Bald'.[22] That said, these nicknames have an oddly sexualised sound to them as well, perhaps hinting that, despite themselves, Southey and Coleridge tacitly registered Barbauld as a sexual being (and Coleridge could apparently not resist contemplating her sex life with her husband). It may well be that other efforts by male writers to stigmatise women as passionless and sexless betray a covert sexual attraction and dread.

The tradition of Enlightenment feminist thought, represented, for example, by Mary Astell, Catharine Macaulay (later Graham), and Mary Wollstonecraft (later Godwin), seems to have further complicated the way that women writers engaged with sex. As Vivien Jones observes,

> Eager to use the humanist rationalist ideal as a means of escape from the sexually-differentiated regime of desire, as well as from the tyranny of unthinking domesticity and reproduction, Enlightenment feminisms typically reject, or ignore, the pleasures of the body so dear to late twentieth-century sensibilities.[23]

Nevertheless, despite partially exemplifying this tradition, Wollstonecraft cannot finally be contained within it. Indeed, Jones argues, this female Romantic writer's great 'originality' lay 'in making female pleasure and desire central to feminism'.[24] Craciun goes further, declaring,

> From prominent Enlightenment feminists like ... Wollstonecraft and Mary Robinson (*née* Darby), to poets like Letitia [Elizabeth] Landon (later Maclean), women writers of the Romantic period always addressed the body when they considered issues of intellect, subjectivity, sexuality, agency, and power.[25]

As Jones reminds us, Wollstonecraft was targeted in Richard Polwhele's *The Unsex'd Females* (1798), not only for her advocacy of the 'rights of women', but also for her recommendation that girls be taught about sex and reproduction more openly. Challenging Wollstonecraft's premise that it is ignorance, not knowledge, which corrupts, Polwhele repeats the old line that corruption lies with knowledge itself, denouncing, in the same breath, the 'botanizing girls' who violate modesty in studying 'the sexual system of plants'.[26] It should be noted that Wollstonecraft's advice on sex education strikingly anticipates male contemporaries such as Thomas Beddoes, with the same anti-masturbation subtext, although, of course, she lacked Beddoes's credentials as a male medical professional.

At least in part, the marginalisation of women writers in the study of Romantic sexuality may be tied to the kinds of sources often favoured in the field of the history of sexuality, namely medical and juridical discourses and institutional histories, which did not give opportunity for the expression of female voices and too often reduced women to the status of objects. As Behrendt points out,

> Because women were routinely excluded from formal education, ... many male critics assumed that they were therefore incapable of writing in informed fashion on 'intellectual' subjects, including ... philosophy ... history ... politics, economics, and science. For women to publish on these subjects seemed to such critics a violation not just of decorum but also of nature: without rigorous formal experience in empirical reasoning, of which many eighteenth-century men believed women were not just temperamentally but *constitutionally* incapable, they could have nothing of value to say.[27]

As such, women who dared to write in the face of general discouragement met with additional strictures regarding what they might say and how they might say it. The least controversial option was, according to Behrendt, to 'write about "what they knew", which implied that their writing must inevitably be essentially autobiographical'.[28]

This relative absence in the scholarship on Romantic sexuality is certainly not due to any shortage of prospective material in female Romantic writing, which features many different kinds of transgressive and perverse sexuality. Particularly abundant are treatments of extramarital sexuality, especially in novels. Some immediate examples that come to mind are Elizabeth Inchbald's *Nature and Art* (1796), Wollstonecraft's *Wrongs of Woman* (1798), Mary Hays's *The Victim of Prejudice* (1799), Amelia Opie's *The Father and Daughter* (1801), and Charlotte Dacre (later Byrne)'s *Confessions of the Nun of St Omer* (1805), *Zofloya; or, The Moor* (1806), and *The Libertine* (1807). Inchbald controversially treats the same subject elsewhere in her drama, most notoriously, in *Lovers' Vows* (1798), whose improprieties serve as a major plot point in Jane Austen's *Mansfield Park* (1814). Female Romantic writers, starting with Caroline Lamb, played their own role in developing the Byronic hero as a type. There are many striking examples of female Romantic *femmes fatales*, such as Anne Bannerman's 'The Dark Ladie' (1802) and Landon's 'The Fairy of the Fountain' (1835) (both texts discussed by Craciun).[29] Mother–son incest figures in Joanna Baillie's dramatic tragedy *Rayner* (1804), while father–daughter incest provides the primary material for the plot of Mary Wollstonecraft Shelley's *Mathilda* (c.1819–20; 1959), a reason it remained long unpublished after her death. Meanwhile, sibling incest and rape are at the heart of

Elizabeth Hands's *The Death of Amnon. A Poem* (1789). Same-sex love is treated less openly, but not infrequently, and female romantic friendship, which Hitchcock observes as on the rise from the mid-eighteenth century onwards and cites as a reaction against the ascendancy of a 'phallocentric' model of sex, is nearly ubiquitous. A number of women who contributed to Romantic literature have been clearly identified as having had female lovers. The best known are perhaps Anne Seymour Damer, a sculptor and a writer, and Anne Lister, the main protagonist of the recent popular BBC series *Gentleman Jack* (2019). Although the exact nature of their relationship has been the subject of much debate, the Ladies of Llangollen, Eleanor Butler and Sarah Ponsonby, visited by Wordsworth, Percy Shelley and Byron, among others, represent other important examples on the Romantic lesbian continuum. In this context, another fascinating figure is Mary Diana Dods, who wrote under a male pseudonym and lived as husband to a woman Isabella Robinson under a different assumed male identity (important for thinking not only about homosexuality but also gender performativity and fluidity, and the possibilities for trans identity in the period).

Female Romantic writers include a significant number with notorious sexual reputations in real life, notably Mary Robinson, Helen Maria Williams, Wollstonecraft, Hays, Mary Shelley, and Landon. Accusations of sexual transgression (substantiated and unsubstantiated) were employed as the frequent rod with which to beat women writers, especially those perceived as radicals, throughout the period. Robinson's highly publicised affair with the Prince Regent and William Godwin's revelations in his posthumous memoir of Wollstonecraft provided powerful ammunition for opponents, and even women writers of otherwise impeccable sexual reputation were sometimes sexualised to neutralise their claims to authority and controversial interventions into politics.[30] The political cartoon *Don Dismallo Running the Literary Gantlet* (1790), which features Barbauld exclaiming, '[T]he most incorrigible Urchin in my School never felt from my hands what this Assassin of Liberty shall now feel!' – with whip raised against a shirtless Edmund Burke – not only exploits her career as a mother-teacher as part of the joke but also arguably targets her sexual character. Together with another female figure in the scene shown baring one breast and the length of one leg, identifiable as Liberty, the representation of Barbauld seems deliberately calculated to generate an uncomfortable sexual *frisson*.

This limited attention paid to women in the study of Romantic sexuality may well have created particular gaps in our knowledge. From the focus on medical literature in the period, we have acquired a good sense of how women's bodies were subjected to the regime of power and knowledge called 'sexuality' ascendant during the late eighteenth and early nineteenth centuries. Taking direct cues from Foucault and Laqueur, Sha establishes how physicians sought to identify signs of sexuality (and sexual deviancy) written on the body during the late eighteenth and early nineteenth centuries. From the evidence he gleans, women were under particular scrutiny, for example, in William Hunter's preoccupation with the clitoris and his brother John Hunter's with the hymen, and masturbation continued to be pathologised in both sexes. Thus, Sha develops another important contribution to the history of sexuality by Laqueur, who has determined that a medicalising and pathologising of bodies and sexualities had already begun during the eighteenth century, especially in relation to masturbation, and, to a lesser extent, lesbianism, in theories that the latter was caused by an enlargement of the clitoris (a few connecting 'onanism' and Sapphism together).[31] Less clear from this line of research is how women of the period contributed to developing the ascendant regime of 'sexuality'.

There is additionally much still to learn about how women resisted sexual discipline. Sha notably identifies an opportunity for resistance created by the same physicians who were pathologising sexuality, as they recognised the unreliability of the body in disclosing sexual secrets, producing what he characterises as an 'epistemological panic' at this historical juncture. In his view, this 'epistemological panic' was intensified by the increasing location of the sex drive in the brain. As such, there was still an opportunity for sex to escape discipline and to escape discipline through sex, explaining, in part, why the Romantics turned to sex as a form of liberation.[32] Sha himself has paid particular attention to how late eighteenth- and early nineteenth-century discussions of masturbation contributed, on the one hand, towards transforming private vices into public virtues, by directing 'sexual pleasure and the somatic experience of that pleasure' towards heterosexuality and marriage and in otherwise regulating sex by prescribing healthy and unhealthy levels and forms of it, and, on the other, towards the 'epistemological panic' cited above. He has also credited Romantic medicine with making its own contributions in the history of sexuality, as late eighteenth-century experiments in artificial insemination encouraged a general divorce of sexual pleasure from reproduction, producing a concept of 'perversion', where pleasure was without function, and, in turn, became a kind of aesthetic experience. Sha suggests that Romanticism 'acknowledged the perverseness of human sexuality, its resistance to reproductive telos and discipline' and that Romantic writers drew on the separation of pleasure from reproduction in order to align aesthetics and sex through their common 'purposiveness without a purpose', infusing an erotic dimension into their art that heightened its appeal and enabled it more effectively 'to engage readers otherwise stupefied by the "savage torpor" of industrialism or encrusted by the weight of custom'.[33] His effort to show how the separation of sex from reproduction during the Romantic period enabled 'Romantics as diverse as Byron, Blake, Anna Seward, the Shelleys, and Wollstonecraft [to] begin to organize their emancipatory politics around the axis of sexuality' opens up new scholarly territory as yet relatively unexplored.[34]

As an aside, it should be emphasised that the gender politics of the one-sex and two-sex models are more complicated than have sometimes been represented by historians of sexuality. While the one-sex model envisioned women as inferior to men, Enlightenment feminists such as John Locke, François Poulain de la Barre and Mary Astell advanced arguments in favour of more intellectually rigorous education and more equal relations between the sexes based on the assumption that women were not fundamentally different from men and that there was no sex in minds, an assumption that was more compatible with the one-sex than the two-sex model. The acceptance that women were more highly sexed than men and that their pleasure was requisite for reproduction gave them some license and agency in sexual matters. At the same time, it left them vulnerable to censure and calls for tight patriarchal control (and discredited them in cases of sexual abuse and rape that resulted in pregnancy). The sense of gender fluidity connected with the one-sex model suggested a fundamentally precarious gender hierarchy, a state either to be lamented or celebrated and exploited. Indeed, the one-sex model theoretically allowed the possibility that men and women might change sexes, although it was considered more likely for women since the process of formerly hidden parts descending and becoming visible appeared more straightforward than that of visible parts ascending and retracting. For its part, the two-sex model could be used to make the case for women as equal to but different from men. However, it might as easily promote an essentialised view of sexual difference that undermined claims to equality, gave sanction to an ideology of separate spheres and the limitation of women's lives to motherhood and household duties and denied their status as sexual beings, placing sexually transgressive women further beyond the pale than before. The two-sex model has been seen as giving a generally stronger foundation to a heteronormative order that punished or excluded all those who defied sexual norms. This perceived group of transgressors included not only sexually assertive women but also men and women who pursued same-sex love and/or sought to pass as members of the opposite sex, and individuals with ambiguous sexual characteristics. That said, several Romantics scholars have seen the ascendancy of the two-sex model as opening up unexpected liberating opportunities to challenge gender hierarchy and heteronormativity.

Other scholars have begun integrating women into the study of Romantic sexuality and laying the groundwork for future research. Andrew Elfenbein connects sexuality and the Romantic concept of genius, arguing that during the Romantic period, genius became an identity category that lent itself directly to transgressive cross-gendering and expressions of same-sex desire in Romantic literature. He cites Damer and Bannerman, who exploited genius's liberating possibilities in allowing escape from prescribed gender and heteronormative rules. Christopher C. Nagle discusses several women writers, notably Charlotte Smith, Williams, Robinson, Austen and Landon, as part of his argument that the male Romantics adopted and adapted a tradition of sensibility, understood as a 'mode of eroticized benevolence', by making it more individualised and heteronormative.[35] Andrea K. Henderson includes Frances (Fanny) Burney (later d'Arblay) and Baillie (whom she specifically discusses in relation to voyeurism) in the case she makes that the late eighteenth and early nineteenth centuries were characterised by a transition from pleasure to desire and a masochistic 'erotics of lack', embodied in the *femme fatale* and Byronic hero who emerged as literary types at this time, lovers who 'keep in suspense' the 'heroes and heroines of Romantic literature' and 'dominate them, and even humiliate them'.[36] In her view, the generation of this Romantic 'erotics of lack' was part of a broader effort to deal with commodity culture, with its constant array of goods for purchase. After beginning his analysis of desire in Romantic literary culture with an extended consideration of Wollstonecraft, Sigler includes chapters on Austen, Joanna Southcott, Robinson and Dacre (focusing in the last instance on masochism). As part of this analysis, he postulates that sexual difference was made visible during the period through the experience of sexual enjoyment and that even as the sexes became 'alien to each other' at this time, the constraints of 'sexual identity open[ed] the door for non-gendered forms of sexual identity'.[37] He concludes that 'the range of possible sexualities within British Romanticism' was 'much broader than the usual binaries, even those of queer theory, can accommodate, and that these atypical sexualities became thinkable because of the period's ideological investment in enjoyment'.[38]

Still, this body of scholarship is not yet sufficient to determine the extent to which female Romantic writing either models and promotes sexual self-control, relegating sexuality to the realm of desire, deferral and lack, or seeks to evade control. Such questions are all the timelier given recent work in eighteenth-century studies on the role of the novel and female novelists in establishing a new disciplinary regime over sexuality. Kathleen Lubey, for one, identifies Eliza Haywood as an essential contributor towards developing the eighteenth-century novel as a means for promoting sexual self-control by presenting readers with scenes of sexual titillation and transgression that encourage them to reflect on and master their own sexual responses. She briefly considers Austen, whom she situates within a long tradition of novelists who 'link intimate description with critical modes of thought over and above impolite curiosities' as part of the project of 'forestall[ing] corrupt reading'.[39] There are already potentially fruitful connections that could be made, for example, between Lubey's account of the eighteenth-century novel and Henderson's theorisation of Romantic aesthetics, as well as with the work of others such as Sha and Sigler. Laqueur contends that during the eighteenth century, cultural anxiety over masturbation and novel-reading centred on women. His insights need to be sifted in the context of Romantic fiction (a line of inquiry that Eve Kosofsky Sedgwick famously initiated) and female novel criticism.[40] Women writers, even those ambivalent about novels and novel-reading, have left us with more substantial reflections on the genre than have male contemporaries.

The study of women writers promises to enrich that of specific 'peripheral sexualities' of increasing interest to Romanticists, such as homosexuality, and to illuminate such questions as when the concept of a homosexual identity first historically applied, keeping in mind Sedgwick's caution against imposing categorical judgements on any historical moment (a danger some historians of sexuality have sought to obviate by focusing on heteronormativity rather than homosexuality). Scholars of the Romantics have already queried the heterosexist biases that have proliferated in later representations of the canonical male Romantics in biography and popular culture even though, as O'Quinn quips, 'none of the big six is a poster boy for normative middle-class sexuality'.[41] Scholars have especially sought to recuperate the significance of Byron and Keats and, less predictably, Blake as queer icons. A literature of queer readings of Romantic writers has begun to accumulate, extending now to all of the big six and well beyond, sometimes in obvious directions, for example, to Beckford, and less obvious ones, including to Ann Radcliffe and Austen, although the queering of Austen, in particular, has met with persisting opposition.[42] Certain literary genres that flourished during the period, notably the Gothic, have invited various queer readings. Indeed, George Haggerty considers that, as a genre, the Gothic at once illustrates an 'erotics of loss' related to an object of homoerotic and incestuous desire and complicates later accepted binaries in the realm of sexuality (homosexuality/heterosexuality, sadism/masochism), with potentially utopian implications.[43] Over the course of his scholarly career, he has supported his thesis regarding the 'queer Gothic' with examples of novels by women writers, including Clara Reeve, Radcliffe, Smith, Sophia Lee and Regina Maria Roche, effectively highlighting how much scope there is for the study of female Romantic literature and sexuality.

Beyond homosexuality, female Romantic writers could well cast additional light on the familiar Romantic theme of incest. Critics have long interested themselves in the possibly sexual dimension of William and Dorothy Wordsworth's relationship, Byron's reported affair with his half-sister Augusta Maria Leigh and brother–sister incest in Romantic literature, not only in Gothic novels such as Matthew Lewis's *The Monk* (1796), but also in works by the canonical male Romantics, including Percy Shelley's *Laon and Cythna* (1817) and *Rosalind and Helen* (1819) and Byron's *Bride of Abydos* (1813) and *Manfred: A Dramatic Poem* (1817). Alan Richardson has usefully identified certain features of Romantic brother–sister incest as distinctive from its representation in other periods, as it is often pursued deliberately with full knowledge of the kinship relationship, as 'an extension and intensification' of 'the normal sibling relation', a union simultaneously celebrated and punished.[44] This scholarship might well be enriched by extending the frame of reference to female Romantic representations of incest, taking into account scholarship on incest in eighteenth-century studies, where consistent connections have been made to the transition from the patriarchal to conjugal model of marriage and the rise of the affective family. Mary Shelley's *Mathilda* has already excited some critical attention, with incest, however, often less emphasised than other themes.[45]

To factor in the work and thought of women writers is potentially to transform our understanding of Romantic-era sexuality as a first step towards a generally more intersectional approach that considers class, ethnicity, race, disability and age alongside gender. At the same time, there are significant implications concerning the ongoing effort to revisit and rethink the once-influential paradigms of 'masculine' and 'feminine' Romanticism. Theorists of 'masculine' and 'feminine' Romanticism have set women writers in opposition to a conception of Romanticism oriented towards idealism and transcendence and aligned them with the material. As noted at the beginning of this chapter, this particular conception of Romanticism has been inimical to the study of Romantic sexuality. However, the same theorists have seen female Romantic writers distancing themselves from imagination and feeling, which so often elided with sexuality in the period, thereby setting limits upon 'desire'. Recognising these tensions, we can already see that the story of female Romantic engagements with bodies and sexualities is more complicated than once supposed.

Notes

1. As Jeffrey Weeks outlines, fundamental to sexuality studies as a field is the recognition of sexuality as 'a social and historical construct' and 'sexual forms, beliefs, ideologies and behaviours' as variable and influenced by many different social and historical factors. Jeffrey Weeks, *Sexuality and its Discontents* (London: Routledge and Kegan Paul, 1985), 29–30. See Tim Hitchcock, *English Sexualities, 1700–1800* (New York: St Martin's Press, 1997) and Foucault and Laqueur references below.
2. Richard C. Sha, 'Romanticism and Sexuality – A Special Issue of *Romanticism on the Net*', *Romanticism on the Net* 23 (2001): n. p., https://doi.org/10.7202/005994ar and Andrew O'Quinn, 'Preface: Romanticism and Sexual Vice', *Nineteenth-Century Contexts* 17, no. 1 (2005): 6.
3. Mario Praz, *The Romantic Agony*, trans. Angus Davidson (London: Oxford University Press, 1933).
4. Praz has left his mark in a few now classic examples of Romantic studies, albeit not necessarily concentrated on sexuality, including Alethea Hayter, *Opium and the Romantic Imagination* (Berkeley: University of California Press, 1968); M. H. Abrams, *The Milk of Paradise: The Effect of Opium Visions on the Works of De Quincey, Crabbe, Francis Thompson, and Coleridge* (New York: Octagon Press, 1971); Morse Peckham, *The Triumph of Romanticism: Collected Essays* (Columbia, SC: University of South Carolina Press, 1971); and Jacques Barzun, *Classic, Romantic, Modern* (Chicago: University of Chicago Press, 1975).
5. See Bradford K. Mudge, 'Romanticism, Materialism, and the Origins of Modern Pornography', *Romanticism on the Net* 23 (2001): n. p., https://doi.org/10.7202/005988ar.
6. This phrase appears on page 38 of Michel Foucault, *The History of Sexuality, Vol. 1: An Introduction*, trans. Robert Hurley (New York: Vintage, 1990), with relevant mention of Sade on page 21.
7. Ibid., 40.
8. Ibid., 37, 38–9.
9. Foucault's theorisation of the emergence of homosexuality as an identity category during the nineteenth century has since been queried and complicated. David Halperin, for example, cites historical evidence for the existence of a homosexual morphology and subjectivity long predating the nineteenth century, although still not corresponding exactly with Foucault's conception of modern homosexual identity. See David Halperin, 'Forgetting Foucault: Acts, Identities, and the History of Sexuality', *Representations* 63 (July 1993): 93–120.
10. Margaret Homans, *Bearing the Word: Language and Female Experience in Nineteenth-Century Women's Writing* (Chicago: University of Chicago Press, 1986).
11. Meena Alexander, *The Poetic Self, Towards a Phenomenology of Romanticism* (Atlantic Highlands: Humanities Press, 1981).
12. Marlon B. Ross, *The Contours of Masculine Desire: Romanticism and the Rise of Women's Poetry* (New York: Oxford University Press, 1989), 119.
13. Ibid., 119.

14. Anne K. Mellor, *Romanticism and Gender* (New York: Routledge, 1992).
15. Susan J. Wolfson, *Borderlines: Shiftings of Gender in British Romanticism* (Redwood City: Stanford University Press, 2006), 3. Besides Wolfson, a number of others have thoughtfully revisited the distinction between 'masculine' and 'feminine' Romanticism. See, for instance, Paula Backscheider, *Eighteenth-Century Women Poets and Their Poetry: Inventing Agency, Inventing Genre* (Baltimore: Johns Hopkins University Press, 2005); Stephen C. Behrendt, *British Women Poets and the Romantic Writing Community* (Baltimore: Johns Hopkins University Press, 2009); Beth Lau, *Fellow Romantics: Male and Female British Writers, 1790–1835* (Farnham: Ashgate, 2009); Devoney Looser, 'Feminist Pioneers, Feminist Classics: Reflections on Age and Generation in Scholarship on Romantic-Era Women's Writings', *European Romantic Review* 23, no. 3 (2012): 349–54; and Kate Singer, *Romantic Vacancy: The Poetics of Gender, Affect, and Radical Speculation* (Albany: SUNY Press, 2019).
16. In addition to the above-cited scholarship of Ross and Mellor, see Margaret Homans, 'Keats Reading Women, Women Reading Keats', *Studies in Romanticism* 29 (Summer 1990): 341–70. Philip Cox notes the long history of associating Keats with the 'feminine', dating back to the nineteenth-century reviewers attempting to dismiss his claims as a poet. As he underscores, this same association in late twentieth-century Romantic studies was taken rather differently, as a sign of gender fluidity and performativity. Philip Cox, 'Keats and the Performance of Gender', *Keats-Shelley Journal* 44 (1995): 40–65.
17. Mellor, *Romanticism*, 11.
18. Adriana Craciun, *Fatal Women of Romanticism* (Cambridge: Cambridge University Press, 2002).
19. Behrendt, *British*, 34.
20. See the review of Edgeworth's *Tales of Fashionable* Life (1809) in *The Quarterly Review*, where the author criticises the representation of a male character's visit to a brothel in the story 'The Dun', claiming that it will teach male readers 'who labour under the same infirmity, ... where a cure is to be had'. 'Art. VII. Tales of Fashionable Life', *The Quarterly Review* 2, no. 3 (August 1809): 153. Mary Poovey has maintained that 'by the last decades of the eighteenth century' it 'was considered unladylike' for women 'even to refer to the body'. Mary Poovey, *The Proper Lady and the Woman Writer* (Chicago: University of Chicago Press, 1984), 14.
21. David Sigler, *Sexual Enjoyment in British Romanticism: Gender and Psychoanalysis, 1753–1835* (Montreal: McGill-Queen's University Press, 2015).
22. Robert Southey, *The Life and Correspondence of Robert Southey*, ed. Charles Cuthbert Southey, 6 vols. (London: Longman, Brown, Green and Longmans, 1850), vol. 2, 175, and Samuel Taylor Coleridge, *Notebooks of Samuel Taylor Coleridge*, ed. Kathleen Coburn, 5 vols. (London: Routledge and Kegan Paul, 1973), vol. 3, 3965.
23. Vivien Jones, 'Advice and Enlightenment: Mary Wollstonecraft and Sex Education', in *Women, Gender and Enlightenment*, ed. Sarah Knott and Barbara Taylor (Basingstoke: Palgrave Macmillan, 2005), 142.

24. Ibid., 144.
25. Craciun, *Fatal*, 4.
26. Richard Polwhele, *The Unsex'd Females: A Poem, Addressed to the Author of* The Pursuits of Literature (London: Cadell and Davies, 1798), 9, 8.
27. Behrendt, *British*, 18. Emphasis in original.
28. Ibid., 18.
29. Craciun devotes additional consideration to Mary Lamb, Wollstonecraft, Robinson, and Dacre, mingling an interest in sex and violence.
30. Barbara Creed discusses continuing examples of this strategy in the context of twentieth-century film in *The Monstrous-Feminine: Film, Feminism, Psychoanalysis* (New York: Routledge, 1993).
31. For Laqueur's most comprehensive treatment of masturbation, see Thomas Laqueur, *Solitary Sex: A Cultural History of Masturbation* (New York: Zone Books, 2003).
32. Richard C. Sha, 'Scientific Forms of Sexual Knowledge in Romanticism', *Romanticism on the Net* 23 (2001): n. p., https://doi.org/10.7202/005993ar.
33. Richard C. Sha, *Perverse Romanticism: Aesthetics and Sexuality in Britain, 1750–1832* (Baltimore: Johns Hopkins University Press, 2009), 16, 1–2.
34. Ibid., 17.
35. Christopher C. Nagle, *Sexuality and the Culture of Sensibility in British Romanticism* (Basingstoke: Palgrave Macmillan, 2007), 64.
36. Andrea K. Henderson, *Romanticism and the Painful Pleasures of Modern Life* (Cambridge: Cambridge University Press, 2008), 1–2.
37. Sigler, *Sexual*, 8.
38. Ibid., 16.
39. Kathleen Lubey, *Excitable Imaginations: Eroticism and Reading in Britain, 1660–1760* (Lewisburg: Bucknell University Press, 2014), 4.
40. See Eve Kosofsky Sedgwick, 'Jane Austen and the Masturbating Girl', *Critical Inquiry* 17, no. 4 (Summer 1991): 818–37.
41. O'Quinn, 'Preface: Romanticism', 6.
42. Less controversial has been the queering of Mary Shelley, for example, in A. A. Markley, 'Tainted Wethers the Flock: Homosexuality and Homosocial Desire in Mary Shelley's Novels', *The Keats-Shelley Review* 13 (1999): 115–33.
43. His most extensive examination of the 'queer Gothic' is in *Queer Gothic* (Urbana: University of Illinois Press, 2006). Haggerty ranges significantly beyond the Gothic and the Romantic period in *Unnatural Affections: Women and Fiction in the later Eighteenth Century* (Bloomington: Indiana University Press, 1998), with consideration of such women writers as Sarah Fielding, Sarah Scott, Burney, Inchbald and Austen.
44. Alan Richardson, 'Rethinking Romantic Incest: Human Universals, Literary Representation, and the Biology of the Mind', *New Literary History* 31, no. 3 (Summer 2000): 554.
45. A notable exception is Frederick Burwick's brief examination of *Mathilda* and Baillie's *Rayner* in 'Romantic Incest Plots: Baillie, Byron, and the Shelleys', in *Decadent Romanticism*, ed. Kostas Boyiopoulos and Mark Sandy (Farnham: Ashgate, 2015), 27–41.

Chapter 3

Reorienting Multi-dimensional Sex with Objects in *Millenium Hall*

Kate Singer

One story to tell about the sexual object of desire is its transit from maternal object (breast) to transitional object (lovey) to *objet petit a*, with some anxieties about the phallic object as well as detours through the psychotic object (fantasy made real) or phobic object (the revulsive other).[1] This trajectory, however, is based upon the psychoanalytic narrative that predicates social and sexual development upon the recognition – or fear – of the lack of the phallus as well as the concomitant discovery of the maternal breast as external to one's self. Not only does the material object increasingly defy the control of the child and adolescent, but it frequently punctures the illusion of omnipotence. As Donald Winnicott would have it, such disillusionment reveals the infant's myth of omnipotence as an infantile belief in the unity of mother-child – what we might recognise more recently as a new materialist primordial fantasy of the 'goo' of materiality and being that pervades and intertwines all things.[2] Yet, from the point of view of the mother, who is indeed no object at all, the 'disillusionment' – which happens when one begins to encourage the child to find freedom, to take the first small steps towards various toys besides the inflatable breast and to find other pathways around the rich ecology of an environment other than the direct course to the maternal body – is not simply a release from false omnipotence. Rather, such play with an object may signal possible liberation from the phallic, not the maternal, object. For play with allegedly substitutive things is accompanied by word play (in the semiotic or slip-sliding around the still unknown symbolic), and such material-semiotic play may find alternate routes from a phallic object that has a teleology towards phallic power – an object that presupposes its own lack to begin with. Sarah Scott's *Millenium Hall* (1762) presents an ecology for such experimentation with objects and narratives loosened from phallocratic power and capering within a mid-century space made safe for women, mothers and young girls.

The novel gathers bodies, spaces, and other objects of play – a collection of women's narratives, their books and their gifts. Scott layers and arranges these toyish things in order to encourage readers to reevaluate objects, both their trajectories within a gendered symbolic system and their mapping of sexual relations along different orientations than the heteronormative.

Women's prostheses, such as toys or books, do not necessarily qualify as either maternal or phallic objects; they are plastic or wood or metal or plant alternatives, whose nonhuman status might be animated by children but not to the exclusion of their thingly, affective natures. They move the very subjects who allegedly move them. Neither do these things represent the sheer difference that would instigate perverse desire for something that is not-mother or not-father. Instead, they offer other worlds, different trajectories and alternative materialities of desire. No fetish or substitution for eluding phallic power or forever lost maternal love, they offer other dimensions of sexuality, in multiple times or mental avenues of semio-material imagination.

Sex toys have a long history in manuals such as the Kama Sutra or in Greek art, and they make a resurgence in particularly interesting ways in eighteenth-century literature concerning feminine or non-normative sexuality. In the Earl of Rochester's 'Signior Dildo', women exchange a personified Priapus to pleasure each other serially – and with a kabbalistic, mutual pleasure that rests with their common member.[3] The condemnatory *Sappho-an* portrays the Greek goddesses on strike from heteronormative love, brainstorming Sapphic forms of pleasure that comprise various strap-ons, including vegetables.[4] Carrots are morphological substitutes for the flesh-and-bone tool. These 'dildonics', as Paul B. Preciado terms the modern sexuality predicated on prostheses, suggest how queer sex rides bareback on modern heteronormativity well before, and perhaps as, England makes the transition from the one-sex to the two-sex model documented by Thomas Laqueur.[5] Similar narratives, in somewhat different forms, echo in the thieving exchanges of Moll Flanders and her mob boss, 'The Governess', as Moll exchanges a life of heteronormative sex work for lucrative objects – a theft of the phallic object if ever there was one. Charlotte Charke's eponymous memoir likewise depicts such skilful cross-dressing at an early age, which might be read as her unique adoption of a particular phallic object – that is, her father Colley Cibber's sartorial, performative prowess.[6]

Yet, the phallocentrism of these narratives masks other sorts of play with things that offer a sexuality resisting domination by the law of the father. We might remember that while laws against sodomy date from the mid-sixteenth century, Sapphic sex was often seen as a warm-up for marriage, a flimsy pleasure, or an illness to be medicalised by preventing masturbation or other 'accidental' stimulus of the clitoris. But written by women, and within a different literary, social and sexual ecology than the medico-juridical discourses discussed by Michel Foucault, there is another genealogy of women's sex with – or sex through – objects. *Millenium Hall*, with its women's pastoral utopia of shared property and things, presents this sort of 'posthuman sex'.[7] The centrality of things in this novel provokes a twisting (compatible with Sara Ahmed's sense of queerness) of the monetary exchange of fabrics, plate and other goods (such as those swived by Moll) into a gift giving and receiving, which pools things for women's intimacy.[8] This gift ecology, set as it is in the pastoral utopia of Millenium Hall, does not easily enact a Maussian-Derridean debt and obligation (itself a symptom of Lacanian phallic lack and fetishistic castration complex). Rather, it offers a space reoriented by alternative relations of things and women, with multiple trajectories and possibilities – be-quests for sex and endowed living. As implausible as it might seem, I want to argue that there exists in the eighteenth century, if only in embryonic form, objects that loosen themselves from the phallus and its associated lack. These objects create sexualities with seeds of feminine and queer sexualities sprung from yonic things – 'things' in Jane Bennett's sense of offering their own affects and powers.[9] Such *euporia* does not place intimacy between people or substitute objects into the climactic narrative of euphoria and quiescence, tumescence and flaccidity, nor in pollyannaish abundance.[10] Instead, these be-quests find women occupying and imagining multiple sexual encounters and sexualities at different times, but always through mutually held things.

Reorienting the Pathways of *Millenium Hall*

Scott's novel presents a firmly allegorical tale of what I am calling multi-dimensional sex with things, which takes root in the novel's narrative structure and especially its narratorial setting or 'story world'. As Broadview editor Gary Kelly suggests, the very name 'Millenium Hall' for both the novel and the story's architectural centrepiece implies a millennialism that would transform the gentry country house into a utopian community (*MH* 53n1).[11] Certainly, the novel harkens back to other feminine utopian spaces, including that of Margaret Cavendish's *Convent of Pleasure* (1668). Yet, rather than a feminine space protectively cordoned off for women and then penetrated by a cross-dressing foreign prince, the faux travel narrative of this novel offers two male ne'er-do-wells on a curative road trip that magically lands them into a space for exploring an entirely different form of relations – a social realm set up by and for women. The narrative consists of two pieces: the men's exploration of Millenium Hall and its environs as a grand experiment in alternative living and a series of narratives telling the stories of the hall's founding members. The temporality of the novel in its entirety – a topic I'll return to later in the essay – is based upon an exploration of a present 'things as they've become' and then of multiple tales that are told sequentially but essentially must be imagined as happening simultaneously in the multiple worlds or dimensions of each of its matrons. In this way, when we read the first part of the novel, we are already reading the intertwinement of multiple twisted, queered *bildungsromane*. Part of the magic of the novel is its ability to present us with a scene of relation that has already reoriented itself around a vaginal hall, symbolically speaking, and which has, in some part, obviated the Gothic haunting of the phallic law of the father.

In her book *Queer Phenomenology* (2006), Ahmed argues that 'orientations involve directions towards objects that affect what we do, and how we inhabit space'.[12] The hall and its environs become the locus of what the founding women might do for each other and the various populations with which they surround themselves – namely young women, agricultural workers, factory workers, animals and those with disabilities. As Ahmed elaborates, 'Form takes shape through the 'direction' of matter towards an action'.[13] Although the novel ends by spotlighting the women's carpet factory and the larger capitalist bent of their economy, nonetheless, the novel begins intently within a pastoral space, a 'female Arcadia' where those women who reside within its grounds are intently focused on each other (*MH* 223). 'Gender', Ahmed theorises, 'could thus be described as a bodily orientation, a way in which bodies get directed by their actions over time'.[14] Millenium Hall's centripetal force reorients its women away from urban dissipation or the London marriage market and towards each other, and towards various communities in need. If, as Ahmed writes, heterosexuality is a 'compulsory orientation', which directs women and men towards biopolitical reproduction, entailed forms of inheritance, domestic tranquillity and penetrative/phallic sexuality, this novel attests to queer reorientations – if not queer sexualities themselves.[15]

The narratorial frame, of two precocious men who get pulled into the trajectory of the hall, redoubles this reorientation away from the phallic. The unnamed speaker roams to ameliorate his constitution after his 'long abode in the hot and unwholesome climate of Jamaica', where he had 'dedicated all his application to mercantile gain' and had 'given up the substance for the shadow' (*MH* 54). His companion is a promising young man whose trajectory of becoming a 'true wit, degenerated into pertness and impertinence' so as 'to render him a coxcomb' (*MH* 55). Thus bound by narcissism's and capitalism's overproduction, the men fend off their fear of castration with an over-abundance of vanity and trade. While it might be titillating to posit this friendship as a sodomitic one, or even a phallic/colonial incursion into the feminine space, they run into a pastoral space that completely arrests that phallic momentum:

> When we had walked about half a mile in a scene truly pastoral, we began to think ourselves in the days of Theocritus, so sweetly did the sound of a flute come wafted through the air. Never did pastoral swain make sweeter melody on his oaten reed … Curiosity now prompted us to walk on; the nearer we came to the house, the greater we found the profusion of flowers which ornamented every field. (*MH* 56)

Clearly lured farther into an unexpected pastoral by the thrills of the reed played by the swain, the love song, played on a phallic flute, curries the men's attention. Just as abruptly, however, the shepherd leaves to do actual work, and our gay men stumble into a different landscape – one given to a 'profusion of flowers'. Phallic allurement gives way to a vaginal ecology.

If such hard-coded Freudian tropology seems too on the nose for modern readers, we might remember that early eighteenth-century Sapphic poetry played with such pastoral figures. Katherine Phillips, Elizabeth Singer Rowe, Anne Finch and Aphra Behn wrote pastoral verse to experiment with alternative world making and female erotic desire.[16] Behn's now-infamous 'To the fair Clarinda, who made Love to me, imagin'd more than Woman' offers such shapeshifting, sexed taxonomies that inhere in body and ecology:

> For sure no Crime with thee we can commit;
> Or if we shou'd – thy Form excuses it.
> For who, that gathers fairest Flowers believes
> A Snake lies hid beneath the Fragrant Leaves.[17]

This poem has been variously read as a poem of same-sex desire and female friendship, as well as an early trans poem. What might be helpful to us here is the poem's simultaneous demarcation of phallic and vaginal figures (snake/fragrant leaves and flowers) as inhabiting the same space. The topographic duality that flavours this poem is redrawn in the novel as one of sequence: the phallic tune fades, giving way to the more material flowers and vaginal ecologies that shape the rest of the novel. The floral, yonic landscape of the feminine pastoral might reorient and engulf even two such libertine figures: in the novel's very last sentence, the speaker declares that the women of Millenium Hall have reoriented him: 'my thoughts are all engaged in a scheme to imitate them on a smaller scale' (*MH* 249).

Rather than understanding this narrative as one of indoctrination, conversion, or contagion, it may be that the hall and its environs even more grandly redirects the travellers' attractions and queers their 'compulsory orientations'. As Ahmed writes in *The Cultural Politics of Emotion* (2014), 'it is through emotions, or how we respond to objects and others, that surfaces or boundaries are made'.[18] Rather than understanding the arrival of the male visitors as a phallic incursion – or the necessary arrival of the phallic law that then defines maternal objects – we might understand the narrative shape as the reshaping of male desire. In this move, of bringing into the novel the ghost of castration only to reorient it completely, Scott answers Julia Kristeva's warnings against (feminist) utopias in 'Women's Time' (1981) for their 'belief in a good and pure substance ... the belief in the omnipotence of an archaic, full, total, englobing mother with no frustration, no separation, with no break-producing symbolism (with no castration, in other words)'.[19] *Millenium Hall*, within its encounters with renegade phalluses (or their castrated, phantom limbs of coxcombs and colonists), questions the need for the phallus at all, and thus the revenant of its lack. It does not, however, naively melt into a fantasy of reunification with the one great mom.

We can more fully see Scott's ecology of queer orientation when the men encounter a crip asylum, which houses disabled people that the women care for but which the men mistake for a zoo of exotic animals. This substitution of one subordinate group for the other intimates a discourse on fetishised objects – and their relation to phallic lack. When Lamont conjectures that the seven-foot-high enclosure made by a fence and evergreen trees must hold a menagerie of foreign animals, Miss Mancel first schools the coxcomb for his colonialist attitudes, admonishing that 'reduc[ing] a fine and noble creature to misery, and confin[ing] him within narrow inclosures whose happiness consisted in unbounded liberty, shocks my nature' (*MH* 71). She resists the fetishising of foreign animals, or really any animal. As Jacques Lacan writes in *The Object Relation* (2021), the fetishist 'finds his object at last' and 'identifies with the object' such that he becomes 'both mother and object'.[20] Pursuing the restoration of his phallus, Lamont fantasises about communing with and thus identifying with exotic and thus dandified animals. Alongside his sartorial peacockery, this creaturely identification masquerades as a grandiose restoration of his 'pertness' and 'vivacity of parts', even though he knows animals to lack a human phallus. The enclosure of such animals speaks to Lamont's need to look to those beings that, like the mother, have no power by their very definition (as animals in an

Enlightenment, humanistic world). The enclosure serves as a redundant sign of the maternal hole – the maternal desire for and simultaneous absence of the phallus, which everyone knows the mother lacks.

Mancel ends her little lecture with the cliched lament for the suffering of animals that we might expect from the discourse of sympathy. Within this speech, however, she also protests the collecting and enclosing of animals at all, as well as the human ability to give (and take away) animal liberty, declaring, 'as it is not in his power to give them any thing so valuable as their liberty, it is, in my opinion, criminal to enslave them in order to procure ourselves a vain amusement' (*MH* 72). Even if men continue to treat animals as commodities with use and exchange value, non-human animals should neither be enclosed nor set free. They cannot, according to Mancel, suitably serve as maternal, fetishistic or phobic objects.

What Lamont has taken for a corral of ready fetish objects is actually a home for the disabled. Mancel relieves Lamont's curiosity by granting him knowledge of what is inside the fenced area with a discursive gesture that reorients the topography and sociality of the hall's environs away from phallic anxieties or even the phobic objects the separation of the disabled might signify:

> It is, then, an asylum for those poor creatures who are rendered miserable from some natural deficiency or redundancy. Here they find refuge from the tyranny of those wretches, who seem to think that being two or three feet taller gives them a right to make them a property, and expose their unhappy forms to the contemptuous curiosity of the unthinking multitude. Procrustes has been branded through all ages with the name of tyrant; and principally, as it appears, from fitting the body of every stranger to a bed which he kept as the necessary standard, cutting off the legs of those whose height exceeded the length of it and stretching on the rack such as fell short of that measure, till they attained the requisite proportion. But is not almost every man a Procrustes? (*MH* 72)

Although the disabled in this asylum might be separated from Millenium Hall proper, Mancel works against the tendency that Lamont might have either to identify with the disabled as figures of castrated humanity or as creaturely objects of revulsion. Mancel's accusation, 'But is not almost every man a Procrustes?' aims at evanishing man's tendency to fixation on castration (maternal or self-) and its remedy in various object substitutions or objectifications. This 'refuge' should not be seen as one predicated on lack (or a prior intellectual/physical 'cutting off') but rather a gathering of like bodies and minds. Their separation from phallic, acquisitive colonialism, Mancel explains, is due to the desire to avoid 'inflicting some of the pains from which they had endeavoured to rescue those poor creatures' (*MH* 73). Like the women of Millenium Hall, with whom the travellers and readers become acquainted just after this passage, the rescued and allegedly 'deformed' members of the asylum become reoriented around and towards each other.

The 'asylum' inhabitants gain pride from the price the women paid for their rescue, bespeaking their financial prowess – as a new-found phallic power. Yet, there is no longer a paternal factotum who ultimately holds such power that the mother desires in this novel. Do the women, then, take over the phallic power of the aristocratic treasury? The sisterhood of the hall encourages their disabled brethren to relinquish such pride in commodification (and thus objectification) for good manners and good works. The women's attempts to reroute both aristocratic treasury and commodity exchange as forms of phallic power become thematised in the four subsequent stories of found women. For it is not merely the exclusion of men from the hall that obviates the phallus, but rather the women/mothers/girls/feminine non-objects that discover a way out, however momentary, of binary, sexed heteronormative relations and that become reoriented, for the duration, towards each other.

Gift Objects, Yonic Things and Bookish Multi-sex

What is the relation, then, between or among the utopian women? Given the women's interplay with the two roving male narrators and the incisive figural commentary on the intrusions of the phallus, it seems unfair to categorise this utopia as naively subscribing to Kristeva's notion of the unifying, archaic maternal force. In that sense, *Millenium Hall* also seems to speak truth to the fantasies of new materialist assemblages, entanglements or moments of transcorporeality as an easy solution to quite fraught forms of relation that must operate within specific gender politics. Neither is the situation so simple as to easily resolve into either some form of celibate sisterhood or a form of proto-lesbian (Sapphic) sexuality within the hall's protected walls. Jean B. Kearn's, Paula Backscheider's and Janet Todd's readings have assumed the women to be celibate; the lack of sex is sometimes seen as freedom from male-imposed sexuality, as Linda Dunne suggests.[21] Yet, as Sally O'Driscoll argues, these relationships are 'characterized not by disappointment [by male suitors] but by an original indifference to men – not even hostility, just a marked lack of sexual interest'.[22] For George Haggerty, the novel's narrative is shaped not by the resistance to or even freedom from male desire but by the love between women.[23] Emma Donoghue's immense archival work on female friendships looks at the 'contradictions' and multiple formations of 'female friendships' in the long eighteenth century, including the 'spinsterism' of *Millenium Hall*.[24] Susan Lanser likewise reads 'all traces of physical relationship to have been erased except ... the physical as a site of suffering' within the novel.[25] The novel's alleged capitalistic conservatism comes, for the many other commentators on its economics, to then reflect upon women's sexuality as one that must lack Sapphic perversion.

Such readings, however, make unnecessary assumptions about (lesbian/Sapphic) sexuality and orientation. The first assumption, based on early eighteenth-century stereotypes, is that sexual experimentation, not only in the form of libertinism but also aristocratic sexual intrigue and Sapphism, frequently goes hand in hand with monarchical/Tory economic conservatism. A second assumption presumes that romantic, erotic or sexual relationality occurs through human, physical touch. Even if that physicality doesn't include penetration, there seem to be unnamed thresholds according to which the friendly or platonic would become romantic or passionate; the romantic, erotic; and the erotic, sexual, between two women. In part, such assumptions are understandable given the thick context furnished by Valerie Traub and others' work on the physically invasive tracts written by medical men that continually isolated the clitoris (and female masturbation) as the pathological, if not etiological site, of Sapphism or tribadism.[26] This model of physicality is born from a heterosexist understanding of reproductive sexuality, and our own notions of sexuality as attached to identity. Kyla Schuller, theorising sex in the nineteenth century, reminds us that sex 'does not necessarily fit the criteria of what we today recognize within the domain of the sexual and may be unrecognizable as such'.[27] Even when we understand sex as a 'mode of relation, a style of affiliation', we too often presume the relation to be between two humans and ignore the function of objects as a part of real, not substitutive, sexuality.[28] Alenka Zupančič argues for the primacy of objects in sexuality, yet even her account understands the object as an often static, coherent, perforated and manipulable item, sexual as it fills the hole of desire. *Millenium Hall* recasts these questions with objects that are not so much objects but things as Bennett describes them, containing a conatus and force within their very matter that is '*loosened off* and on the loose' from human representation or teleological control.[29] These things are promiscuous, making connections between and among women, redirecting them via their own orientations and vibrant attractions.

The relationship of many of the women in the novel, but particularly the relationships between Miss Mancel and Mrs Morgan that receives the longest treatment, revolve around the exchange and mutual use of things. After acquaintance with each other's good manners at their Frenchified boarding school, they begin to give each other knowledge and books:

> and when by a further knowledge of her, she perceived her uncommon share of understanding; her desire to learn; the strength of her application; the quickness of her apprehension; and her great sweetness of temper, she grew extremely fond of her; and as Miss Mancel's melancholy rendered her little inclined to play with those of her own age, she was almost always with Miss Melvyn, who found great pleasure in endeavouring to instruct her; and grew to feel for her the tenderness of a mother, while Miss Mancel began to receive consolation from experiencing an affection quite maternal. (*MH* 87–8)

Miss Melvyn (later Mrs Morgan) and Miss Mancel form a mother–child attachment through, on the one hand, Miss Mancel's desire to learn and, on the other, Miss Melvyn's desire to instruct her. If Melvyn temporarily substitutes for Mancel's mother, she, too, has already had the experience of living with a stepmother. The new Lady Melvyn had developed a rivalry with her stepdaughter, attempting to dominate Miss Melvyn by establishing a greater feminine lack, wielded as a power to lure phallic attention. However, this second maternal relationship between Miss Melvyn and Miss Mancel models an intellectual bonding between them that occurs not through creating greater lack or need but through altering the nature of relationality. Such education, particularly of the bluestocking sort, has been typically understood as a feminine grasping for phallic power, which often satirises the learners as masculine women. To understand the relationship this way, however, is to repeat the phallic ideology that the hall has already redirected at the novel's start. That frame encourages readers to twist away from a view of learning as symbolic of only masculine, static power.

The women's relationship, born through the exchange of knowledge, or a mutual process of education, transforms twice in the short course of this narrative. First, Mancel gives Melvyn a library – that is, a very different kind of object from the phallic or fetish object we might assume it to be. The library as a concrete, printed archive might offer a phallic silo of intellectual treasures – including accounts of orientalised, medical, and romantic fetishes of all sorts that could substitute for masculine power, cultural capital, or property. Yet, the nature of these objects (as property or as even discrete possessions) changes through this exchange. Mancel's guardian, ominously named Mr Hintman, leverages his ward's affection, and eventually her virginity, via various gifts to her and those that show her 'any particular civility' (*MH* 90). As Julie McGonegal writes, this gift exchange reveals the violent underpinning of generosity that obliges the recipient to reciprocate with symbolic capital.[30] Yet, there is also something of a female inheritance, since Hintman's books are a library left to him by his sister, and Mancel eventually donates them as a 'present' to the hall's gentlewomen (*MH* 196). This shared library garners both a 'considerable increase of happiness', and Mancel's uncommon intellectual opening: her 'greatest improvement was from reading with Miss Melvyn', such that 'her understanding opened to a surprising degree' (*MH* 91). This intellectual narrative of development – the inheritance of books, joint seminar reading, the education of a young woman's mind – is characterised by a surprising enlargement and opening. It is not merely that Miss Mancel and Miss Melvyn become educated or educate one another (despite the elder Melvyn originally knowing more than her young companion). Rather, the women's books, reading, and understanding constitute a form of intimacy and physical/ metaphysical touching that opens them both. Instead of widening any phallic holes of lost mothers, fathers or longed-for lovers, the bookish present, like its voluminous pages, opens a *euporia* of experiences, ideas and intimacies. The book becomes a yonic thing – generative, affecting, additive and recombinant. Books become mutually dexterous erotic toys that lay bare multiple scenes where shared acts of reading touch and entangle both parties at once, but not with exact similitude.

We can see the results of this psychic-figural turn in the narrative when, shortly after this description of the mutual *jouissance* of reading, Miss Mancel decides she'd like to 'treat her friend with masters for music and drawing' (*MH* 92). Whether we want to see such triangulation as a feminine version of Eve Kosofsky Sedgwick's homoerotic love triangle, where two women now become simultaneously excited and stimulated by a master,[31] what the text emphasises is the change in affect and discourse revolving around the thingly nature of knowledge:

> she ran to Miss Melvyn with some of the impatience in her countenance, though she endeavoured to conceal it, with which her heart was filled, and tried every tender caress, every fond and humble petition, to obtain a promise from that young lady, that she would grant her a request she had to make. She hung round her neck, and endeavoured to prevail by a thousand engaging infantine arts; and when she found they would not succeed, she knelt down before her, and with all the grace and importunity of the most amiable suppliant, tried to win her to compliance. (*MH* 92)

The idea of treating her companion to lessons creates the most physical intimacy of the narrative, and maybe the entire novel. The caressing, hanging around the neck and especially the kneeling before Melyvn veers towards a proposal scene. Rather than the offer of a patronymic, though, Miss Mancel offers an additional 'opening' to touch knowledge together.

Even more radical within this chain of exchanges is Miss Melvyn's thinking on whether she should accept such a gift from her younger friend. She muses,

> Had Louisa been of the same age with herself, she would have felt a kind of property in all she possessed; friendship, the tenure by which she held it; for where hearts are strictly united, she had no notion of any distinction in things of less importance, the adventitious goods of fortune. The boundaries and barriers raised by those two watchful and suspicious enemies, Meum and Tuum, were in her opinion broke down by true friendship; and all property laid in one undistinguished common. (*MH* 92–3)

For Melvyn, boundaries of 'Meum and Tuum' collapse through 'true friendship', and all property, including the affective, is held in common. These things are played with in a conversation of giving and receiving that heightens what Silvan Tompkins calls affective and thingly density – its intensity and duration.[32] Such commoned things include not only the books and lessons, dowries and inheritances, but also the minds and perhaps bodies of this dyad and, eventually, those of other women who live within the hall. Miss Melvyn at this point in the story asserts that age difference inserts a power differential that makes such an 'undistinguished common' impossible. Yet, Mancel does convince her by a similar but differential commoning of affect: 'I should not envy you the joy of giving, because I as receiver should not have the less share of that satisfaction, since by reflecting on yours I must partake of it, and so encrease my own' (*MH* 93). The recipient shares the joy in the giving, partaking in its increase, such that if giving and taking do not themselves come in common, they amplify and excite one another in a feedback loop of affective sharing. What it means to touch and teach another's bodymind is to teach and amplify one's own. The nature of property – objects and symbolic capital that one might have or lack – becomes reoriented through the commoning of things, affects and the bodies that play with them.

This language of female friendship that obviates boundaries can be found in poetry both earlier and later than this novel. Katherine Phillips's poems, which address the members of her Society of Friendship, repeatedly adapt metaphysical conceits to figure the intermixture of souls or beings. In 'Friendship's Mystery, To My Dearest Lucasia', she writes,

> Here Mixture is Addition grown;
> We both diffuse, and both ingross:
> And we whose Minds are so much one
> Never, yet ever, are alone …[33]

Minds, Hearts and Souls are often already mixed or intermixed so as to become 'one'. The hint of financial language ('both ingross') suggests a large scale or quantity that is not available for individual or retail sale. In Scott's novel, this 'undistinguished common' takes on the semblance of land prior to enclosure – or ontologically unavailable to enclosure, sale or private agriculture. The ontology of this materiality – 'both diffuse, and both ingross' – suggests both dispersal and mutual impregnation that deconstruct capitalistic exchange or phallic penetration with an infusion that cannot be bounded by property, body or asynchrony.

The boundaryless aspect of such post-property bodies likewise features in Percy Bysshe Shelley's imagining of non-penetrative, non-phallic, queer sexuality in *Prometheus Unbound* (1820)'s dream sequence involving Prometheus, Panthea and Ione:

> His presence flow and mingle through my blood
> Till it became his life, and his grew mine,
> And I as thus absorbed, until it passed,
> And like the vapors when the sun sinks down,
> Gathering again in drops upon the pines,
> And tremulous as they, in the deep night
> My being was condensed ...[34]

Panthea later goes on to give Ione a hot kiss that arguably transfers such material-affective intermingling.[35] As Shelley imagines such dreamy intermixture of materialities as a series of dynamic processes ('flow and mingle', 'grew', 'absorbed', 'passed', 'gathering again', 'condensed'), he emphasises the trespass – and really disregard of – bodily boundaries. In both these examples, however, the dreamy space of the metaphysical or perhaps causeless desire instigates these intermixtures and post-body inter-trembling. In Scott's first narrative of female friendship, however, books and lessons magnetise the space of the boarding school, rerouting and establishing the circuits of desire, which, in turn, overwrite their status as property or capital. They put and are put into motion as non-phallic intermingling of being and mutual frisson, however asymmetric.

While Mancel's language of giver and recipient invokes the inequities of debt, obligation and gift exchange, her formulation resembles that of theorist Karen Barad, who thinks of reciprocity not as necessarily an exchange of gift for obligation but rather as a reciprocal partaking, touching and increasing of the other in oneself. As Barad writes in her essay on touching, 'All touching entails an infinite alterity, so that touching the Other is touching all Others, including the "self", and touching the "self" entails touching the strangers within'.[36] For Barad, this Levinasian absorption offers a plenitude of space-times and shared beings (what she calls intra-active phenomena): 'every finite being is always already threaded through with an infinite alterity diffracted through being and time'.[37] Books, in particular, might be said to instigate or house such infinite spaces, beings and times; as yonic things of queer intimacy, they generate the mingling of Miss Mancel and Melvyn's intellectual, symbolic and bodily property (including, I would argue, their own bodies). This commoning, moreover, opens other space-time-beings as the novel subsequently diffracts the multiple stories of Lady Mary Jones, Mrs Selvyn, and Mrs Trentham, and even Scott's sequel, *The History of Sir George Ellison*. This archive of stories creates a multi-temporal and multi-dimensional axis engendered by Miss Mancel and Miss Melvyn's bookish queer pleasures.

Multi-dimensional Narratives, Multi-layered Genius Sex

The second part of the *Description of Millenium Hall* stacks several narratives of other founding members of this 'female Arcadia'. 'The History of Miss Mancel and Mrs. Morgan' briefly pauses while the women have dinner, tell their visitors the 'rules' of Millenium Hall, and sleep. The next morning their history resumes with Mrs Morgan's marriage and what ensues is a somewhat separate story. Then, we listen to the stories of Lady Mary Jones, Mrs Selvyn and Mrs Trentham. These 'origin stories' of the founders give the hall not one but several backstories, many occurring synchronically, although they are told diachronically. Such a tension between the synchronic and diachronic becomes apparent when the characters meet each other and then reappear in multiple narratives. For example, Mrs Selvyn counsels Mary Jones to resist the seductions of Lord Robert St George, who later, after his failures with Lady Mary, attempts a seduction of Miss Selvyn, in her subsequent narrative. This six-degrees-of-separation aspect of the novel's larger plot evidences the incestuous nature of the London-based aristocratic class. Yet, it is the intense endogamy of women's relations that further queers the temporal dimension of these four parallel-yet-looping narratives.

The use of a frame story to tell a set of tales of multiple characters has a whiff of Geoffrey Chaucer's *The Canterbury Tales* (c. 1400) or Giovanni Boccaccio's *The Decameron* (c. 1353). However, in this collection, a temporal simultaneity of the stories (as they occur) resounds with the figure of the hall as a space of lyrical pause within a pastoral refuge. The younger women that the founders adopt or aid may choose to move forward on a path of chrononormativity, advancing from adolescence to an adulthood of marriage and child-bearing. Yet, the space of the hall pointedly resists the necessity of linear biopolitical reproduction and offers a temporal space of contingent non-chrononormativity.[38] Located in the lyrical genre of a *Description*, not *Travels*, readers begin by dwelling in a queer horizon of temporal contingency, which only later moves repetitively backwards and forwards in time to offer multiple queer narratives of chrononormative resistance. Such stacked narratives are not infrequent in the works of Romantic women writers, such as the ending of Mary Wollstonecraft's *Maria*, with its successive stories of Darnford, Maria and Jemima, which do not move towards any teleology but end in multiple possible endings yet-to-be-written. As I have written elsewhere, the iterative acts of reading, writing and retelling in that novel offer a feminine *jouissance*.[39] That this *jouissance* revolves around notes written in shared books and the exchange of stories not only scrambles normative time, but also suggests that the book's materiality – as well as the storytelling voice – has something to do with queer time and, therefore, queer orientation.

Work by theorists such as Elizabeth Freeman and José Esteban Muñoz as well as Romanticists Emily Rohrbach and David Sigler has accustomed us to think of temporal play when looking at the narratives of women and queer subjects.[40] Scott's novel juxtaposes temporal dimensionality with the spatial extension of the hall and its pastoral spaces, as a vaginal space that takes up space, furnishing a multi-dimensionality of synchronic tales, each with its own varied diachronies. Multiple reorientations occur in space (bodies enclosed, asylumed, commoned) and in time (backwards and forwards along a timeline that has already paused), as well as in psychic, social, historical, political, sexual and financial dimensions. To attempt to rematerialise this multi-dimensionality, especially its multi-dimensional sex, I want to return to the allegedly lost maternal object within these four, layered narratives composing the last half of the novel. For the reiterative returns of the maternal figure – whether through the reappearance of an allegedly lost mother, through the doubled mother of the aunt or grandmother, and finally through the reconnoitre of the founders with each other – adumbrate this multi-dimensional reorientation of a phallic unidirectional, one-dimensional plot.

Let me quickly rehearse the novel's last four narratives. (1) After Miss Melvyn marries (and becomes Mrs Morgan) and after Sir Charles refuses to let his wife have any 'intimates' other than himself, Miss Mancel hires herself as a companion for Lady Lambton, who becomes a guardian of a sort until her son Sir Edward and Mancel fall in love. Barred from marriage by her status and poverty, and then by Sir Edward's death at war, Mancel becomes a companion to Mrs Thornby, who is in fact Mancel's mother! Thornby eventually dies and leaves

Mancel her fortune, and Mancel goes to help Morgan care for her sick husband, and the two are reunited, finally. (Sir Charles's dying body ostensibly becomes the object that gives the women new life.) (2) In the next (and simpler) narrative, Lady Mary Jones is adopted by her wealthy but overly lively and frivolous aunt, Lady Sheerness. Thanks to a carriage accident, she escapes elopement with Mr Lenman, whom she finds out to have been previously married, then has a second escape from seduction by St George (thanks to Mrs Selvyn's counsels). After Sheerness passes on, Lady Mary is adopted by Lady Brompton, the widow of her half-brother, and given both an annual livelihood and, eventually, a bequest/inheritance. (3) Mrs Selvyn's 'father', a poor tutor, moves his ward into the neighbourhood of Lady Emilia Reynolds, who adopts her upon his death. Eventually, on her own deathbed, she admits to being Selvyn's mother (having given birth to her outside wedlock)! (4) Finally, Mrs Trentham is adopted by her grandmother, Mrs Allworth. She develops a platonic relationship with her first cousin, and they are set to marry when he falls in love with a frivolous woman, realises his error, and falls passionately in love with Miss Allworth (otherwise known as Trentham), only to be rebuffed.

The women's indifference eventually stymies all roads to heteronormativity; all avenues to independence are provided by the return of the mother (that is, Mrs Thornby and Lady Emilia Reynolds) or through adoption by an aunt, a half sister-in-law or a grandmother (that is, Lady Brompton and Mrs Allworth). These maternal inheritances, emotional and financial, offer a rewriting of mid-eighteenth-century sociability as largely without need of, which is to say without the lack of, male financial or familial prowess. Within the symbolic chain, moreover, the multiplicity of founding 'mothers' doubles (and here more than triples) the 'imaginary exchanges'. As Lacan points out, such repetition of the 'maternal ideal is precisely what offers a certain type of way out and positioning in the relation between the sexes'.[41] The grounding of the relationship between the sexes becomes unmoored through this symbolic play. Here, we have a form of relation that reconstitutes itself by relation to many mothers, themselves with multiplying relations to power, which are oriented towards and around each other.

Mothers and daughters (as well as intimates) find each other through the love of books, through similar attitudes, and through the 'response-ability', where an '"us" … is constituted as responsible for the other, as the other'.[42] This maternal communing – both the Phillipsian additive intermixture of being and the commoning or ingrossing of resources – more than 'displaces the radical relation to a certain essential alterity'.[43] Rather than an alterity consistently bound to and by lack, women in these narratives, in the 'luckiness of the overturn', turn away from becoming 'an imaginary object of the other'.[44] Instead, they become an other touching others, anticipating not fearful lack but the admixture of mutual stories, knowledge and vibrant things.

These recursions likewise recompose the plot of sex as non-phallic touching. Each return of the mother materialises a woman with books and a reading practice, and her physical and mental stimulation revolve around book-generated 'genius', that natural aptitude for a queer inclination. Interestingly, this centrality of the maternal does not go the route of Kristeva's semiotic, in finding voices that echo the primordial wombish 'commoning' of mother and child within the maternal body.[45] Judith's Butler's account of the lesbian phallus, as plastic, iterable, variable comes closer to the bookish genius and the genius for books as something not necessarily so flexible as generative – that is, able to take sexuality to multiple dimensions, not all of them manifested through bodily contact.[46]

The word 'genius' recurs in these narratives, and it returns all these women to a multi-dimensional symbolic slippage held open by the enjambed pages and sprawled bindings of books. As Andrew Elfenbein argues in his seminal work *Romantic Genius* (1999), 'a woman labeled a female genius was at risk of being perceived not only as masculine but also as a sapphist'.[47] The first hint of the rhetoric of the Sapphic genius arrives in Mary Jones's narrative, where Mrs Maynard (the narrator) notes that the founders added those women to their number who displayed an 'uncommon genius' (*MH* 160). Readers may retroactively reflect on Mancel and Morgan's own commoned genius, their bodies, books and learning a similarly shared inclination. Later in the narrative we hear that the ladies 'watch their geniuses with great care' (*MH* 197). Upon meeting her second adopter, Lady Mary Jones notes, 'She had often heard Lady Brumpton ridiculed under the appellation of a genius, and a learned lady' (*MH* 191). Jones gets tutored by Brumpton, but not before her half-sister-in-law offers her a settlement of a hundred pounds a year in her dressing room, such that the redistribution of wealth seems metonymically connected to the bookish lessons and mutual reading Jones likewise receives at the Lady's hands. Brumpton marries her wealth and mental proclivities to her husband's half-sister. When Jones joins her Lady's friends, she expects to come upon a 'superior race of beings' and, indeed, at first feels 'as if they had talked another language' (*MH* 190, 192). Mrs Selyvn, thanks to her tutor-guardian, 'was bred a philosopher from the cradle', and her 'tenderness' with her unbeknownst mother Lady Emilia Reynolds is made through reading: 'They were both extremely fond of reading, and in this way they spent most of their time' (*MH* 200, 205). Mrs Trentham, too, 'was well instructed in the ancient and modern philosophy, and in almost every branch of learning' (*MH* 227). While these attributes certainly characterise the women as bluestockings, the absence of the Sapphic label is not particularly unusual either, since, as Elfenbein argues, for women to 'associate themselves with the cultural category of sapphism … meant taking on its bad associations'.[48]

The absence of passion might likewise seem to undermine a queer reading, yet the last story of the Allworth cousins seems to suggest otherwise – that wild passion, in the obsessive and narcissistic sense that it was understood mid-century, may also intimate a heteronormative relation. When the married Allworth finally falls violently in love with Harriot (Trentham), she resists his adulterous advances, undertakes a reconciliation between husband and wife, then takes joy in educating their daughter, ultimately becoming a surrogate mother herself. In its scepticism of temporary passion, *Millenium Hall* anticipates Wollstonecraft's critique of fleeting passion and recommendation of something more companionate; but this earlier novel goes further in sketching out a new form of queer relationship – platonic, romantic or sexual – built through mutual reading, learning and being. The lack of passion, through this alternative, might therefore be diagnosed as a critique of heteronormativity's propensity for violent, penetrative affect. The cycle of lack-excess speaks to a bodily passion based upon the alternation of tumescence and flaccidity arising from phallic models – and perhaps the lusted-after surplus values and credit of developing capitalism and, concomitantly, the novel genre itself.

The dyads end up together with 'an intimacy so desirable' that neither 'appeared to want any conversation than' the other, and whom neither 'loved with a tenderness so justly due to her merit' (*MH* 203, 205). This kind of queerness may be founded, at its core, on queer platonics that arise from the ability to read, storify and fantasise together. Erotics are created through literal mutual 'exercise', but likewise through the sensual excitements of reading and conversing that offer the possibility for multiple stories, space-times, new imaginaries and things of resonant affection. The women's reading – as a processual act of playing with, conversing about, and iteratively contemplating both pages and the fantasies/ideas they produce – cues the material-symbolic dimensions of the novel's reorientation. These are processes of mental, physical and metaphysical touching. Mutual, intense female reading becomes entangled with a durable relationality among women and their play things, which have material, imaginary, and ever-shifting symbolic dimensions. These later stories therefore reiterate the bookish commoning of Mancel and Melvyn by bringing back the yonic book as itself a semi-imaginary thing that offers a multi-dimensional sexual experience different from phallic sexuality or even phallic-directed platonic relationship. This genius for play with the toys of books does not simply bind lesbianism to intellectualism but rather connotes reading as a process of queer reorienting of many possible sorts of touching.

Notes

1. I am compiling here some accounts of subject-object relations starting with Freud's discussion of the fort-da game in *Beyond the Pleasure Principle*, Donald Winnicott's notion of the transitional object, and Frantz Fanon's account of the phobic object in *Black Skin, White Masks*. I could have likewise included Julia Kristeva's maternal abject, as the thing that occupies the liminal, horrifying space between womb and world, among others.
2. Donald Winnicott, *Collected Papers: Through Pediatrics to Psycho-Analysis* (London: Tavistock Publications, 1958). For discussions of new materialist primordial materiality see Diana Coole and Samantha Frost, eds., *New Materialisms: Ontology, Agency, and Politics* (Durham, NC: Duke University Press, 2010); for a critique of the primordial 'goo' of flattened materiality, see, for example, Graham Harman, 'Agential and Speculative Realism: Remarks on Barad's Ontology', *rhizomes* 30 (2016), https://doi.org/10.20415/rhiz/030.e10.
3. John Wilmot, Earl of Rochester, 'Signior Dildo', in *The Poems of John Wilmot, Earl of Rochester*, ed. Keith Walker (London: Oxford University Press, 1984), 186.
4. 'The Sappho-An, c.1735 or 1749', in *Homosexuality in Eighteenth-Century England: A Sourcebook*, ed. Rictor Norton, 26 August 2017, http://www.rictornorton.co.uk/eighteen/sapphoan.htm.
5. See Paul B. Preciado, *Countersexual Manifesto*, trans. Kevin Gerry Dunn (New York: Columbia University Press, 2018) and Thomas Laqueur, *The Making of Sex* (Cambridge, MA: Harvard University Press, 1992).
6. See Daniel Defoe, *Moll Flanders* (New York: Norton, 2003) and Charlotte Charke, *A Narrative of the life of Mrs. Charlotte Charke*, ed. Robert Rehder (Burlington, VT: Pickering & Chatto, 1999).
7. Michel Foucault, *The History of Sexuality, Vol. 1: An Introduction*, trans. Robert Hurley (New York: Vintage, 1990).
8. Sara Ahmed, *Queer Phenomenology: Orientations, Objects, Others* (Durham, NC: Duke University Press, 2006).
9. Jane Bennett, *Vibrant Matter: A Political Ecology of Things* (Durham, NC: Duke University Press, 2009). I use yonic here and throughout the essay to evince a spatial orientation toward something that is not phallic but also not necessarily defined against the phallic, as 'non-phallic' would be. This quest for alternative metaphoric forms is part and parcel of the feminist, queer, and arguably Lacanian symbolic, and it is a project of Scott's novel as well.

10. I use the word '*euporia*' to denote a material richness, which Giorgio Agamben reads through Deleuze as a political and material alternative to deconstructionist and post-structuralist understandings of abundant (textual) materiality. See Leland Deladwrantaye, 'Agamben's Potential', *diacritics* 30.2 (2000): 7–9.
11. All references will be to this edition, Sarah Scott, *Millenium Hall*, ed. Gary Kelly (Orchard Park, NY: Broadview, 1995). Further references to this text given parenthetically, with *MH*.
12. Ahmed, *Queer*, 28.
13. Ibid., 47.
14. Ibid., 60.
15. Ibid., 84.
16. Heidi Laudien, 'Reading Desire in the Pastorals of Elizabeth Singer Rowe', *Women's Writing* 19, no. 4 (November 2012): 602–21. For other discussions of the lesbian pastoral see Elizabeth V. Young, 'Aphra Behn, Gender, and Pastoral', *Studies in English Literature, 1500–1900* 33, no. 3 (Summer 1993): 523–43; Valerie Traub '"Friendship so Curst": Amor Impossibilis, the Homoerotic Lament, and the Nature of Lesbian Desire', in *Lesbian Dames: Sapphism in the Long Eighteenth Century*, ed. Caroline Gonda and John C. Beynon (London: Routledge, 2016): 605; and Harriette Andreadis, *Sappho in Early Modern England: Female Same-Sex Literary Erotics, 1550–1714* (Chicago: University of Chicago Press, 2001).
17. Aphra Behn, 'To the Fair Clarinda', in *Poems Between Women: Four Centuries of Love, Romantic Friendship, and Desire*, ed. Emma Donoghue (New York: Columbia University Press, 1999): 4–5, lines 14–17.
18. Sara Ahmed, *The Cultural Politics of Emotion*, 2nd ed. (London: Routledge, 2014): 10.
19. See Julia Kristeva, 'Women's Time', *Signs* 7, no. 1 (Autumn 1981): 29.
20. Jacques Lacan, *The Object Relation: The Seminar of Jacques Lacan, Book IV* (New York: Polity, 2021): 77. My many, many thanks to Capricornian editor David Sigler for Zooming through the Foucault-Kristeva-Lacan crux of object-related sexuality with me and for generously sending me excerpts from this book to help with this essay.
21. See Jean B. Kern, 'The Old Maid, or "to grow old, and be poor, and laughed at"', in *Fetter'd or Free? British Women Novelists, 1670–1815*, ed. Mary Anne Schofield and Cecelia Macheski (Athens: Ohio University Press, 1986), 201–15; Linda Dunne, 'Mothers and Monsters in Sarah Robinson Scott's *Millenium Hall*', in *Utopian and Science Fiction by Women: Worlds of Difference*, ed. Jane L. Donawerth and Carol A. Kolmerten (Syracuse: Syracuse University Press, 1994), 54–72; Paula Backscheider, '"I Died for Love": Esteem in Eighteenth-Century Novels by Women', in *Fetter'd or Free? British Women Novelists, 1670–1815*, 152–68; and Janet Todd, *The Sign of Angelika: Women, Writing, and Fiction, 1660–1800* (New York: Columbia University Press, 1989).
22. Sally O'Driscoll, 'Lesbian Criticism and Feminist Criticism: Readings of "Millenium Hall"', *Tulsa Studies in Women's Literature* 22, no. 1 (Spring 2003): 69.
23. George Haggerty, '"Romantic Friendship" and Patriarchal Narrative in Sarah Scott's *Millenium Hall*', *Genders* 13 (Spring 1992): 108–22.

24. Emma Donoghue, *Passions Between Women: British Lesbian Culture, 1668–1801* (London: Scarlet Press, 1993).
25. Susan Lanser, *The Sexuality of History: Modernity and the Sapphic, 1565–1830* (Chicago: University of Chicago Press, 2014), 139.
26. Valerie Traub, 'The Psychomorphology of the Clitoris', *Gay and Lesbian Quarterly* 2 (1995): 81–113.
27. See Kyla Schuller, *The Biopolitics of Feeling* (Chapel Hill: Duke University Press, 2018), 29.
28. Peter Coviello, *Tomorrow's Parties: Sex and the Untimely in Nineteenth-Century America* (New York: New York University Press, 2013), 22. Quoted in Schuller, 29.
29. Bennett, 3. Emphasis in the original.
30. Julie McGonegal, 'The Tyranny of Gift Giving: The Politics of Generosity in Sarah Scott's *Millenium Hall* and *Sir George Ellison*', *Eighteenth-Century Fiction* 19, no. 3 (Spring 2007): 291–306.
31. While Sedgwick clearly argues that erotic triangles cannot occur among two women and a man due to the continuity between female friendships and lesbianism as well as the male homophobic, violent force that necessitates a female third, I am influenced by Kate Turner's work in progress, presented at the International Conference for Romanticism 2021. She attempts to establish a long history of female Gothic triangles that has been erased by misunderstandings of platonic female friendship, female-female violence, and the dominance of the scopophilic male narrator. See Eve Kosofsky Sedgwick, *Between Men: English Literature and Male Homosocial Desire* (New York: Columbia University Press, 1985) and Kate Turner, 'Mirrors and Queer Doubling: Paired Women, Queer Rivals, and the Female Gaze' (Honours thesis, Mount Holyoke College, 2021).
32. Eve Kosofsky Sedgwick and Adam Frank, *Shame and Its Sisters: A Silvan Tompkins Reader* (Chapel Hill: Duke University Press, 1995).
33. Katherine Philips, *Katherine Philips (1631/2–1664) Printed Poems 1667: Printed Writings 1641–1700: Series II, Part Three*, ed. Paula Loscocco (London: Routledge, 2017): 43–4, lines 12–16.
34. Percy Bysshe Shelley, *Shelley's Poetry and Prose*, 2nd ed., ed. Donald H. Reiman and Neil Fraistat (New York: Norton, 2002), lines II.i.80–6.
35. Shelley, *Shelley's*, ll.
36. Karen Barad, 'On Touching – The Inhuman That Therefore I Am', *differences* 23, no. 5 (2012): 215.
37. Ibid., 215.
38. For more on chrononormativity see Elizabeth Freeman, *Time Binds: Queer Temporalities, Queer Histories* (Durham, NC: Duke University Press, 2010).
39. Kate Singer, '"I feel it coming in the air tonight": Mephitical Vapors, Pestiferous Plagues, and the Psychosis of Materiality in Wollstonecraft', in *Romantic Psychosis*, ed. Elizabeth Fay, *Romantic Circles Praxis* 2022.
40. José Muñoz, *Cruising Utopia: The Then and There of Queer Futurity* (New York: New York University Press, 2009), Emily Rohrbach, *Modernity's Mist: British Romanticism and the Poetics of Anticipation* (New York: Fordham University Press, 2015), David Sigler, *Fracture Feminism: The Politics of Impossible Time in British Romanticism* (Albany: SUNY Press, 2021).

41. Lacan, *Object*, 408.
42. Barad, 'Touching', 215.
43. Lacan, *Object*, 423.
44. Ibid., 178, 476.
45. Julia Kristeva, *Desire in Language: A Semiotic Approach to Literature and Art* (New York: Columbia University Press, 1980).
46. Judith Butler, *Bodies That Matter* (New York: Routledge, 1993), 89.
47. Andrew Elfenbein, *Romantic Genius: The Prehistory of a Homosexual Role* (New York: Columbia University Press, 1999), 92.
48. Ibid., 94.

Chapter 4

The Necrophilia of Wollstonecraft's 'The Cave of Fancy'

David Sigler

It has been easier to read Mary Wollstonecraft as a champion of sexual liberation and women's rights than as a promoter of sexual transgression. Seldom does necrophilia, for instance, come up in discussions of her writing. A reminder might therefore be warranted that 'The Cave of Fancy', an unfinished short story of hers, commends the wisdom of a man who painstakingly covets corpses on a desolate beach, to the point of fetishisation. The aptly named Sagestus is a hermit, living, as hermits do, cordoned off from the world; he emerges from his cave occasionally to inspect, with smug satisfaction, the corpses of the rich washed ashore. One day, he meets the sole survivor of a shipwreck, a young girl weeping for her dead family. He dubs her, equally aptly, Sagesta, and brings her to the eponymous cave for tutelage in the ethic of sensibility; together they philosophise about the sexual pleasures that can be derived from the dead. Sagestus, like a nonagenarian version of Dolmancé from the Marquis de Sade's *Philosophy in the Bedroom* (1795), presents necrophilia as something supremely exquisite; Sagesta, more knowing than Sade's Eugénie, explains that loving a dead person may open new and more expansive modes of being, enabling one to explore fantasies of immortality. Such a plot makes it possible to claim Wollstonecraft as an icon of sexual transgression, in addition to her well-earned status as a feminist icon. This sexually transgressive Wollstonecraft is the one who spent the 1780s in league with a notorious pornographer;[1] whose lifelong defiance of sexual norms would destroy her reputation posthumously;[2] and whose *magnum opus* guardedly looks to *jouissance* rather than love as a catalyst for the feminist cause.[3]

Wollstonecraft wrote the story in 1787, leaving it unfinished. She planned it as a fictional accompaniment to *Thoughts on the Education of Daughters* (1787), which she was writing concurrently. Yet, the story was not published until 1798 in her *Posthumous Works*, edited by her widower William Godwin.[4] The delay is fitting since the story relentlessly explores both the eroticisation of the dead and the possibility of writing, speaking and thinking after one's death. It is a curiously erotic story, with an unexpected eagerness to cling to death and an investment in fetishising corpses. Its paraphilia could, perhaps, be attributable to Sagestus and Sagesta rather than to Wollstonecraft; that is, it could be ironic. But we could just as easily interpret the fantasy as an aspect of Wollstonecraft's radicalism in the context of 1780s and -90s France. In that context, a taste for sexual perversion, and even libertinage, was understood to signal one's zeal for the era's 'new political upheavals', as Élisabeth Roudinesco explains in her history of perversion. Wollstonecraft was closely affiliated with these upheavals as their advocate and contemporary-future historian.[5]

Can an attachment to death be a search for vitality, for visibility? As Sagesta explains to her mentor, 'My passion [for my dead lover] seemed a pledge of immortality; I did not wish to hide it from the all-searching eye of heaven ... [T]hough darkness might reign during the night of life, joy would come when I awoke to life everlasting' ('CF' 205). From her point of view, eroticism involves bringing secret, transgressive sex acts into the field of public recognition to ensure that what is supposed to be an 'all-searching eye' really is so. She yearns, then, to fill in the lack in the Other. She pursues such a 'passion' not as a matter of piety, religious devotion nor fidelity to either her master or her now-dead lovers, but specifically for its exquisite *jouissance*: such love makes possible a 'voluptuous sorrow [which] was superior to every gratification of sense' ('CF' 205).

As Julie Peakman notes, 'while attitudes towards sodomy, homosexuality, lesbianism, sadomasochism and bestiality have changed [over the centuries], necrophilia stands out as being continually condemned as a "perversity"' – and specifically, one that connects with the history of consent and women's bodies in complex ways.[6] It is, in a way, the quintessentially perverse form of desire. Meanwhile, Wollstonecraft may be considered, in a way, the Romantic period's quintessential woman writer (as such). What this combination means, I think, is an open question and one that I would like to hold open to the extent possible. After all, to consider the place of such enjoyment within Wollstonecraft's oeuvre is to reconsider the meaning of that oeuvre. Wollstonecraft is known as a thinker for whom 'reason is the basis for morality' and who tends to embrace a Kantian stance towards moral questions.[7] To read the 'The Cave of Fancy' in terms of its ardent necrophilia requires us to reinterpret that Kantian vision of morality in the mode of Lacan's 'Kant with Sade', such that we can see unlimited sexual gratification as part of Wollstonecraft's commitment to reason, Enlightenment and the literary culture of sensibility – that is, as one of the 'rights of woman'. Yet, I find such an interpretation hard to sustain, as the perversion in the story tends to unsettle, rather than to clarify, the meaning of the text and muddy the substance of its author's mighty cultural intervention.

Caves within Caves

In typical Wollstonecraftian fashion, the story is told through elaborate narrative frames. In the outermost frame, Sagestus finds the girl among the shipwrecked dead. He takes her to the Cave of Fancy, intending to impart moral lessons. The tables turn, though, when Sagesta begins to tell Sagestus the sad story of her upbringing, only to be interrupted by a female 'spirit', which, too, begins to relate its own sad story of an oppressive childhood and marriage ('CF' 199). There is some ambiguity here as to the identity of the spirit, and it is even slightly implied, given the hints of Sagesta's own death in the cave, that the spirit may be her own emanation – an odd scenario given her apparent young age and tales of marriage. The story abruptly ends just as a fourth inset frame narrative begins, in which the spirit remembers soliciting the 'simple tale' of 'a girl, who stood weeping on the common', for reasons that are never explained ('CF' 205). Given the lack of additional details, it is certainly tempting to see the weeping girl as Sagesta's and Wollstonecraft's double, a madwoman-on-the-common. Just as Sagesta has been brought to the cave, this girl has been entombed within the layers of narration that render her unknowable. The site of her lamentations makes her private grief a matter of public interest; in this way, she also becomes a figure for 'the rights of woman' generally. She may seem to be the navel of Wollstonecraft's dream, an innermost chamber of 'The Cave of Fancy' that the reader is given no opportunity to spelunk. Yet, I would caution against such a reading since the outermost layer of the story, with its perverse and inappropriate accumulation of details, presents the more disquieting and pressing aporia, and its mystery arises out of excessive narrative detail rather than too little.

In the outer frame, the two main settings, the beach and the cave, represent death in different degrees: the beach is the scene of death construed chaotically, and the cave represents chaos adapted into a form of living death in which death can be raised to the level of a categorical imperative. Hence, the alternative to death, the outermost layer of the story suggests, is not life, but a better, more fully inhabited death. With its privileged space of the eponymous cave, the frame story showcases the space between these two deaths. The cave permits the sagely duo to live in death and speculate from within the space of death, when they would otherwise have been walking around on the common, weeping and learning. In an inversion of Plato's parable of the cave, one must go ever further into the Cave of Fancy, further into necrophiliac perversions, to arrive at true knowledge. Likewise, the reader must go ever further into 'The Cave of Fancy' and its nested layers of narration to gain a broader vantage on history and contemporary affairs. As I suggested in the introduction to this volume, the literature of sexual transgression transgresses not by going beyond epistemological limits, but by burrowing relentlessly into them. In this way, the story's narrative structure allegorises literature itself.

Read with the outermost frame foremost in mind, 'The Cave of Fancy' is not at all a story about making women's private grief public, but rather one about learning to follow the path of one's desire, even at the expense of living within human society. As the scene of narration, the Cave of Fancy is a severely private space, accessible only through proper training, and located as far as possible from the 'common'. In this, Wollstonecraft seems to prefigure Georges Bataille's suggestion that 'eroticism is a solitary activity, ... it cannot be public'.[8] To the extent that this story develops a politics, which frankly any reader would expect given its author, it does so only by staging repeated acts of withdrawal and disengagement from the public. It iterates a politics of 'undeadness', to borrow a term from Eric L. Santner, according to which 'a strange state of immortality' emerges as the ghostly excess of meaningful public life to produce its own *jouissance*.[9] Such a form of life does not involve rising above one's life conditions; it consists of nestling deeply enough into a life that death appears to be happening already, until more life – the life of decay – can proliferate from within. Necrophilia becomes a way of confronting this excess. As Jolene Zigarovich suggests, the tendency for eighteenth-century texts to eroticise the dead may represent the period's literary response to whatever surplus would seem to inhere within the dead, a nugget of transgressive enjoyment that would resist becoming, along with the rest of the dead body, an inert object ready for scientific analysis.[10]

Julie A. Carlson, in the most extended reading of 'The Cave of Fancy' to date, has focused on the keyword 'Fancy' to highlight the 'life force' running through the story. As Carlson sees it, 'The Cave of Fancy' clearly establishes that Wollstonecraft is ever 'on the side of life', a life that pursues 'futurity' as 'its object'.[11] 'Fancy', she explains, connoted a temporal experiment as it was used in the 1790s, functioning as 'a dead term, a signifier of past times and of art as mere pastime', and yet, as a concept ever in the process of passing. Thus 'the histories that fancy tells, especially about fixity and deadness, have designs on futurity in determining where life resides'.[12] Carlson's reading is important and compelling, but I would caution against aligning eroticism with vivacity too quickly when it comes to 'The Cave of Fancy'. After all, futurity is not the object of 'life'; it would be more accurate to say that death is the aim of futurity, both in Wollstonecraft's perverse storyworld and in the world generally. As an alternative or supplementary reading to Carlson's, I propose that 'Fancy' functions in the story not as a master signifier but as a concept surrounded and crisscrossed with others, many of which exalt death rather than life.

When Sagestus first encounters the girl, she is on the beach, weeping and clinging to her dead (or possibly dying) mother. Corpses are strewn across the sand. The girl begs Sagestus to try to revive her mother, but instead, shockingly, Sagestus drugs the girl so that she too can be 'asleep'. The narrator reports this alarming decision with a tone as flat and practical as could be. The story does not seem to register this drugging and abduction as something monstrous, instead praising the ploy as an efficient one: 'Sagestus had a quicker method to effect his purpose; he took out a box which contained a soporific powder, and as soon as the fumes reached her brain, the powers of life were suspended' ('CF' 193). Once the girl is unconscious, he takes her to the Cave of Fancy, presumably the same subterranean lair that he can only access at 'midnight', to begin her erotic education. He offers her, we are told, 'more instruction than mere advice', a phrase which lends an authoritarian tone to his, and the story's, didacticism ('CF' 200).

The narrator tends to focus on Sagestus's affect and advice rather than his deeds, which raises the possibility that his deeds are going unreported. For instance, we hear of Sagestus's emotional reactions to the shipwreck rather than a report of the disaster itself: 'The blood flew rapidly to his heart; it was flesh; he felt he was still a man, and the big tear paced down his iron cheeks, whose muscles had not for a long time been relaxed by such humane emotions' ('CF' 193). The passage presents Sagestus as a man of feeling – as if he were beneficently rescuing the orphan girl and trying to mentor her. Yet, the constant focus on the sage's sexual desire tends to undermine any sense that this scene is a rescue or the beginning of an earnest pedagogical project. Examining the corpse of Sagesta's mother, Sagestus unwittingly confronts the caves of his own fancy, that is, his unexpected sexual desire for the corpse. Hence the narrator suddenly pivots from a description of the mother's body to an account of Sagestus's desire: 'he turned to the lily that had been so rudely snapped, and, carefully observing it, traced every fine line to its source. There was a delicacy in her form, so truly feminine, that an involuntary desire to cherish such a being, made the sage again feel the almost forgotten sensations of his nature' ('CF' 197).

It would seem impossible that Wollstonecraft would be recommending this pathway to enlightenment in earnest. Or might it not? The core issue in the 'lily' passage is to what extent a corpse may be considered 'a being', and it is here that Bataille, the infamous theorist of necrophilia, can be of help. 'The verb to be', explains Bataille, is always the mark of an erotic relation, 'the vehicle of amorous frenzy'.[13] Yet, the eroticisation of death, far from celebrating annihilation, is a way of orienting one's being towards living. He explains that the meaning of death, 'rather than to be, is to expect to be' until the cessation of life fills eroticism with 'the anticipation of being'.[14] Death, in this way, is the condition of any eroticism and 'the most luxurious form of life'.[15] In Bataille's argument, a coincidence of opposites enacts a shift in the opposition itself: 'Death is really the opposite process to the process ending in birth, yet these opposite processes can be reconciled', he explains.[16] In a proto-deconstructive fashion, what appears to be a reconciliation of opposites occurs only through placing the binary terms one inside the other. It is akin to naming one's charge 'Sagesta', to emphasise how both generational and gender difference can disappear through their very demarcation once the difference becomes internal. The naming of Sagesta seems to imply multiple forms of connection between the two, from the hermit's perspective: it marks her as his prospective student, his partner-in-crime, his self-projection, his would-be-lover, his inductee into unknown pleasures. To covet one's own mother may be Oedipal; to covet the mother of the orphan one has taken in, and who will be fashioned into one's double, after one has refused to save the mother, is to turn oneself into the instrument of the Other's Oedipal enjoyment.

A similar displacement of binaries appears at the end of Wollstonecraft's story, when, very surprisingly and without further explanation, Sagesta seems to indicate that the womb-like Cave of Fancy has all along been a metaphor for death. She says, enigmatically, 'a few days ago I entered this cavern; for through it every mortal must pass; and here I have discovered, that I neglected many opportunities of being useful, whilst I fostered a devouring flame' ('CF' 206). We should infer from this metaphor that the wise Sagestus, a sentimental figure who has served as this girl's moral guide, had refused to administer first aid on the girl's mother and has additionally murdered Sagesta for his own gratification. Yet, nothing in the tone of the story indicates that he is less than beneficent, generous and wise. The lack of alarm registered by either the narrator or implied author separates 'The Cave of Fancy' from other Gothic tales of necrophilia popular around that time, such as Matthew

Lewis's *The Monk* (1796), which aim to titillate and alarm the reader. It is the flat tone of outright perversion, one familiar to readers of Sade. It is precisely Sagestus's eagerness to acknowledge his own perverse desire, and to offer it to Sagesta as a curriculum of study, that enables him to 'overleap[] the boundary prescribed to human knowledge' in the cave ('CF' 191). If a boundary is being overleaped, it is that between sexual transgression and perversion.

Beachy Dead

The story, which offers scant guidance for its preferred interpretation, often presents dead bodies as puzzles to be explored philosophically. Much of the word count is taken up with Sagestus scrutinising corpses, and the implied author never undermines the sage's interpretations. Returning to the scene of the shipwreck the next day, for instance, the narrator says without judgment that Sagestus 'walked leisurely among the dead, and narrowly observed their pallid features' ('CF' 194). Sagestus's main impression is that the victims were quite rich – an unexpected observation from someone who, being a hermit, normally eschews an exchange economy ('CF' 194). Perhaps their deaths would seem to vindicate his choice of the hermit lifestyle. Yet, the emphasis is more on their particular features than the fact of their deaths, and the adverb 'leisurely' would seem to align him with the rich rather than differentiate him. The word does, though, differentiate Sagestus from the other hermits of Romantic-era poetry, be they found in the poems of Charlotte Smith, Samuel Taylor Coleridge or William Wordsworth. Kari Lokke sees Sagestus as 'a strange and suggestive precursor to Smith's hermit' in *Beachy Head* (1807) and finds that Wollstonecraft's settings and moral lessons 'correspond strikingly' to Smith's.[17] But Smith's hermit Darby is associated with industry rather than leisure, austerity rather than abundance, and he 'administered assistance to ship-wrecked mariners' – precisely the act that Sagestus refuses to do when asked.[18] Smith also doesn't give her hermit a ward, which in contrast can seem to be a brilliantly paradoxical supplement on Wollstonecraft's part: after all, is a hermit who lives with another person, and who instructs them how best to socialise, still really a hermit?

Sagesta is being trained to evaluate people (and spirits) through snap judgment – a skill that particularly befits those whose sexual partners are to be static objects instead of living people. Sagestus encourages her to judge people right away based on their appearance: 'Try to remember the effect the first appearance of a stranger has on your mind', he sagely offers, 'and, in proportion to your sensibility, you may decide on the character' ('CF' 199). He recommends this strategy not because it enables moral perceptiveness but rather because it abundantly generates *jouissance*. Those who develop such techniques, he promises, find that 'exquisite pain and pleasure is their portion' ('CF' 201). With this, the paraphilia at the heart of this story becomes clear. Sagesta's invagination in the eponymous cave clearly suggests the reconciliation of gestation and death ('CF' 191). And the narrator, gleaning lessons from the situation from even before the outset of the narration, enjoins the reader to live 'at the dawn of wisdom' ('CF' 191). This is effectively another way of affirming the Bataillean 'anticipation of being'. If eroticism and death find their purest convergence, says Bataille, in our sexual attraction for corpses and the desire to murder our lovers,[19] then it is noteworthy that Sagestus devotes himself so thoroughly to both! When Wollstonecraft conjoins these forms of necro-eroticism in 'The Cave of Fancy', she suggests that intense feeling can lower us into total annihilation, from which a broader perspective on desire might be achieved.

Death, Bataille says, is 'that shipwreck in the nauseous' that is ever aligned with 'the purulence of anonymous infinite life, which stretches forth like the night'.[20] Note how Bataille's words essentially recap the plot of 'The Cave of Fancy': the story begins with a shipwreck and finds, through the alluring brutality of that event, a way to imagine oneself living interminably and unnoticed. Sagestus cultivates a way of life-in-death neither inside nor outside of the disastrous world of cosmopolitanism and commerce, as metonymised by the shipwreck. The shipwreck is not merely the story's deadly initiating event; it is also a symbol of death per se.

Wollstonecraft's interest in the victims of shipwrecks seems to have arisen from a challenging event in her life, in which she had to persuade a ship's captain, through the threat of shaming him, to rescue people who were drowning.[21] Wollstonecraft adapted this traumatic experience into a key episode in her novel *Mary: A Fiction* (1788), roughly written concurrently with 'The Cave of Fancy'. As the eponymous protagonist of *Mary: A Fiction* rescues survivors of a shipwreck, they clamour for an afterlife in the name of 'futurity', as David Collings has analysed in exquisite Kantian detail.[22] In 'The Cave of Fancy', quite dissimilarly, the shipwreck brings the future into the diegetic present by eroticising the dead. The difference is a crucial one. If, as Collings holds, the quintessential Wollstonecraftian lesson is that satisfaction can only ever be deferred, which is why her texts so often appeal to an afterlife,[23] then we can only see 'The Cave of Fancy' as a significant exception to this rule. It identifies a loophole of sorts in the problem of deferred satisfaction. It does not belong, as does the shipwreck in *Mary*, to 'the mini-genre of the exemplary episode focused on an ethical decision'; rather, it dramatises a cut in the ethical field, to open the possibility of an ethics of the Real.[24] Wollstonecraft assures the reader that 'he who formed the human soul, only can fill it, and the chief happiness of an immortal being must arise from the same source as its existence' ('CF' 206). The 'must' contained in this advice is more vexing than it would first appear. It appears as an injunction, a kind of plenitude derived from an extimate point in a set, as a way of pretending that the Other is not lacking by standing in their place. Wollstonecraft makes the dead alluring by showing the reader how to identify with them. This is consistent with Lisa Downing's suggestion that necrophilia may not be so much a perversion of mourning as a 'wishful identification with the dead', a way of living on in tribute to the memory of what one will eventually become.[25] This perversion, however shocking, opens the possibility for desire to be fulfilled even as it remains embroiled in loops of deferral and repetition. Thus, as some critics have done, we should not see 'The Cave of Fancy' as an author's early attempt to explore themes that would soon be articulated more fully in *Mary*.[26] Instead, 'The Cave of Fancy' is uniquely a story about how eroticism and enlightenment conjoin in death as a sexual practice. Because these principles are so thoroughly intermingled in the text – one thinks, once more, of Sade's *Philosophy in the Bedroom* as a point of literary comparison – the story's moral and philosophical world seems incredibly slippery, even implausible.

In 'The Cave of Fancy', the pedagogical aims are mainly about *jouissance*, turning the eponymous cave into a scene akin, *avant la lettre*, to the chalet in Sade's text. Sade's and Bataille's subsequent works cast a darkness over 'The Cave of Fancy' that renders the narrator's account of Sagestus's desires quite mysterious, as Sagestus evaluates bodies on the beach. Sagestus's desire is a mystery yet more profound than that of the weeping girl on the village common – whose rageful grief, after all, makes perfect sense when read retroactively in the context of the author's overall career. At the very core of the narrative, appearing only as a half-retrieved memory, the girl on the common can sit recognisably, if not sustainably, as the key traumatic encounter of Sagesta's experience. Sagestus's perversity, in contrast, gets purposelessly narrated at curious length, refusing to accommodate itself to any part of Wollstonecraft's overall thought.

Bataille warns that 'the prohibition concerning the dead is not designed to protect them from the *desire* of the living'.[27] Luckily for lovers of Bataille, no one in 'The Cave of Fancy' is thus shielded. 'The Cave of Fancy' offers an account, six pages long in the original printing, of Sagestus's gazing at, and evaluating, the corpses on the beach one by one, 'indelibly fixed by death', finding some of them 'exquisite'. He evaluates their musculature, their faces, their lips, their 'every feature and limb'; he strokes the corpses' hair, 'measur[ing]' and 'weighing' their bodies until he is caught up in 'the mazes of fancy' ('CF' 195). He notes the bodies that are 'round and fleshy', that seem to offer a 'vital spark ... buried deep in a soft mass of matter', as these make possible an experience with the body 'so equivocal, that it only appears a moister part of the same body' ('CF' 195). This is a clear example of what Rebecca E. May calls 'the necro-gaze', the discourse of which proliferated through the eighteenth century and into the nineteenth. The necro-gaze, says May, is a 'masculinized impulse' that, in pursuing 'the ideal of receptivity', reveals 'disconcerting manifestations of control and excitement' in the arrangement and anatomisation of corpses.[28] Sagestus moves beyond the medicalising-pornographic necro-gaze, though, in then grouping those bodies into imagined tableaux that could be said to mock eighteenth-century discourses of family, fixating as he does on the corpses' respective roles as mother, husband or brother ('CF' 196). There at what Jacques Derrida would call the 'unbordered and unbounded arrhythmy on a beach that is a continuation of the sea', Sagestus develops an instructional space of interruption and delimitation, through which death can be valorised as if it were an erotics, an ethos and a kinship structure.[29]

The Family Tableau

As Sagestus surveys the scene, 'he turned his step towards the mother of the orphan: another female was at some distance; and a man who, by his garb, might have been the husband, or brother, of the former, was not far off' ('CF' 196). Innumerable mysteries are encoded in this sentence, and I will beg the reader's indulgence as I enumerate some of them. I wonder: what about a man's garb would indicate that he might have been either the woman's husband or brother? Would the term 'garb' be thought to include, say, a wedding ring that matches hers, perhaps – and wouldn't that seem to bear mentioning in particular, if so? But would a 'brother' wear such 'garb'? How did husbands and brothers become so interchangeable, equivalent? Do husbands wear the same sort of clothes as brothers do, in a way that is different from the preferred style of men generally? Or are brothers just another form of husband, an extension of the same concept? Why does Sagestus rely upon clues from the victims' clothes, rather than Sagesta's firsthand knowledge, to determine these relations? Why would we so readily assume that Sagesta had a father or uncle? She had not mentioned them – the previous day, she had been crying specifically over her mother, not, more broadly, her parents or family. What leads Sagestus to single these three out and to see in them the picture of a family? What could make these three corpses a 'family', if not Sagesta's willingness to identify one of them as her mother? Note that they are not grouped together on the beach: the male body is 'not far off' but not adjacent either, and the second female is 'at some distance' – so, what leads Sagestus to conclude that these three, but not the others, are related? And what does he suppose is the relation of the distant body to the other two? Why would Sagestus create a constellation out of these three points when other bodies are lying everywhere around and between them? Why focus on the woman, and thus worry about which corpse was her husband or brother, instead of who might be the father, stepfather or uncle of little orphaned Sagesta, a person he now knows, and who seems to be mostly alive? Why, in painting the picture of a dead couple, would Sagestus present them as linked to this unknown third person, a 'female', whose body is 'at some distance'? What leads Sagestus to incorporate this far-away body into the tableau? Is this female an adult or a child? She does not seem to be connected to the scene through any spatial arrangement and nor, it would seem, through her 'garb'. The link, I would suggest, must be an affective one, as relayed through Sagestus's desire: what we have here is an erotics. We might call it a gender-inverted necro-homosocial tableau. To discuss the dead couple, or siblings, one needs to place another woman's corpse between them, fantasmatically and syntactically, but not actually, to establish their intimacy. Only through this arrangement can Sagesta be considered an orphan and thus require Sagestus's care and tutelage. It is as if to assert that a family is made out of desire. This statement is, of course, conventionally true in an obvious way, through sexual intercourse and conception; Sagestus, though, performs this work of family-making on the bodies of the dead.

It is as if Wollstonecraft is suggesting that while desire requires a family for its original constitution, family as such can only ever exist at the level of fantasy and so must be constructed retroactively out of any materials ready to hand. Downing argues that necrophilia is a form of desire that develops outside of kinship structures, offering instead 'the fetish of entire loss, of complete absence'.[30] Yet, Sagestus specifically fetishises these bodies by imagining them as kin to one another, and by making himself the family of some members of that family. He mocks the idea, derived from Thomas Gray's 'Elegy in a Country Church-yard' (1751), that working-class bodies would have more to give: 'How little, he exclaimed, did that poet know of the ways of heaven!' ('CF' 196).

The bodies of the poor could only be fit for 'mediocrity' or 'a dunghill', while the bodies of the wealthy may become family, once they are dead and remediated through fantasy. His notion is quite reminiscent of 'Kant with Sade', in which Lacan warns that 'the object of desire, where we see it in its nakedness – is but the slag of a fantasy in which the subject does not come to after blacking out. It is a case of necrophilia.'[31] That is, desire can require the death of the object to give it, retroactively, its meaning, once it has been caught up in a network of desire. Sagestus presumes that, in death, the full potential of these people has been realised at last, through the very fact that they do not 'come to after blacking out'. Without the intervention of his fantasy, they could only be mourned as 'the heterogenous mass' ('CF' 196). Not everyone is wise enough to be an ancient sage, he submits – thus, it is best to make of the dead what one will in the current circumstances, instead of thinking of them as possible geniuses lost before their contributions had been made. Having focused on their unrealised creative potential in life rather than their erotic potential in death, Gray seems to have misunderstood the uses to which dead bodies can be put.

Not Very Unfortunate

The question, then, is how literature can or should memorialise the dead. David McAllister stresses the conceptual difference between literary memorials to the particular dead and memorials to the mass of dead within nineteenth-century British literature. Even as Victorian literature endeavoured to memorialise the particular dead, McAllister says, it nevertheless sought 'to *unmake* this group of the dead: to eliminate them from the social body, disenchant their physical remains, police their cultural representation, and aestheticize their material traces'.[32] Wollstonecraft seems to be responding to this particular cultural problem, using Sagestus's desire as the mechanism through which she can move the reader between these parallax registers.

Part of what makes this story difficult to interpret is the bizarre flatness of the narrator's tone: though liberally splashed with admiration for Sagestus and his forms of moral instruction, the narrator leaves the context for his observations (that is, beaches of dying people frantically attempting to dig their own graves) without commentary or pathos one way or the other. The extraordinary detail that Sagestus shows in evaluating the features of each dead face and scrutinising the contours of each dead body might, at first, seem like an effort to recognise the dignity of each life – an attempt to offer tribute to each lost life specifically.

Yet, Sagestus knows nothing about any of these victims. The narrator's tone is flatly evaluative rather than memorialising. Sagestus even mocks the idea that each might have had separate contributions to make and relishes instead in the very deadness of their bodies as a spur to his desire, which alone can serve as a meaningfully creative power. In the narrator's deadpan, descriptive tone, excessiveness of detail and overabundance of example, Wollstonecraft seems to be providing the sort of 'breviary of bodily deconstruction' that would shortly characterise Sade's work.[33] If the narrator creates any point of emphasis in this scene, it is that Sagestus is highly attentive to the dead, offering a blazon of each corpse and its features. One could say, following Lacan, that he envies the corpses for their capacity to 'keep what gave the living its character: body'.[34]

Although the story seems earnestly to admire Sagestus, it can also seem like this must be some sort of satire about his indifference and thus a commentary on the cruelty inherent in the ethic of sensibility. Why else would Wollstonecraft have Sagestus, gazing a second time at the sexy dead body of Sagesta's mother, conclude that

> He was now convinced that the orphan was not very unfortunate in having lost such a mother. The parent that inspires fond affection without respect, is seldom an useful one; and they only are respectable, who consider right and wrong abstracted from local forms and accidental modifications. ('CF' 198)

The passage is vexing, to say the least. To be clear, the narrator is mocking a dead woman for not being 'abstract' enough. In a gesture akin to the tutelage of Sade's Dolmancé, he is about to teach a young girl how better to enjoy the dead by offering her the corpse of her own mother. The text does not seem to notice that this is strange or unusual. To adapt from 'Kant with Sade', we could say that the 'monstrous' pathways of desire outlined by Sagestus come to seem 'more respectable' and 'purer in their valences', than 'more ordinary jouissances encountered in life'.[35] This commitment to abstraction as a pathway to respectability is Wollstonecraft at her most Kantian and Sadean.

Sagestus concludes, looking at the brother-husband's face, that the man had been dimwitted, given 'the expression it must have had'. The verb tense implies that the deceased man does not show the expression in question at present. When Sagestus sees what he presumes to be the corpse of Sagesta's father-uncle, Wollstonecraft contrasts his quickness of perception with the dead man's slowness; this seems an unfair fight, given that the man is dead. Note the emphasis on quickness of perception: 'Sagestus quickly discerned the expression it must have had' ('CF' 196). Having assured himself of his intellectual superiority over the woman's deceased husband-brother, he turns to look at Sagesta's dead mother and observes that she was intelligent but educated poorly. It is unclear why this would matter to Sagestus now that the woman is dead. He can see that she is a woman: would that not be enough, given the insights of Wollstonecraft's wider oeuvre, to enable him to conclude that her education would have stunted her development? Yet, we can assume that Sagestus, having lived alone in a cave for decades, may not have much knowledge of contemporary British or European education systems. What he observes is more subtle than simply the mother's gender expression or her access to the pathways of self-realisation. Wollstonecraft emphasises the closeness of his inspection and the phases of his determinations:

> On observing her more closely, he discovered that her natural delicacy had been increased by an improper education, to a degree that took away all vigour from her faculties. And its baneful influence had had such an effect on her mind, that few traces of the exertions of it appeared on her face, though the fine finish of her features, and particularly the form of the forehead, convinced the sage that her understanding might have risen considerably above mediocrity, had the wheels ever been put in motion. ('CF' 197)

Here we have another outrageously insulting passage. Surely it cannot be Wollstonecraft's own view. Yet, it has recognisably Wollstonecraftian themes: Sagestus's concern is that a deficient education has stunted a woman's potential. (He had just rejected this same idea moments before, in looking at the dead on the beach.) He draws many conclusions, based only on physiognomy, about the status of her mind and her position in the world. And he looks at her as if she were dead, despite Sagesta asking him to save her life.

Sagesta's story, which takes up the second half of the text and ambiguously crosses into, or yields to, the voice of a spirit, shows a similar preoccupation with necro-eroticism. Sagesta or the spirit relates how 'the dear object of my fondest affection, said farewell, in dying accents', while she was married to a visually impaired merchant whom she did not love ('CF' 204). The situation is a surprising one: up to this point, we had known Sagesta only as 'a blooming child' with 'a weak infantine voice', helpless without her mother, a combination which had seemed to suggest someone much younger than the spirit ('CF' 193). The spirit describes how it developed her capacity to fantasise about the dead man as a way of coping with the disappointments of marriage. As it explains,

> I smoothed my mothers [sic] passage to eternity, and so often gave my husband sincere proofs of affection, he never supposed that I was actuated by a more fervent attachment. My melancholy, my uneven spirits, he attributed to my extreme sensibility, and loved me the better for possessing qualities he could not comprehend. ('CF' 205)

There is a lot that is surprising in this story: for instance, one would not have expected the spirit, who may be the spirit of the orphan girl, who has seemed to be a child, to have been married for several years before the shipwreck, or that it was she who had proposed marriage, out of pity, to the merchant ('CF' 203). Yet, the most surprising thing of all is this murderous 'smoothing' of the mother's 'passage to eternity', given how Sagesta's mother was in the process of dying on the beach in the frame tale. Between the ambiguous crossing of Sagesta and the spirit, one could say that Sagesta's mother dies twice in this brief narrative. It is as if she were caught in a space between two deaths, such that her second death can be the death of death itself.[36] As a narrative flourish, it 'is simply an excess, an excess to make our heads reel, but the excess of our own extravagance', as Bataille would say, because the twice-dead mother quickly becomes the basis of a complicated love quadrangle.[37] The quadrangle is constituted through the pathways of desire that have emerged between (in the first place) Sagesta, as a grieving daughter, (in the second) her mother, dying for a second time, (in the third) the merchant fiancé, whom she calls 'my more than father', for whom she 'felt ... all the affection of a daughter' ('CF' 203, 202), and (in the fourth) the man she really loves. Each term finds its erotic significance in the mother's deaths, which come after them in the plot, if not the narration. And so, the fourth term is understood to be a perverse and excessive element, out of keeping with propriety, despite its being the story's most socially acceptable attachment: this longing for 'the other friend' was, she explains, 'the passion I too fondly nursed, ... an affection, which seemed twisted in every fibre of my heart' ('CF' 202). Here, the excessive death of the mother becomes the 'excess of [the daughter's] own extravagance'. It is an excess in which, per Bataille, 'the fullness of horror and joy coincide'.[38]

The text dares us to acknowledge with open eyes its brutal perversity, which it presents as a certain twistedness of heart. If one were to read 'The Cave of Fancy' without knowing the author's identity, it would seem a shocking proclamation of libertinage. If we wanted to say that such a reading is implausible given Wollstonecraft's wider oeuvre, then we could try to see the above passage as ironic – the narrator's voice could mark, for instance, Wollstonecraft's silent indictment of the sage's cruelty. Surely there must be some irony at work, we would say, knowing what we know of Wollstonecraft and her decent, progressive values and respect for human dignity. Yet, there are no signs to indicate that the passage is ironic. The other possibility would be to learn to see 'The Cave of Fancy' as evidence of its author's unexpectedly broad sexual range, as a thinker of sexual transgression and as a writer of fiction. It would be to posit that the moral lessons of the story may be perverse and monstrous and offered to the reader as a pathway to unlimited *jouissance*. I would like to raise that possibility. With all due respect for Lokke's work – and I mean that very sincerely, as she is one of my favourite scholars to read – in this case, I find it inadequate to say that 'The Cave of Fancy' has a 'strong moral' and a 'moralistic conclusion'.[39] True, it does not hesitate to offer lessons in sympathetic feeling. But nothing about its vision of sensibility is familiar from other eighteenth-century literature, except maybe from the oeuvre of Sade.

The Voice of Experience

Collings, provocatively, has argued that Wollstonecraft's *Mary* seems to require the presence of a Sadean sovereign, against whom her protagonists can react and thus to whom they are indirectly indebted.[40] 'The Cave of Fancy' would seem to go yet further in its libertinage, tapping directly into the *jouissance* of death as the basis for an apparent code of ethics. In 'The Cave of Fancy', it is not merely that perversity lends moral virtue to the protagonists; the protagonists are themselves, rather, outrageous perverts. Sagestus imagines himself as the guarantor of Sagesta's desire in order to ensure his own *jouissance*, yet does so defensively, as a bulwark against his own desire. Such is the basic structure of perversion, according to Lacan.[41]

We can now consider the motto that opens 'The Cave of Fancy', which distinctly echoes and subverts the opening of Samuel Johnson's *Rasselas* (1759). Johnson's version specifically warns the reader against 'fancy' and implies that time will not compensate for any lack in the present.[42] Wollstonecraft's version, quite to the contrary, says,

> Ye who expect constancy where every thing is changing, and peace in the midst of tumult, attend to the voice of experience, and mark in time the footsteps of disappointment, or life will be lost in desultory wishes, and death arrive before the dawn of wisdom. ('CF' 191)

In Wollstonecraft's formulation, which would seem to befit a sarcastic motivational poster, 'the voice of experience' urges us not to find wisdom before we die, but rather to focus on delaying death until after wisdom has arrived. It is a strange bit of advice, especially at the beginning of a story: its booming voice of universal wisdom informs us that wisdom will never come for those who seek universal wisdom. By apostrophising the reader as 'ye', the narrator intrudes into the scene of reading before any text has appeared. Functioning seemingly as an epigraph, given its second-person address to the reader but contained within the first body paragraph of the story, its status as 'part' of the story is disquietingly indeterminate. In ambiguously standing as a parergon to the main text, an allusion to another text and wildly crossing between levels of textuality before any levels are established, the motto serves to undermine the nested structure of narration that this text wants to rely upon. The irony becomes more meaningful if we take seriously its instruction to 'mark in time the footsteps of disappointment'. It is difficult, to be sure, to mark any distance, even a footstep, 'in time': it depends upon a category error, whereby we measure one dimensional axis by another – what is a footstep but a fantasmatic past event discovered in the present? We are being asked to convert temporal features into spatial ones. It is likewise impossible to 'mark [anything] in time', because the act of marking, *qua* event, is itself temporally bound and thus beholden to the timeline it is supposed to annotate. There is no metatemporality possible. Is the narrator asking us to note when disappointment left its trace upon the world, or simply asking us to defer our consideration of that disappointment – in the sense that we should mark the disappointment sometime, but not right now? The ambiguity directly combines a deferral with a difference, showing these movements to be inseparable within the motto. And yet, this specific deferral and difference, if properly 'marked in time', is supposed to be the only thing that can save us from premature death. There are two consequences of a refusal to mark these footsteps in time: first, life will be lost, and second, death will arrive. By presenting these as two separate consequences, or by using the 'and' to suggest a difference, or a lag, between the loss of life and the arrival of death, Wollstonecraft carves out a space between life and death adequate to impart an ironic lesson, possibly. And this space between 'me' and 'my death' is the very soil in which necrophilia can take root, fantasmatically. 'Wisdom' had been coming for us all, reliable as the dawn, but like those who were shipwrecked, we readers may not live long enough to receive it. And as the opening of a story chock full, at each of its narrative levels, with dead people – indeed, as I have said, Sagesta's mother dies at least twice in the story and possibly three times if we are to take Sagesta's request for assistance after the shipwreck seriously – the advice seems like a cruel moral condemnation: if death arrives, it's because of your own stupid false expectations. One can, it seems, either defer death or experience it too soon: the disappointment is that it can never arrive on time. And yet, we are enjoined to mark that disappointment 'in time', as death, coming later and too soon, seduces us into and beyond its boundary. In generating the *jouissance* that exceeds bourgeois limits, necrophilia indicates one's temporal enlightenment and inducts one into a circuit of repetition and deferment.

It has been suggested that the concept of literature requires a written corpus representing a 'framed unity', for which the demand for life serves as the necessary supplement, and an authorial 'I' that arrives, only ever incompletely, through the promise of its eventual death.[43] Wollstonecraft's *Posthumous Works* presents an interesting test case in that regard, much as Wollstonecraft's body, which was not interred within her grave, has sometimes symbolised a similar disjuncture.[44] 'The Cave of Fancy' appears to the reader only as a retroactive construction of Godwin's, that is, as an originally and only ever a 'posthumous work'. I say this not because Godwin seems to have departed from the manuscript or marketed the text in any particular way, but simply because the publication of the *Posthumous Works* represents Godwin's attempt to close the author's oeuvre and secure its range of possible meanings – an analogous gesture, one might say, to his burying an empty coffin for his wife. Yet, the eroticism and structure of 'The Cave of Fancy' pushes back, basically, in the opposite direction. Announcing itself both as a fragment and a posthumous effort, it advises the reader to burrow deeper into a life that has already transpired until life reveals, as its internal disavowed condition, new forms of deathliness lusted after and immeasurable. In making its explorations of lifelessness in an erotic key, the story becomes a way of theorising not only death's relation to literature but also necrophilia. Its interest in necrophilia – and its reluctance to pursue necrophilia beyond the limits of its narrative frame – mark the story as an outlier in the Wollstonecraft canon, a fragment of something inassimilable under its author's name. It seems impossible to think about Wollstonecraft as the advocate for such an unsavoury perversion, yet the function or purpose of its possible irony is indeterminate. With its strangely flat tone, the story itself gives us very few clues about how best to interpret its perverse content; Wollstonecraft's life and other works present even fewer. It is in many ways an uninterpretable text when detached from the project of the *Posthumous Works*, and its endeavours to shore up and destroy reputations. At best, we have a text, like Herman Melville's *Billy Budd* (1891/1924), that asks us to take sides in an interpretive dispute but gives us no basis for doing so.[45]

Notes

1. Gary Kelly, 'Mary Wollstonecraft as *Vir Bonus*', *ESC: English Studies in Canada 5*, no. 4 (Spring 1979): 276–7; Susan Laird, *Mary Wollstonecraft* (New York: Bloomsbury, 2014), 16–17. The pornographer in question,

Henri Fuseli, himself can be said to have cultivated a necrophiliac aesthetic in his work as a painter.
2. Anna Clark, *Scandal: The Sexual Politics of the British Constitution* (Princeton: Princeton University Press, 2004), 126–47; Angela Monsam, 'Biography as Autopsy in William Godwin's *Memoirs of the Author of* A Vindication of the Rights of Woman', *Eighteenth Century Fiction* 21, no. 1 (Autumn 2008): 109–30, https://doi.org/10.1353/ecf.0.0029. It would be interesting further to consider William Godwin's acts of tribute to the dead Wollstonecraft, including the publication of 'The Cave of Fancy', as erotic acts in their own right.
3. Tom Furniss, 'Nasty Tricks and Tropes: Sexuality and Language in Mary Wollstonecraft's "Rights of Woman"', *Studies in Romanticism* 32, no. 2 (Summer 1993): 177–209, https://doi.org/10.2307/25601005; David Sigler, *Sexual Enjoyment in British Romanticism: Gender and Psychoanalysis, 1753–1835* (Montreal: McGill-Queen's University Press, 2015), 3–8.
4. Julie A. Carlson, 'Fancy's History', *European Romantic Review* 14, no. 2 (2003): 167.
5. Élisabeth Roudinesco, *Our Dark Side: A History of Perversion*, trans. David Macey (Cambridge: Polity, 2009), 30; Mary Wollstonecraft, *An Historical and Moral View of the French Revolution*, in *The Works of Mary Wollstonecraft*, ed. Janet Todd and Marilyn Butler, vol. 6, 7 vols. (London: William Pickering, 1989), 1–235.
6. Julie Peakman, *The Pleasure's All Mine: A History of Perverse Sex* (London: Reaktion Books, 2013), 268.
7. Eileen Hunt Botting, 'Mary Wollstonecraft, Children's Human Rights, and Animal Ethics', in *The Social and Moral Philosophy of Mary Wollstonecraft*, ed. Sandrine Bergès and Alan Coffee (Oxford: Oxford University Press, 2016), 103, 110–11.
8. Georges Bataille, *Erotism: Death and Sensuality*, trans. Mary Dalwood (San Francisco: City Lights, 1986), 252.
9. Eric L. Santner, *On the Psychotheology of Everyday Life: Reflections on Freud and Rosenzweig* (Chicago: University of Chicago Press, 2001), 78.
10. Jolene Zigarovich, 'Courting Death: Necrophilia in Samuel Richardson's *Clarissa*', *Studies in the Novel* 32, no. 2 (Spring 2000): 113.
11. Carlson, 'Fancy's History', 168.
12. Ibid., 163.
13. Georges Bataille, *Visions of Excess: Selected Writings, 1927–1939*, ed. and trans. Allan Stoekl, Theory and History of Literature Series 14 (Minneapolis: University of Minnesota Press, 1985), 5.
14. Georges Bataille, *The Accursed Share: An Essay on General Economy, Volumes II and III*, trans. Robert Hurley (New York: Zone Books, 1993), 81.
15. Bataille, *Accursed II–III*, 84.
16. Bataille, *Erotism*, 55.
17. Kari Lokke, 'The Figure of the Hermit in Charlotte Smith's *Beachy Head*', *The Wordsworth Circle* 39, no. 1–2 (Winter-Spring 2008): 40.
18. Charlotte Smith, *Beachy Head*, in *The Poems of Charlotte Smith*, ed. Stuart Curran (Oxford: Oxford University Press, 1993), 245n.

19. Bataille, *Accursed II–III*, 97.
20. Ibid., 81.
21. Janet Todd, *Mary Wollstonecraft: A Revolutionary Life* (New York: Columbia University Press, 2000), 70–1; David Collings, *Disastrous Subjectivities: Romanticism, Modernity, and the Real* (Toronto: University of Toronto Press, 2019), 32.
22. Mary Wollstonecraft, *Mary: A Fiction*, in *Mary/Maria/Matilda*, by Mary Wollstonecraft and Mary Shelley, ed. Janet Todd (London: Penguin, 1992), 37; Collings, *Disastrous Subjectivities*, 31–55.
23. Collings, *Disastrous Subjectivities*, 34.
24. Ibid., 33.
25. Lisa Downing, *Desiring the Dead: Necrophilia and Nineteenth-Century French Literature* (Oxford: Legenda, 2003), 58.
26. Barbara Taylor, 'The Religious Foundations of Mary Wollstonecraft's Feminism', in *The Cambridge Companion to Mary Wollstonecraft*, ed. Claudia L. Johnson (Cambridge: Cambridge University Press, 2002), 115.
27. Bataille, *Accursed II–III*, 97. Emphasis in the original.
28. Rebecca E. May, 'Morbid Parts: Gender, Seduction and the Necro-Gaze', in *Sexual Perversions, 1670–1890*, ed. Julie Peakman (Basingstoke: Palgrave Macmillan, 2009), 168–9.
29. Jacques Derrida, 'Living On', in *Deconstruction and Criticism*, ed. Harold Bloom, trans. James Hulbert (New York: Continuum, 1979), 121.
30. Downing, *Desiring the Dead*, 52.
31. Jacques Lacan, *Écrits: The First Complete Edition in English*, trans. Bruce Fink (New York: Norton, 2006), 658.
32. David McAllister, *Imagining the Dead in British Literature and Culture, 1790–1848* (Cham: Palgrave Macmillan, 2018), 3. Emphasis in the original.
33. Roudinesco, *Our Dark Side*, 38.
34. Jacques Lacan, 'Radiophonie', interview by Robert Georgin, trans. Jack W. Stone, June 1970, 5.
35. Lacan, *Écrits*, 658.
36. Jacques Lacan, *The Seminar of Jacques Lacan, Book VII: The Ethics of Psychoanalysis, 1959–1960*, ed. Jacques-Alain Miller, trans. Dennis Porter (New York: Norton, 1992), 280–3.
37. Bataille, *Erotism*, 192.
38. Ibid., 268.
39. Lokke, 'The Figure', 40.
40. Collings, *Disastrous Subjectivities*, 38.
41. Lacan, *Écrits*, 699.
42. Samuel Johnson, *The History of Rasselas, Prince of Abissinia*, ed. Jessica Richard (Peterborough: Broadview, 2008), 43.
43. Derrida, 'Living On', 142, 120.
44. Thomas W. Laqueur, *The Work of the Dead: A Cultural History of Mortal Remains* (Princeton: Princeton University Press, 2015), 365–6.
45. Barbara Johnson, 'Melville's Fist: The Execution of Billy Budd', *Studies in Romanticism* 18, no. 4 (Winter 1979): 567–99.

Chapter 5

Sexual Violence, Sexual Transgression and the Law in Mary Hays's *The Victim of Prejudice*

Kathleen Emily Hurlock

Mary Hays uses part of the early feminist treatise *An Appeal to the Men of Great Britain in Behalf of Women* (1798) to theorise the source of patriarchal power in British society. In what Eleanor Ty calls an evocation of 'Godwinian' theories of human development, Hays argues that women are not biologically or essentially inferior to men, but that patriarchal oppression is socially constructed, based on 'external circumstances'.[1] According to Hays, men derive their social power from 'the same law by which the strong oppresses the weak, and the rich the poor', meaning that the gender hierarchy operates akin to a class system. She goes on to write that, for women, 'it is to man alone to whom they owe their humiliating state in society', indicating that women's current condition is not inherent but could be changed or reversed.[2] She proceeds by comparing gender relations to empire and, as noted by Ty, other 'political [activities]'.[3]

Hays's second novel, *The Victim of Prejudice* (1799), explores the institutions that help to construct and maintain patriarchal power in more detail. The novel raises a particular concern with the law and how it impacts gender relations, giving men power and subordinating women. Because of this bias in favour of men, the law can absolve Sir Peter Osborne of the rape of Mary Raymond if she is willing to marry him. It further ensures that Mary Raymond has little opportunity for a livelihood when she refuses that marriage proposal. The same laws had oppressed Mary Raymond's mother, also named Mary (and hereafter referred to as the elder Mary). Because the elder Mary cannot find any legitimate support for herself and her child after her sexual transgression, she turns to sex work, a criminal enterprise, initiating a chain of events that ends in her execution.

Although both mother and daughter experience sexualised trauma related to the law, there is one significant difference: the elder Mary is sexually transgressive, whereas her daughter is sexually transgressed against. Several essays in this collection consider women writers who employ sexual transgression as a form of feminist resistance, as in the case of the elder Mary, who openly chooses and enjoys her transgressive sexuality until she is disciplined for it. In contrast, the younger Mary is the unconsenting victim of a legally and culturally transgressive sexual act. Thus, Mary Hays's novel could, in theory, offer a look into what happens when women with overlapping yet distinct experiences in relation to sexual transgression and the law claim solidarity with each other, finding commonalities in their experiences as a means to raise consciousness about the different kinds of experiences women have, with a view towards feminist reforms of men's laws. However, the novel equally acknowledges an obstacle in the face of forming this kind of solidarity: the woman transgressed against can gain some, flawed recognition as a sympathetic figure through legal institutions, while the willingly transgressive woman cannot.

In this chapter, I consider the centrality of this difference between Mary Raymond and her mother to uncover the feminist message of *The Victim of Prejudice*. Many critics, including Ty, Ian Ward and Marilyn Brooks, are concerned with the kind of social prejudices against transgressive women that prevent them from re-entering society, with Ward, in particular, defending the elder Mary.[4] Still, few critics take note of the major difference between the two 'victims' in the novel. I intervene in this secondary literature by underscoring that the younger Mary can understand her mother's traumas only through her experience of the legally recognised trauma of sexual violence. I come to this insight by considering the ways the younger Mary envisions her mother as a victim of violence in pseudo-flashbacks to the latter's life prior to execution. In other words, the younger Mary reconceives her mother's willing transgression of societal expectations for women as a form of sexual victimisation similar to that acknowledged within the context of juridical law. I develop my argument through a framework indebted to the feminist theorist Susan Brison, whose book *Aftermath: Violence and the Making of a Self* (2001) articulates a theory about the way intergenerational trauma between women operates concerning sexual violence. Ultimately, I contend that *The Victim of Prejudice* interrupts cultural scripts, which, underpinned by androcentric law, assume that women can only be victimised by one thing, what gets legally labelled 'rape', an assumption that, in turn, helps to expose the limits of the law as a lens for understanding female trauma.

Indeed, the trauma of the elder Mary's experience comes mainly from social 'prejudice' against sexually transgressive women, not from being victimised by the legally recognised crime of rape. Moreover, the elder

Mary's actions become legally transgressive when she turns to sex work for livelihood, but this decision results from the prejudice she faces after her earlier social transgression. Her downfall follows the script of seduced or fallen women much more closely than that of her daughter, whose subversion of gender roles mainly occurs in the way she resists patriarchal expectations after her own rape. Instead, 'seduction' and a refusal to have a heteronormative, married relationship catalyse the elder Mary's downfall. The elder Mary appears conscious of her failure in acceding to an appropriately feminine gender role, writing to her daughter, 'I rejected the manly address and honest ardour of the man ... whose affection would have supported me; through whom I might have enjoyed the endearing relations, and fulfilled the respectable duties, of mistress, wife, and mother'.[5] This Mary understands the political, gendered dimension of her transgression. She suffers and dies prematurely not merely because she was a criminal but because she rejected 'respectable' expectations for women, and she knows this well. She castigates herself, blaming her seduction on 'my weak judgement' and 'the mingled intoxication of my vanity and my senses', supposing the abbreviation of her life to be a function of her personal failings (*VP* 63). Again, she underscores her personal failings as a catalyst for her life cut short.

These self-chastisements happen quite early in the elder Mary's correspondence. However, as the letters go on, the elder Mary suggests that such gestures have been, as gender roles often are, a bit of a self-conscious performance. Ty notes how the younger Mary learns throughout the novel that the constraints of femininity are not indicative of a 'woman's experience, but rather are ideological representations or cultural scripts which transmit a set of assumptions or values of patriarchal society'.[6] That is, Mary Raymond comes to understand her gendered experiences with stalking, sexual violence and trauma as not merely features of her own experience, but as replications of how a larger patriarchal society hurts women. This conclusion is enabled by her various communications with other women, including through the reading of her mother's letters. To some extent, the elder Mary's letters portray her as a young woman who has internalised those 'cultural scripts' about what it means to be a woman, one who is regretful regarding her promiscuity and rejection of heteronormative marriage. Yet, as the letters go on, the elder Mary becomes increasingly unable to accept her 'fault' in her situation. For instance, she points out how her parents treated her 'as an abandoned wretch, whom it would be criminal to relieve and hopeless to attempt to reclaim' (*VP* 64). Her hyperbolic use of the word 'criminal' stands out here, as, in contrast to her own future as a sex worker and accomplice to murder, nothing about her parents taking her in would be unlawful. This word choice underscores the elder Mary's dissatisfaction with her own parents, who she believes care more about the adverse social impacts if they take in her in than her actual welfare.

The elder Mary becomes even more pointed as the correspondence continues, explaining her descent into criminality as the result of her 'victim of prejudice' status: 'I perceived myself the victim of the injustice, of the prejudice, of society, which, by opposing to my return to virtue almost insuperable barriers, had plunged me into irremediable ruin' (VP 66). She thus succinctly expresses how her society offers sexually transgressive women like herself no rehabilitation, only retribution. She perhaps downplays the radicalism of her challenge to the patriarchal status quo, noting that she 'perceived' herself as a 'victim', emphasising the subjective appraisal of her situation. This caveat indicates that she might be aware she is not technically supposed to think this way. The elder Mary subtly reveals that she takes similar issue with any perception of her as transgressed against as a 'ruined' woman in sexual relationships that were freely chosen and consensual, perhaps criticising even the need for her rehabilitation in the first place. At no point does the elder Mary suggest that the non-marital sex with her seducer was traumatic in and of itself or that she thinks she was objectively wrong for engaging in it. She merely indicates that she is critical of the social and ideological forces preventing her from living a normal life afterwards.

The elder Mary even describes her time with the seducer as 'months' that 'revolved in a round of varied pleasures'. This statement indicates that she fully enjoyed her time with her seducer, including perhaps many different sexual pleasures, and that her problems post-dated his departure, when she no longer had any means to support herself. As she relates, 'I found myself suddenly deserted, driven with opprobrium from the house of my *destroyer*, thrown friendless and destitute upon the world, branded with infamy, and a wretched outcast from social life' (VP 63, emphasis in original). Her life as an unmarried, sexually active woman is joyful until she faces abandonment and realises that nobody will help her, underscoring that her victimisation comes not from engaging in extramarital sex itself but from its stigmatisation. The elder Mary even enjoys life as a single mother, finding it a distraction from her circumstances. Writing about her infant daughter, she notes that 'I forgot for awhile its barbarous father, the world's scorn, and my blasted prospects: the sensations of the injured woman ... were absorbed for a time in the stronger sympathies of the delighted mother' (VP 65). Again, she will not criticise the life path she has chosen, suggesting that the problem is society's views of her choices are the problem, not her transgression per se. Had her community accepted her instead of castigating her as irredeemable, her life would have been different.

The elder Mary also draws a direct link between her status as an outcast who cannot be rehabilitated and her subsequent criminality, writing that, due to this perception of her, her 'mind became fiend-like, revelling in destruction, glorying in its shame', and noting that her sex work, the only way she could support herself at this point, 'eradicated from my heart every remaining human feeling' (*VP* 66–7). Ian Ward notes how the elder Mary even explicitly critiques 'jurisprudential prejudice, the embedded, institutional prejudice of the law'[7] in the following passage:

> Law completes the triumph of injustice. The despotism of man rendered me weak, his vices betrayed me into shame, a barbarous policy stifled returning dignity, prejudice robbed me of the means of independence, gratitude ensnared me in the devices of treachery, the contagion of example corrupted my heart, despair hardened and brutality rendered it cruel. A sanguinary policy precludes reformation, defeating the dear-bought lessons of experience, and, by a legal process, assuming the arm of omnipotence, annihilates the being whom its negligence left destitute, and its institutions compelled to offend. (*VP* 68–9)

The elder Mary's critiques here go beyond just the law, demonstrating her concerns with morality ('vices') under patriarchy, and, especially, 'prejudice', or the cultural scripts surrounding seduced women that prevented her from rehabilitating her reputation and re-entering society. Still, the elder Mary centres 'law' in her critique, as Ward underscores. The law 'completes the triumph of injustice', which most stridently prevents a rehabilitation in the end, and she directly attributes her lack of 'reformation' to the 'legal process'.

The elder Mary's criticism of law centres around its 'assumed' 'omnipotence', underscoring her belief that the law is artificially elevated to be all powerful and pointing out the myriad ways the law ignored her and caused her further harm. When she is victimised by prejudice, the law neglects her and is, by its own dictates, 'compelled' to do further harm to her due to her sex work. Ultimately, as a falsely omnipotent social construct, the law 'annihilates' her through execution. The elder Mary's words here anticipate twentieth-century and later feminist critiques of androcentrism in law and other supposedly objective or neutral social structures. One can see connections between her words and broad critiques of androcentrism, for example, by Donna Haraway and Sandra Harding, as well as specific critiques of the law as a structure of patriarchal power, for example, by Catharine A. Mackinnon.[8] The elder Mary's most salient experience with the law as a form of patriarchal power over women rather than as an institution for the 'objective' determination of justice occurs during the period when she is a sex worker. When Mary threatens men's power to control women sexually through marriage and suffers the consequences, she turns to sex work, effectively her only chance to alleviate some of the hardship imposed by her current lack of means to economic support. But, because men have outlawed sex work, she opens herself up to still harsher punishment, descending into criminality that eventually leads to her execution.

That being said, the elder Mary's worst experiences with the law are, in a sense, not directly gendered. She is executed for being an accomplice to murder, not because of her sex work or previous sexual transgressions. What draws more attention to the law's gendered dimensions is Mary Raymond's experience of a legally recognised form of sexual violation. Osborne's rape of the younger Mary falls precisely into the category of what MacKinnon calls 'a strange ... man knowing a woman does not want sex and going ahead anyway' and identifies as the only kind of sexual violation that law, given its male bias, can recognise.[9] Osborne is aware of Mary's non-consent, as Hays makes clear: he 'besought [Mary's] forgiveness for an outrage' (*VP* 117). He accepts, then, that what he did was criminal. Mary states that Osborne 'solemnly assured me, he was far from attempting to justify' his behaviour, and that he was 'to consider the best means of future reparation' for what he did (*VP* 117). Unlike her mother, Mary Raymond does have some recognition as a victim: a sympathetic figure under the law. Of course, the rest of the novel's plot reveals the limitations of sexual violence laws for Mary Raymond. Osborne's idea of reparation – marrying Mary – would render his attack legally consensual, retroactively absolving him of his crime of rape. When she refuses this option, she has few resources or institutions to which she can turn. In 'Rape and the Rise of the Novel', Frances Ferguson describes this form of marriage as a corrective of sorts to legal rape. According to Ferguson, marriage being the 'legal recompense for rape' suggests that, when proposed by a sexual assailant and accepted by the victim, marriage confers 'consent to intercourse that was previously lacking ... recasting rape so that marriage is a misunderstanding corrected, or rape rightly understood'.[10] Ferguson is referring to how rape gets used as a plot device in eighteenth-century novels, considering what Samuel Richardson's Pamela does in marrying the man who has previously attempted to rape her and what his later heroine, Clarissa, refuses to do when her rapist Lovelace offers marriage as amends. Mary's rejection of Osborne's proposal, her subsequent refusal to be an extramarital 'mistress' or a sex worker like her mother, and her ability to continue living independently, albeit briefly, represent acts of feminist resistance to the misogynistic solution to rape enshrined in law: marriage to one's rapist, a scenario which is, as Marilyn Brooks argues, analogous to the kind of unfair dilemma her mother faced.[11]

Mary Raymond's feminist resistance to these kinds of outcomes stands out because of the way she knows, from her childhood, that she will be violently victimised in some way due to her gender. Initially, her feelings do not suggest an unusual power of premonition, but instead a typical sense that women and girls, in the eighteenth century and today, possess: the feeling of being always already susceptible to sexual violence and, in turn, always already traumatised by the future expectation of that violence. Susan Brison characterises this feeling in terms of prememory and postmemory of sexual violence:

> Girls in our society are raised with so many cautionary tales about rape that, even if we are not assaulted in childhood, we enter womanhood freighted with postmemories of sexual violence ... Postmemories (of other women's rapes) are transmuted into prememories (of one's own future rape) through early and ongoing socialization of girls and women, and both inflect the actual experiences and memories of rape survivors.[12]

Brison then explains that postmemories of rape are 'not primarily inherited from one's parents, but, rather, absorbed from the culture', meaning that the younger Mary's postmemory of sexual violence, in general, does not emerge directly from, for instance, her mother's experience with 'seduction' and grave warning to this Mary to avoid the same fate, but rather from growing up in a profoundly patriarchal society.[13]

Prior to reading her mother's letters, when Mary Raymond first experiences sexual violence, she demonstrates remnants of women's societal postmemories of sexual violence and prememory of what will happen to her. These scenes will sharply contrast with later moments of trauma in the text. The first such moment occurs early in the text when William puts Mary up to stealing some of Peter Osborne's 'forbidden fruit':

> Having seized and secured the tempting bait, I was about to retreat with the spoil, when a burst of mirth from behind a thicket, accompanied with loud shoutings, suspended my steps, and fixed me motionless with surprise. I held in my hand the proof of my guilt, the consciousness of which shook my frame with a trepidation to which it had been little accustomed. A tumultuous party of young men issues from a grove, and advanced hastily towards me: I attempted not to fly, but, rallying my spirits, firmly waited their approach. (*VP* 14)

At first, Mary does not try to run away, instead 'firmly' waiting for the men to approach, suggesting that she thought she could stand up to these young men. Mary's first reaction shows a youthful unawareness of the danger facing her, one perhaps compounded by the fact that, though Mr Raymond educates her, she does not seem to have much exposure to popular print media or novels, which might show her what sexual violence actually looks like.

Mary very suddenly discovers how she is demarcated as a woman, though, when Osborne grabs and restrains her, calling her 'a true daughter of Eve!' (*VP* 14). Ty highlights the biblical implications here: Mary, equated with Eve and literally taking 'forbidden fruit', becomes 'a figure of temptation in the eyes of men'.[14] In fact, what happens to Mary after Osborne grabs her recalls ideas about 'seduction' and sexual violence in other eighteenth-century fiction:

> As I struggled to disengage myself from his hold, a large straw hat, which shaded my face from the sun, fell back, and, suspended by the riband, hung upon my shoulders; over which, my dishevelled hair streamed in wild disorder. (*VP* 14)

Suddenly, Mary moves from non-sexualised little girl to tempting object of desire with 'dishevelled hair', a sexualised description that recalls how Lovelace describes Clarissa prior to an act he characterises as 'seduction' but which is actually rape: 'Thou has heard me also describe the wavy ringlets of her shining hair, needing neither art nor powder; of itself an ornament, defying all other ornaments; wantoning in and about a neck that is beautiful beyond description'.[15] Clarissa's hair 'wantoning' and 'needing neither art nor powder' indicates its looseness as part of what 'tempts' Lovelace, something that connects her, the paradigmatic, eighteenth-century 'seduced' victim, to Mary Raymond.

Lovelace projects this sexualisation onto Clarissa as a fantasy. In contrast, Mary Raymond perceives her own sexualisation in real time while she is being assaulted. Notably, Mary 'struggle[s]' against Osborne when he initially grabs her but states that she only truly panics after her hair becomes dishevelled: 'Shocked and frightened by a brutality of a manner so novel and unexpected', she recounts, 'with a sudden spring I evaded his grasp, and, winged by terror and disgust, flew towards the boundaries of the park with inconceivable swiftness' (*VP* 14). Although the loosening of her hair appears to be an accident, not an intentional part of Osborne's attack, Mary registers this moment as a more dangerous, 'novel and unexpected' instance of violence, perhaps because of the general societal association between loosened hair and the sexual act. Even though Mary has no knowledge of someone with direct experiences of sexual violence or 'seduction' at this point in the novel, she has an 'odd familiarity' or 'prememory' of her own, potential future sexual assault, to use Brison's terminology, that she is in danger.

Similarly, during the scene in which Osborne forcibly kisses Mary, she only reacts with fear after realising the sexual nature of the attack. At first, when Osborne tries only to physically harm her and William with his whip, she stands defiant:

> My neck and arms bore marks of the rough discipline I had received, yet I neither uttered a complaint nor shed a tear: indignation inspired me with a sullen fortitude; while, in the smart of blows acquired in the cause of humanity and friendship, I found only a source of triumph. (VP 22)

Once again, Mary thinks of herself as a brave subject, unaware, at first, that patriarchal society expects her to be lesser and weaker as a young woman. As soon as Osborne grabs Mary and violently kisses her, she reacts differently, noting, 'I shrieked, struggled, and fought, with all my strength' (V 22). Mary is not scared of being whipped, but she screams and attempts to get away from what she clearly understands as a sexual attack, again underscoring that she knows that sexualised violence, specifically, is something she needs to fear. As in the forbidden fruit scene, she has a fearful prememory of her own potential future assault. Particularly since Mary's fear of a sexual attack interrupts her subversive defiance to Osborne, this scene highlights how the feared future of a sexual attack supports patriarchal oppression and disrupts women and girls' lives.

Thus, Hays deftly shows how a young woman can come to understand the cultural expectations surrounding her, internalising the assumption of victimised status and, in turn, regulating her actions. What separates Mary from other girls is that she has a victimised woman in her family about whom she will come to learn in vivid detail. While the fate of the elder Mary diverges from Brison's idea of societal postmemory, the personal connection she has with her daughter allows it to operate on the latter in much the same way. The younger Mary experiences multiple, vivid pseudo-flashbacks of the trauma her mother went through, up to and including at the moment of her own, unambiguous rape. Despite not being there herself, the younger Mary repeatedly demonstrates a sort of 'postmemory' of her own mother's trauma, with a deft, intimate understanding of what that trauma must have looked like. For example, shortly after reading her mother's correspondence, she visualises her mother in a moment of trauma, one that is more graphic than anything included in the letters:

> I recalled to my remembrance the image of my wretched mother: I beheld her, in idea, abandoned to infamy, cast out of society, stained with blood, expiring on a scaffold, unpitied and unwept. I clasped my hands in agony; terrors assailed me till then unknown; the blood froze in my veins; a shuddering horror crept through my heart. (VP 72)

The younger Mary's thought process reads like a modern depiction of post-traumatic stress disorder. The idea of an unwanted pseudo-flashback comes through in the description of how she 'recalled' the 'image' of her 'mother' to her remembrance'. Moreover, the novel emphasises the physical symptoms of trauma, in the way that Mary clasps her 'hands ... in agony', her 'blood' freezes in her 'veins', and 'a shuddering horror' creeps 'through ... [her] heart', serving to connect her closely with her mother's own embodied experience. This powerfully felt a response is one that indicates far more than Mary's simple shock at discovering the truth of her illegitimate birth.

Mary Raymond's embodied sense of her mother's shock and pain, a postmemory of another woman's experiences, becomes the frame through which she interprets Osborne's actions. These postmemories of her mother never turn into prememories of fearing a future similar fate, perhaps not only because they are of experiences she never really had but also because they are a reinterpretation of her mother's experiences as like those of a victim of sexual violence rather than of social prejudice. The two references to blood, for instance, in Mary Raymond's pseudo-flashback to her mother's life, evoke a sense of trauma linked to sexual victimisation. The image of blood 'staining' her mother's body, as opposed to merely her 'hands', as would better fit with her role as an accomplice to murder, conveys the idea that the elder Mary is herself a victim of violence. The younger Mary's description of her own 'blood' frozen in her 'veins' significantly picks up the description of her earlier experience of one of Osborne's attempts at sexual assault, after which he leaves her with 'hands and arms bruised and scratched, and streaming with blood' (*VP* 14). Clayton Carlyle Tarr notes that Hays also repeatedly refers to blood when describing Mary's awakening sexual attraction to William Pelham, further blurring the lines between consensual transgressive sexual desire (which has such unhappy consequences for her mother) and rape in the text.[16]

Mary Raymond's reinscription via pseudo-flashback of her mother as a survivor of sexual violence intensifies after her own rape. During three weeks of depression following her assault, Mary has repeated pseudo-flashbacks to her mother's experiences:

> One moment, methought I beheld her in the arms of her seducer, reveling in licentious pleasure; the next, I saw her haggard, intoxicated, self-abandoned, joining in the midnight riot; and, in an instant, as the fantastic scene shifted, covered with blood, accused of murder, shrieking in horrible despair. (*VP* 123)

Mary Raymond does not deny that her mother enjoyed 'pleasure', stymied later by her status as a 'ruined' woman who has had premarital sex.

Notably, though, this Mary uses the loaded term 'seducer' (which contrasts with different vocabulary she employs elsewhere in calling William her 'lover'). Arguably, the term 'seducer' more clearly communicates trauma surrounding the sexual encounter, indicating a potential lack of full consent or, at the very least, power differential. This term is further significant when considering parallels with *Clarissa*, a novel rife with characters misunderstanding the lines between seduction and rape. While literally referring to murder, the phrase '[c]overed with blood' serves a similar purpose for Hays in highlighting sexual trauma and presenting the elder Mary as akin to a victim of physical/sexual violence.

The fact that Mary Raymond has a flashback to this moment in her mother's life shortly after her own sexual assault intensifies the connection between the symptoms of her rape trauma and the fate of her mother. To her audience, the younger Mary confides, 'imaginary terrors, broken recollections, strange phantoms, wild and wandering thoughts, harassed and persecuted me. In some of these terrible moments, the visionary form of my wretched mother seemed to flit before me' (*VP* 122–3). Thus, she blurs the lines between her traumatic experience of rape and her mother's consensual transgressive sex. Her flashbacks here suggest almost a reverse of Brison's model of postmemory and prememory. Instead of transmuting 'postmemory' or cultural memory, other women's, or even a single other woman's, experience with sexual trauma or violence into 'prememory' of her own sexual assault, the younger Mary projects a memory of her own, that of rape, back onto her mother, revising via pseudo-flashback and fantasy the 'postmemory' she has of her mother's experiences. She 'remembers' her mother's experiences, despite not being there, just like women and girls acquire a 'memory' of sexual violence they have not (yet) experienced, in order to recast her mother into a victim of violence rather than of prejudice.

Beyond the pain of feeling what her mother felt, Mary Raymond makes a discernibly feminist gesture in imagining her mother as a victim, against the general view of her as outcast and criminal. Society, including family members, rejected the elder Mary, refusing to rehabilitate her and exhibiting disturbing complacency over her final fate. Mary Raymond helps to validate the elder Mary's experiences by acknowledging them as deeply traumatic.

At the same time, Mary the daughter largely erases her mother's experience by projecting an entirely different kind of victimhood onto her. I do not mean to suggest that Mary Raymond deliberately rewrites the story of her mother via fantastical memories with an intent to write a more sympathetic story. Instead, lacking a culturally and legally intelligible way to validate her mother's sexual choices and acknowledge her victimhood simultaneously, Mary makes sense of her mother's trajectory by aligning it with the only terms available to her at this historical moment, the 'strange ... man knowing a woman does not want sex and going ahead anyway'.[17] Recall that even the elder Mary herself is not as direct in blaming the society around her for her downfall as she could be, indicting her own 'vanity' and conceding to misogyny in labelling her experiences as mere 'perception'. Only one type of sexual trauma against women, like what Osborne does to Mary Raymond, is legitimised in official law underpinned by a patriarchal perspective.

In turn, Mary's recharacterisation of her mother's trauma as if it were trauma from sexual violence makes sense, as the most intelligible cultural script related to women's trauma available to her. She turns to this interpretation of events not because recognition as a victim under the law necessarily betters women's lives, as reflected in her own experience of rape and the consequences of rejecting Osborne's marriage proposal, but perhaps because the legally sanctioned victim category that comes with an act of unambiguous sexual violence is an intelligible way of understanding and conveying that her mother is a trauma victim. Brison writes that 'in not telling one's narrative [of sexual violence], one risks acting out the trauma – and causing others to act it out via their postmemories'.[18] The elder Mary lacks a broadly culturally intelligible way of describing her trauma, though she tries in her letters. But because her letters will find only a limited posthumous audience, she lacks the necessary level of empathetic connection that might have prevented the 'act[ing] out' of trauma. *The Victim of Prejudice* casts light on how the focus on legally sanctioned sexual violence as the only culturally intelligible avenue for understanding women's trauma also harms women like the elder Mary who transgresses sexual and social norms to have pleasurable non-marital sex and an illegitimate child. Nobody can seemingly appreciate that the social rejection for living this life is traumatic enough to lead to Mary's criminality and subsequent death.

The text's final moments offer a respite from this bleak picture, allowing the novel to be not only a commentary on the limits placed on cultural understandings of women's trauma, but also, a least briefly, a utopic text offering a glance at what true, women-centred justice could look like. When facing a premature death similar to her mother's, the younger Mary can properly name the kind of 'prejudice' that cut both of their lives short. Unlike her mother, she speaks affirmatively in characterising the past, not couching any of her language:

> The victim of a barbarous prejudice, society has cast me out from its bosom. The sensibilities of my heart have been turned to bitterness, the

powers of my mind wasted, my projects rendered abortive, my virtues and my sufferings alike unrewarded, *I have lived in vain!* unless the story of my sorrows should kindle in the heart of man, in behalf of my oppressed sex, the sacred claims of humanity and justice. (*VP* 174, emphasis in original)

Why is the younger Mary able to so clearly identify and castigate 'prejudice' in the moments before her death, recalling her mother's letter from right before the latter's execution? The suggestion is that when faced with the most direct and drastic consequences of 'prejudice', women can better understand forms of non-legally sanctioned traumas and clearly articulate them. The younger Mary is not as directly concerned with her rape trauma right before death, even though the rape itself was undoubtedly traumatic, as demonstrated in her three-week period of night terrors and flashbacks. Recalling her mother's concerns with prejudice, not her sexual choices, at the end of her life, Mary Raymond is, too, now primarily concerned with the 'barbarous prejudice' that shut her out of society. Importantly, like her mother, this Mary gets to tell her story of experiencing prejudice, both to Mr and Mrs Neville, who care for her at the end of her life, and, of course, to the novel's readers.

Therein lies the novel's hopeful feminist message. Although women have to suffer because of culturally unintelligible trauma, or 'prejudice', women are able to identify that trauma and speak out against it. Regretfully, only Mary Raymond bears witness to her mother's trauma, and she is not able to conceptualise it outside of cultural scripts until the end of her own life. What is powerfully feminist about Hays's novel, though, is that readers receive these direct messages about the problems of 'prejudice' against women, including sexually transgressive women such as the elder Mary, and, because of the directness of Mary Raymond's final testimony, will understand exactly what is traumatic for the women. In this way, *The Victim of Prejudice* delivers on its initial feminist potential, showcasing a profound solidarity between a sexually transgressed victim and a willingly sexually transgressive woman, both of whom are victimised by social 'prejudice' and the law. Mary Raymond uses her final moments to castigate the way 'prejudice' hurt not only herself but her mother, bringing attention to the fact that the sexually transgressive woman suffers just as the transgressed upon woman does, even though the law only registers the latter as a victim and actively disciplines and punishes the former. Although neither Mary could be saved, perhaps readers can walk away from the novel with their consciousness raised about the distinct, yet interrelated traumas women experience under patriarchy, interrupting the standard 'postmemory' internalisation of women's outcomes under patriarchy and working towards reforming androcentric juridical and cultural laws.

Notes

1. Eleanor Ty, *Unsex'd Revolutionaries: Five Women Novelists of the 1790s* (Toronto: University of Toronto Press, 1993), 47–8.
2. Mary Hays, *Appeal to the Men of Great Britain in Behalf of Women*, ed. Gina Luria (New York: Garland Publications, 1972), 28.
3. Ty, *Unsex'd*, 48.
4. Ian Ward, 'The Prejudices of Mary Hays', *International Journal of Law in Context* 5, no. 2 (June 2009): 136–9.
5. Mary Hays, *The Victim of Prejudice*, ed. Eleanor Ty (Toronto: Broadview, 1998), 63. Further references to this text will be given parenthetically, with VP.
6. Eleanor Ty, 'The Imprisoned Female Body in Mary Hays's *The Victim of Prejudice*', in *Women, Revolution, and the Novels of the 1790s*, ed. Linda Lang-Peralta (East Lansing: Michigan State University Press, 2000), 136.
7. Ward, 'The Prejudices', 138.
8. Donna Haraway, 'Situated Knowledges: The Science Question in Feminism and the Privilege of Partial Perspectives', *Feminist Studies* 14, no. 3 (1988). Sandra Harding, 'Strong Objectivity: A Response to the New Objectivity Question', *Synthese* 104, no. 3 (1995). Catharine A. MacKinnon, *Toward a Feminist Theory of the State* (Cambridge, MA: Harvard University Press, 1989).
9. Catharine A. Mackinnon, 'Feminism, Marxism, Method, and the State: Toward Feminist Jurisprudence', *Signs* 8, no. 4 (1983): 653.
10. Frances Ferguson, 'Rape and the Rise of the Novel', *Representations*, no. 20 (Autumn 1987): 92.
11. Marilyn Brooks, 'Mary Hays's *The Victim of Prejudice*: Chastity ReNegotiated', *Women's Writing* 15, no. 1 (2008): 27.
12. Susan Brison, *Aftermath: Violence and the Remaking of a Self* (Princeton: Princeton University Press, 2002), 87.
13. Ibid., 87.
14. Eleanor Ty, introduction to *The Victim of Prejudice*, ed. Eleanor Ty (Peterborough: Broadview, 1998), xx.
15. Samuel Richardson, *Clarissa: or the History of a Young Lady*, ed. Angus Ross (London: Penguin Books, 1985), 399.
16. Clayton Carlisle Tarr, 'The Loss of Maidenhead: Rape and the Revolutionary Novel', *Eighteenth Century Fiction* 21, no. 3 (Spring 2019): 568.
17. MacKinnon, 'Feminism, Marxism', 653.
18. Brison, *Aftermath*, 98.

Chapter 6

'Thoughts that Breathe and Words that Burn': Barbauld, Masturbation and the Novel

Kathryn Ready

Against a persistent image of Anna Letitia Barbauld as a paragon of feminine propriety and, as younger male contemporaries such as Samuel Taylor Coleridge would have it, passionless and sexually frigid, William McCarthy argues that she was in fact 'one of very few' of her generation 'who granted teenage girls an erotic life and acknowledged their fantasies', perhaps 'remember[ing] her own'.[1] As evidence, he cites a little-known short prose piece entitled 'Allegory on Sleep', first published in *A Legacy for Young Ladies* (1826). In this piece, the narrator chastises a young female friend for her enthralment by a secret lover. She accuses this friend of abandoning her 'most sprightly and once-loved amusements' to her lover's 'soft enchantment', noticing that in his absence she appears 'languid' and 'pale', with 'the marks of his power' all too visible in her 'eyes and ... whole carriage'.[2] McCarthy remarks, '[b]esides their ostensible reference to effects of oversleeping, "languid" and "pale" may suggest the supposed evil effects of masturbation', a subtext that at least one reviewer seems to have picked up on in questioning the 'propriety' of this piece.[3] McCarthy treats 'Allegory on Sleep' essentially as a one-off, barely mentioning the subject of masturbation again in his lengthy biography of Barbauld. However, his take on this piece indirectly raises questions about the potential relevance of masturbation as a theme elsewhere in Barbauld's writings. Given the recurring association between the novel and masturbation in the extensive body of anti-masturbation literature produced throughout the eighteenth century and Romantic period, with which Barbauld was clearly familiar, McCarthy raises questions most immediately with respect to her novel-criticism.[4] Indeed, there are indications in Barbauld's novel-criticism of a tacit (and sometimes not so tacit) response to contemporary discourse around masturbation and the novel. While Barbauld concedes some of the risks that French romances and novels had run for readers as fuel for autoerotic fantasy, she denies that English prose fiction posed the same problems and defends the general respectability of the novel as a form. Moreover, she resists the idea that modernity and novel-reading had introduced any fresh danger related to the masturbatory application of literature and ultimately can be seen as not heavily condemning masturbation, in her own writing playing freely with masturbatory tropes, including in 'Allegory on Sleep', perhaps another reason it was considered improper.

The Dangers of Dreamy Readers

Within the study of the history of sexuality, the most substantial treatment of masturbation remains Thomas Laqueur's *Solitary Sex* (2003). Laqueur draws, in turn, on Michel Foucault's argument that the nineteenth century was characterised by a process of medicalising and pathologising bodies and sexualities under a new regime of sexual discipline that increasingly replaced external mechanisms of control with internal ones.[5] Laqueur points to evidence that this process had already begun during the eighteenth century in relation to masturbation because, he speculates, it seemed to embody, more than any other form of sexual activity, the dangers of an emergent modern capitalist system.[6] In his view, those who condemned masturbation worried that 'it was motivated not by a real object of desire but by a phantasm'.[7] As such, this activity 'threatened to overwhelm the most protean and potentially creative of the mind's faculties – the imagination'.[8] Laqueur sketches a parallel here with contemporary anxiety concerning the operation of credit, which was central to the financial revolution underpinning commercial capitalism and a 'magically promised undreamed-of abundance, shakily linked to the concrete reality of real goods and services'.[9] He posits that masturbation was further vilified because it was private. As he observes, 'privacy and secrecy ... had ... positive associations ... as sites of truth and as foundations of the real self' capable of agency and self-control but were linked equally with solipsism, selfishness and self-indulgence.[10] Masturbation generated additional fears, so Laqueur contends, because of the suspicion that 'unlike other appetites [for pleasure], the urge to masturbate could be neither sated nor moderated', in the same way that consumption constituted a never-ending self-perpetuating phenomenon (as anti-luxury writers had warned since ancient times).[11]

Laqueur further chronicles how fears regarding masturbation became intertwined in the eighteenth century with cultural anxiety over novel-reading, which was similarly pathologised in the period. The connection between novels and masturbation appears to have been made partly in response to historical developments in print culture and reading practices, as printed material exponentially increased to meet consumer demand. People were reading more and more to themselves, silently and privately, than to others out loud (a circumstance presumed to heighten the impact of the reading experience, raising the stakes involved in a rapidly expanding consumer print market, which was enabling the spread of different kinds of socially dangerous material, including 'heresy, politically and religiously dangerous thoughts, romances, erotica').[12] While acknowledging that 'warnings about the dangers of private reading of imaginative literature had a long history', Laqueur posits that such warnings now took on a different inflection, as commentators focused on the masturbatory danger inherent to the solitary reading of novels, especially when they explored 'sexual themes'.[13] Drawing on a wide range of sources from the period, he shows how onanism and novel-reading were assumed to have similar negative consequences on physical and mental health.

As scholars have equally shown, anxiety over novel-reading during the eighteenth century centred consistently on women. According to Laqueur, 'women were thought by men – and by some women – to be the prototypical absorbed readers' and 'the woman reader was the gold standard of the moral corruption latent in all fiction'.[14] Another scholar, Alexandre Wenger, notes the popularisation in eighteenth-century French visual culture of '*lectrices-rêveuses*': women depicted in the act of suspended reading and abstracted dreaming.[15] The faces of these *lectrices-rêveuses* characteristically register a state of blissful ecstasy, and their clothing often appears suggestively dishevelled. Among the prominent anti-masturbation writers who condemned female novel-reading was Samuel-Auguste Tissot, author of *L'Onanisme. Dissertation sur les maladies produites par la masturbation* (1760). In another treatise, *De la santé des gens de lettres* (1768), Tissot blames '*la multiplication infinie des romans depuis cent ans*' (the endless multiplication of novels in the last hundred years) as the principal cause of ill health in women.[16] Another eighteenth-century anti-masturbation writer, Christoph Wilhelm Hufeland, complains that women's habitual reading of novels had corrupted the imagination ('*a corrompu l'imagination*'), as they have heated their minds with voluptuous and lascivious images ('*images voluptueuses et lascives*'), falling into 'moral onanism' ('*onanisme moral*'), presumably the next step down the slippery slope towards literal masturbation.[17]

We know from her correspondence that Barbauld read James Fordyce's *Sermons to Young Women* (1766), a popular example of conduct writing for young women that can be seen taking up contemporary anti-masturbatory concerns regarding female novel-reading. This treatise contains the following memorable admonition to young female readers:

> We consider the general run of Novels as utterly unfit for you. Instruction they convey none. They paint scenes of pleasure and passion altogether improper for you to behold, even with the mind's eye. Their descriptions are often loose and luscious in a high degree; their representations of love between the sexes almost universally overstrained.[18]

While Fordyce makes no direct mention of masturbation, he clearly conveys the idea that 'scenes of pleasure and passion' and 'loose' and 'luscious' descriptions in novelistic 'representations of love' were dangerous provocations to autoerotic fantasy.

Another relevant conduct writer with which Barbauld was undoubtedly familiar is Vicesimus Knox, who anthologised a number of her poems in his *Elegant Extracts ... for the Improvement of Young Persons* (1796). In his *Essays, Moral and Literary* (1778), Knox writes that '[i]f it be true, that the present age is more corrupt than the preceding, the great multiplication of Novels has probably contributed to its degeneracy'.[19] More pointedly still, he warns that novels 'often pollute the heart in the recesses of the closet, inflame the passions at a distance from temptation, and teach all the malignity of vice in solitude', taking particular aim at sentimental fiction.[20]

Barbauld was also a personal acquaintance of Thomas Beddoes, a medical practitioner who saw himself inheriting the anti-masturbation mantle of Tissot.[21] In *Hygeia, or Essays Moral and Medical* (1802–3), Beddoes allows that different kinds of writing had historically provided fuel for masturbation but singles out female novel-reading, which made up the bulk of 'circulating-library literature', for special condemnation.[22] As he supposes, 'the sensations to which all these melting tales immediately give rise, and the voluptuous reveries, which they leave behind, may without injustice, be regarded as part of the concealed fountain, from which the NILE of female unhealthiness derives its origin'.[23] Despite his professed admiration for male novelists such as Alain-René Le Sage, Samuel Richardson, Pierre de Marivaux, Laurence Sterne, Johann Paul Friedrich Richter 'and their equals', Beddoes expresses the hope and conviction that 'as science is a little more improved, and morals a little better understood, many admired novels will be banished in a body to the same shelf with *Jack the Giant-killer* and *Tom Hickathrift*', renounced in favour of more scientific reading, which, significantly, he views as a remedy for the modern epidemic of masturbation.[24]

Conceding Novelistic Dangers

In her most substantial contribution to novel-criticism, 'On the Origin and Progress of Novel-Writing', the prefatory essay composed for her multi-volume series, *The British Novelists* (1810), Barbauld reiterates the concerns expressed by Beddoes and others over the modern growth of the novel-market and the negative influence of novel-reading, especially on young women.[25] As she observes, 'till the middle of the last century, theatrical productions and poetry made a far greater part of polite reading than novels', for confirmation referring her readers to Joseph Addison's *Spectator* No. 37 (12 April 1711). In *Spectator* No. 37, Addison describes the private library of a recently widowed lady, 'Leonora', who now devotes herself to 'Books and Retirement'.[26] Barbauld reminds us that nowhere in this library or anywhere else in the *Spectator* does there 'occur ... the name of one English novel ... [Delarivier Manley's *The New*] *Atalantis* [1709] only excepted; though plays are often mentioned as a favourite and dangerous part of ladies' reading'.[27] She goes on to recount how the success of writers such as Richardson, Henry Fielding and Tobias Smollett generated an unappeasable appetite 'for this kind of entertainment, that it had ever since been furnished from the press, rather as a regular and necessary supply, than as an occasional gratification'.[28] As a result of this expanding novel-market, she notes, '[t]he indiscriminate passion for ... [novels] and their bad effects on the female mind ... became the object of ... satire ... in a sprightly piece entitled *Polly Honeycomb*' [sic], a text which Laqueur cites directly to corroborate his argument about coalescing attitudes around the novel and masturbation during the eighteenth century.[29] Laqueur understands the main point of George Colman the Elder's *Polly Honeycombe: A Dramatick Novel of One Act* (1761) as that 'novels, like seductive whispers and dirty talk, turned women on, made them forget their honor, and led to every sort of deviant social practice'.[30] Barbauld subsequently laments the continued exponential growth of the novel-market, so that 'a great deal of trash is every season poured out upon the public from the English presses' and into the 'circulating library'.[31] She expresses specific disappointment that novels tend to 'paint' the 'passion of love, the most seductive of all the passions', 'too high'.[32]

At the same time, throughout 'On the Origin and Progress of Novel-Writing', Barbauld associates masturbatory danger most closely with French romances and novels. She repeatedly dwells on the 'bad effects' of 'the romances *de longue haleine*, which originated in France, and of which ... [Gauthier de Costes, seigneur de la Calprenède] and ... [Madeleine de] Scudery were the most distinguished authors'.[33] As she acknowledges, the French romances adhere to a 'principle' of 'high honour, impregnable chastity, a constancy unshaken by time or accident, and a species of love so exalted and refined, that it bore little resemblance to a natural passion'.[34] Notwithstanding this acknowledgement, she regrets the dangerous influence that 'the romances *de longue haleine*' had on 'the seductive, the passionate' Jean-Jacques Rousseau.[35] Drawing directly on the account that Rousseau himself provided in his *Confessions* (1782–9), she observes that 'his childhood was conversant in these romances, (a course of reading which no doubt fed and inflamed his fine imagination)'.[36] Although she never makes a direct connection between this reading and Rousseau's notorious disclosure regarding his boyhood practice of the '*supplément dangereux*', it is not a far leap for her readers to make. Nor is it easy to miss the subtext in her subsequent ambivalent tribute to Rousseau's own writing. While she regards Rousseau as the foremost French novelist and 'the most eloquent writer in the most eloquent modern language', she admits,

> whether his glowing pencil paints the strong emotions of passion, or the enchanting scenery of nature in his own romantic country, or his peculiar cast of moral sentiment, – a charm is spread over every part of the work, which scarcely leaves the judgment free to condemn what in it is dangerous and reprehensible. His are truly the 'Thoughts that breathe and words that burn'.[37]

As Barbauld implies, Rousseau produces writings that partake in the same masturbatory danger as his once favourite romances despite his own injunctions to the contrary.[38]

While Barbauld cites *Spectator* No. 37 principally as a testimony to the state of the early eighteenth-century British novel-market, her quotation of the passage in which Addison describes '[t]*he grand Cyrus*, with a pin stuck in one of the leaves' and '*Clelia*, which opened of itself in the place that describes two lovers in a bower', again evokes the masturbatory danger of French romances.[39] In this passage, Addison underscores Leonora's sexually oriented interest in Scudéry's works, *Artamène, ou le Grand Cyrus* (1649–53) and *Clélie* (1654–6), and raises the possibility that they are being employed as masturbatory aids (with the image of the pin stuck in one of the book's leaves evoking, in itself, the act of sexual penetration, either phallic or digital).

Looking at *Spectator* No. 37 as a whole, we see much that resonates with Laqueur's account of emergent anxiety around masturbation.[40] Mr Spectator distrusts the solitary and private aspect of Leonora's reading and the effect of too many 'Books' in the library of 'little more use than to divert the Imagination'.[41] Bradford K. Mudge notably regards Leonora as exemplifying a '"Passion[ate]" ... rather than ... "Understanding" reader who reads to indulge her "Imagination"'.[42] Among the other books on Leonora's shelves are many above reproach: a translation of Virgil and various works of history, philosophy and science. There are also moral and spiritual writings, including by Jeremy Taylor. Yet, details such as the 'Paper of Patches' in Leonora's copy of John Locke's *Essay Concerning Human Understanding* (1690) and the 'Bottle of Hungary Water' in her prayer book, and the set of wood mock-ups of 'Classick Authors', undermine any claims to intellectual or moral seriousness.[43] Equally consistent with Laqueur, Leonora's reading is conflated with uncontrolled (and perhaps uncontrollable) desire, a point underscored metaphorically in the references to consumerism: Mr Spectator notes the 'great Jars of *China*' serving as bookends for Leonora's folios, the 'delightful Pyramid' of 'Vessels' separating the '*Quarto[]s ... from the Octavo[]s*', and the 'Tea Dishes' forming an arrangement around the octavos, as well as 'a thousand other odd Figures in *China* Ware' adjacent to an enclave 'designed for the Reception of Plays and Pamphlets, and other loose Papers' and 'a little Japan Table, with a Quire of gilt Paper upon it, and on the Paper a Silver Snuff-box made in the Shape of a little Book'.[44]

Defending Novelistic Pleasures

While registering fears concerning French fiction, however, Barbauld raises no comparable objections to English writers. She has nothing negative to say about English romances such as Sir Philip Sidney's *Arcadia* (1593), simply admiring its 'great beauties, particularly in poetic imagery'.[45] She also consistently defends the character of English (and other British) novels, celebrating her contemporary countrywomen for having brought the form to a pinnacle of development.[46] Indeed, she insists that 'in general ... [English] novels are not vicious' and that the 'chief harm' of the 'circulating library' in England was the encouragement of 'frivolity' and 'loss of time'.[47] She grants that occasionally 'a girl perhaps may be led ... to elope with a coxcomb; or if she is handsome, to expect the homage of a Sir Harry or My lord, instead of the plain tradesman suitable to her situation in life', but she pointedly adds that such a girl 'will not have her mind contaminated with such scenes and ideas as Crebillon, Louvet, and others of that class have published in France', referring to Claude Prosper Jolyot de Crébillon and Jean-Baptiste Louvet de Couvray, best known for *Le Sopha conte moral* (1742) and *Les Amours du Chevalier de Faublas* (1786–91) respectively.[48] Regarding the works of Crébillon and others that had been 'sold *sous le manteau*', Barbauld affirms, 'These are not merely exceptionable, they are totally unfit to enter a house where the morals of young people are esteemed an object', identifying 'gross sensual pleasure' as 'the very heart of them'.[49] The phrase '*sous le manteau*' evidently refers to the clandestine mode of sale, but also incidentally calls to mind the first plate in William Hogarth's *A Harlot's Progress* (1731), where a man (reportedly inspired by the controversial real-life figure of Colonel Francis Charteris) has been identified as masturbating beneath his coat as he leers from afar at the young country maiden, Mary or Moll Hackabout, being procured for him by a middle-aged bawd.[50]

Indeed, Barbauld frequently glosses over moral lapses among English writers. She rather mildly characterises Manley's sexually graphic amatory fiction as 'filled with fashionable scandal'.[51] After pronouncing the novels of Aphra Behn 'licentious' and 'fallen', she enjoins us to remember 'that [Thomas] Southern[e] borrowed from her his affecting story of *Oroonoko*'.[52] If she condemns the 'earlier novels' of Eliza Haywood, she commends her as 'a very prolific genius' whose 'later works are by no means void of merit'.[53] There are further generous allowances made for male writers whose moral tendencies had been widely criticised. On the one hand, she regards the 'indelicacies' of Sterne as 'very reprehensible'.[54] On the other hand, she allows him 'much originality, wit, and beautiful strokes of pathos'.[55] This same spirit of generosity extends to other critical essays in *The British Novelists*. In her introduction to *Tom Jones* (1749) in volume nineteen, Barbauld rebukes Fielding for the 'indelicate pictures' he presents 'to the imagination'.[56] Nevertheless, she declares, '[t]here is perhaps no novel in the English language so artfully conducted, or so rich in humour and character', lavishing additional praise on his 'scenes that interest the heart'.[57] This overall assessment and inclusion of *Tom Jones* as one of the selections in *The British Novelists* suggest that Barbauld had a higher tolerance for novels that featured 'indelicate pictures' than, say, Samuel Johnson, on record as having stated that this 'corrupt work' is one that 'no modest lady' ever ought to admit to having read.[58] According to Claudia L. Johnson, the first critics who compared Barbauld's *The British Novelists* with a later competing novel-series edited by Sir Walter Scott 'described the difference … as one of emancipated sexual morality', crediting Scott, because he was a man, as able 'to include … the marvelously full-blooded, ribald English novels, supposedly passed over by Barbauld because she was "a stickler for feminine decorum"'.[59] Yet, such an assessment does not square with Barbauld's inclusion of *Tom Jones* in her lineup, and this same critic wonders whether 'Scott's interventions have more to do with politics and gender than … with sexual morality'.[60]

There is additionally much to soften Barbauld's negative commentary on French fiction. Barbauld fully credits the contributions of Scudéry, La Calprenède and Marie-Madeleine Pioche de La Vergne, comtesse de La Fayette, towards the development of a modern tradition of literary realism. She specifically praises *Cassandra* (1642–5 or 1650) for inspiring a memorably 'affecting incident in [Rousseau's *Julie, ou la*] *Nouvelle Heloise*' (1761).[61] Warnings against the novels of Rousseau and Germaine de Staël pay simultaneous tribute to their powers. According to Barbauld, these authors represent 'to the young mind in glowing colours' 'passions, which all have felt, and few are even desirous to resist', 'awaken[ing] and increas[ing] sensibilities, which it is the office of wise restraint to calm and to moderate'.[62] The assessment of Le Sage resembles that of Fielding, as Barbauld finds the 'dubious morality' of Le Sage's writings in some measure offset by the 'entertainment', 'exquisite humour' and 'lessons of life' they provide.[63] Other French writers receive only approbation, including Marivaux, Françoise de Graffigny, Jacques-Henri Bernardin de Saint-Pierre and Isabelle de Montolieu, prompting an acknowledgement that '[f]or the expression of sentiment in all its various shades, for the most delicate tact, and a refinement and polish, the fruit of high cultivation, the French writers are superior to those of every other nation'.[64]

Setting aside her views on individual works, Barbauld signals clearly that her overarching aim is to defend the novel as a literary form. In her opinion, novels demanded 'talents of the highest order', ranking alongside other works that had 'made a part of the polite literature of every age and nation'.[65] With a nod to Fielding, she adds that '[a] good novel' is essentially 'an epic in prose'.[66] Indeed, she privileges novels over other literary forms in the breadth of their appeal, remarking that the 'leaves of novels are seldom found unopened, and they occupy the parlour and the dressing-room while productions of higher name are often gathering dust upon the shelf'.[67] Although the point of the novel is, for her, to entertain, rather than 'to call in fancy to the aid of reason' and 'to deceive the mind into embracing truth under the guise of fiction', she stresses the value of novels as widely available 'innocent pleasures'.[68] In striking contrast to those who fretted over the use to which novels might be put in solitude, she characterises the experience of novel-reading as fundamentally social even when done alone. Indeed, there is a hint that she regards novels as a potential prescription against masturbation (if so, perhaps quietly answering Beddoes). As she emphasises, 'the humble novel is always ready to enliven the gloom of solitude, to soothe the languor of debility and disease, to win the attention from pain or vexatious occurrences', and 'to take man from himself (at many seasons the worst company he can be in)'.[69] The phrases 'gloom of solitude' and 'languor of debility' recall the presumed adverse effects of masturbation during the period, in which Barbauld at least partially implicates the novel. However, the assurance that the novel will 'enliven' and 'take man from himself' intimates that this kind of reading, far from exacerbating any symptoms of weakness associated with masturbation, will improve the state of mind by bringing the reader again into the social world, if only in the imagination. A valuable moral benefit of the novel she sees for female readers is notably in providing knowledge of the world 'with less danger ... than by mixing in real life'.[70]

Foundational to Barbauld's defence of the novel against those who worried about its masturbatory dangers was her view that the novel was, in fact, not particularly new. While recognising issues around an expanding novel-market, Barbauld emphasises continuity between the modern novel and ancient 'fictitious adventures', whether in prose, poetry or drama. She conspicuously refers to the ancient prose fictional *Milesian Tales* as 'novels', and Heliodorus's *Theagenes and Chariclea* as 'romance or novel'.[71] As she underscores in another critical piece, 'On Romances' (1773), romances and novels had no unique claim as literary works in compelling human interest and stimulating an appetite for more. In this piece, she asserts that all 'narrations of feigned events, descriptions of imaginary scenes, and delineations of ideal characters' 'are perused' with 'insatiable avidity' as compared with other writings.[72] The verse quotation Barbauld employs in 'On the Origin and Progress of Novel-Writing' to sum up the effect of Rousseau's fiction is significantly taken from 'A Progress of Poesy: A Pindaric Ode' (1757), in which Thomas Gray pays tribute to fellow practitioners of the Pindaric ode. The original passage develops the distinct image of poet as masturbator, Gray describing poets whose 'hands the lyre explore' (107), causing 'Fancy' to scatter 'from her pictur'd urn / Thoughts that breath[e], and words, that burn' (109–10).[73] Whether or not Barbauld was picking up on this image, the application of Gray's line to Rousseau serves, at the very least, to undercut any too great distinction between novels and poetry.

The recognition that love and sex were literary themes of enduring popularity seems to have further diminished any particular fears that Barbauld might have had regarding the novel. Beddoes and others saw the preoccupation with love in the novel as what chiefly made it dangerous (Beddoes allowing that other kinds of literature, including even Homer and the Bible, had provided an incentive to masturbation with the odd titillating passage but still regarding the threat posed by novels as uniquely serious).[74] Barbauld insists in 'On the Origins and Progress of Novel-Writing' that 'the effect of novel-reading must depend, as in every kind of reading, on the choice which is made' and that, so long as 'looser compositions ... are excluded ... and the sentimental ones chiefly perused ... the danger lies more in fixing the standard of virtue and delicacy too high for real use, than in debasing it' and in setting up young women for disappointment in a world where love played very little part.[75] At the beginning of the same essay, she demonstrates clearly that readers had always needed to be discerning and careful, lamenting the *Milesian Tales* as 'loose love stories' nevertheless 'very popular among the Romans'.[76] As she notes further, enemies blamed these stories for having effeminised Roman soldiers (an accusation that parallels eighteenth-century and Romantic-era anxieties about the effects of masturbation and novels on male readers).[77] In 'The Origin of Song-Writing', a poem written decades earlier for her brother's collection *Essays on Song-Writing* (1772), she invents a mythological origin story that explains the fixing of love as a literary theme in poetry.[78] The narrator of this poem recounts how Venus was 'vex'd' (9) to see the small and haphazard influence of her son Cupid, who spent his days roaming about the countryside, ignored by the heroes.[79] We are told that to remedy this situation Venus took Cupid to the Muses on Mount Olympus, urging them to 'receive the child' (39) and '[c]onduct him thr'o ... [their] fav'rite bowers' (47), their 'solemn shades and springs that lie / Remote from each unhallow'd eye' (49–50). The speaker goes on to describe how Venus's 'rosy breath perfum'd the air / And scatter'd sweet contagion there' (41–2), overpowering the Muses and causing '[r]elenting nature ... to languish' (43) and sicken 'with delightful anguish' (44). Having acquired sway over the Muses through his mother, Cupid tunes their lyre '[t]o languid notes of soft desire' (64). The rest of the poem provides a brief history of love poetry, from Sappho's 'soft infectious page' (67) to modern song. As an aside, it should be noted that this poem serves indirectly to put into historical perspective contemporary worries about solitary novel-reading and masturbation. As hinted at in Cupid's retreat into the Muses' 'bowers', novels were not the only form of literature to have been associated historically with privacy and solitude. Love poetry had already long had this association. The poem also raises questions about whether masturbation and novels deserved to have a particular pathology attached to them, given that, for millennia, love had been recognised as an illness and cause of disease and love poetry as a primary vector of transmission.

Playing with Masturbation

Other poems Barbauld wrote for *Essays on Song-Writing* invite doubts that she was ever too seriously worried about the masturbatory danger of novels or any other kind of literature. In 'Song I', she reworks a masturbatory trope with a long history in literary representations of love, as she adopts the perspective of a forlorn male lover who seeks a solitary spot in nature to bemoan the unattainability of his mistress and to fantasise about a union with her. Through the voice of this male lover, she pronounces,

> If when the darling maid is gone,
> Thou dost not seek to be alone,
> Wrapt in a pleasing trance of tender woe,
> And muse, and fold thy languid arms,
> Feeding thy fancy on her charms,
> Thou dost not love, for love is nourish'd so. (31–6)

After making this pronouncement, Barbauld's speaker then challenges other male youths to 'strive whose fancy shall be lost / In dreams of fondest passion most' (45–6). As such, Barbauld arguably legitimises and licenses indulgence in romantic and sexual fantasy as a sign of the capacity for true love.

A version of this same masturbatory trope appears in 'Allegory on Sleep'.[80] Here, the narrator pictures her addressee Miss D**** caught up in autoerotic reverie, 'reclined on … [her imaginary secret lover's] bosom, on a soft carpet of flowers, on the banks of a purling stream', enjoying 'the murmuring of the waters, the whispering of the trees, the silence and solitude of the place, and the luxurious softness of everything around … [her]'.[81] This scene incidentally invites parallels to settings in French seventeenth-century romances and English romances, for example, book II of Edmund Spenser's *The Faerie Queene* (1590–6), where hapless knights dally with the sorceress Acrasia in her 'Bower of Blisse'. Like Spenser, Barbauld mixes allegory and romance throughout this piece, characterising Miss D****'s lover as a 'powerful enchanter' who has an aristocratic pedigree predating the reign of William the Conqueror, explicitly conjuring up the chivalric romances of King Arthur and the Knights of the Round Table. Barbauld's identification of the lover as the half-brother of Death is consistent with Greco-Roman mythology, where Hypnos/Somnus and Thanatos/Mors are brothers, reflecting obvious resemblances between the state of sleep and that of death. At the same time, it fits with contemporary assumptions regarding the potentially deadly consequences of masturbation.[82] Still, any sense of real danger is arguably undercut at the end of 'Allegory on Sleep', as the narrator admits her own enthralment to the very lover she has been counselling her young friend to be wary of all along. 'I myself', she discloses, 'though my situation affords a thousand reasons to resist him which do not take place with you, have been but too sensible of … [this lover's] attractions'.[83] Tellingly, she concludes by retracting her advice, as she reflects that her own act of composition and Miss D*****'s attention to it are proof that the lover's power is only intermittent. Indeed, if 'Allegory on Sleep' recognises female autoerotic fantasy as potentially dangerous, it implies that it can be managed, controlled and transformed into a source of female creativity as material for Barbauld's own literary excursion here.

Barbauld thus emerges as appropriating and subverting an eighteenth-century and Romantic tradition of anti-masturbation writing and challenging the still consolidating regime of sexuality that Laqueur has outlined. In questioning the status quo on masturbation, she equally lends weight to Richard C. Sha's argument that this period exhibits a fundamental uncertainty on the subject of masturbation, producing an 'epistemological panic' that allowed potential escape from discipline. Part of Sha's project has been to trace how late eighteenth- and early nineteenth-century medical discussions of masturbation contributed towards the regulation of sex and direction of 'sexual pleasure and the somatic experience of that pleasure' towards heterosexuality and sex within marriage for the purpose of procreation.[84] However, he points to many instances in which physicians were forced to confront the unreliability of the body in disclosing sexual secrets, which acquired yet greater inscrutability with the increasing location of the sex drive in the brain. While aware of and not entirely willing to discount contemporary fears on the subject of masturbation and novel-reading, Barbauld excuses and even indulges in a degree of autoerotic fantasy in her own writing, discovering in it a source of creative and imaginative vision (a particularly striking move for a woman writer). It may be that a similar lesson to the one Eve Kosofsky Sedgwick draws concerning Jane Austen applies to Barbauld. In her well-known article, 'Jane Austen and the Masturbating Girl' (1991), Sedgwick posits that the success of the disciplinary discourse that Foucault documents has historically obscured an erotics of masturbation in Austen's novel *Sense and Sensibility* (1811), published a year after Barbauld's *The British Novelists*. By her account, *Sense and Sensibility* features in the story of its two sister-heroines, Elinor and Marianne Dashwood, testimony to the power of this erotics in Elinor's 'one-directional visual fixation with her sister's specularized, desired, envied, and punished autoeroticism'.[85] However, as Sedgwick observes, readings of this novel have focused on the disciplining and punishing of Marianne in ways that have been, despite their ostensibly '*anti*repressive' agenda, 'frankly repressive' or 'structured by what Foucault calls "the repressive hypothesis"' (with similar shortcomings discernible in much general scholarship on Austen, fixated, all too frequently, on 'the spectacle of the Girl Being Taught a Lesson').[86] Sedgwick identifies indirect remnants of this disciplinary discourse in persisting attitudes towards masturbation in her own times. While today masturbation is widely accepted as a normal and healthy practice, it still tends to be relegated to a presumed immature stage in sexual development and to carry persisting connotations of 'hilarity' and self-indulgence (evident, as Sedgwick points out, in the initially dismissive and, even alarmist, response to her own scholarship on Austen and masturbation, cited by some as a purported illustration of 'degeneracy' in the academic humanities).[87] Barbauld, like Austen, furnishes an opportunity to recover a lost female erotics of masturbation in the eighteenth century and Romantic period, with potential connections to be made elsewhere in the era.[88] The recovery of such a tradition is of conceivably more value than simply historic curiosity.

Notes

1. William McCarthy, *Anna Letitia Barbauld: Voice of Enlightenment* (Baltimore: Johns Hopkins University Press, 2008), 504. For Coleridge's statement to this effect, see Samuel Taylor Coleridge, in *Table Talk*, ed. Carl Woodring, 2 vols. (Princeton: Princeton University Press, 1990), 1: 564–5.
2. Anna Letitia Barbauld, 'Allegory on Sleep', in *A Legacy for Young Ladies: Consisting of Miscellaneous Pieces, in Prose and Verse by the Late Mrs Barbauld*, ed. Lucy Aikin (London: Printed for Longman, Hurst, Rees, Orme, Brown and Green, Paternoster Row, 1826), 214–15. Another passage suggestive of the dangers of masturbation is the narrator's lament that her friend has apparently renounced 'the pursuit of knowledge and pursuit of pleasure', except for 'the enervating indulgence of ... [her] passion' (216). McCarthy tentatively identifies Barbauld's addressee, Miss D****, as her friend Judith Dixon (afterwards Beecroft), and, on this basis, posits a possible composition date to much earlier on in Barbauld's literary career, perhaps around 1780.
3. McCarthy, *Voice*, 504, 669.
4. As an afterthought, McCarthy tantalisingly closes his discussion of 'Allegory on Sleep' in an endnote with the claim that '[s]ince masturbation was associated more or less openly with novel reading, ALB's defense of novels in 1810 did ... verge on defending the erotic'. McCarthy, *Voice*, 669.
5. Michel Foucault, *The History of Sexuality, Vol. 1: An Introduction*, trans. Robert Hurley (New York: Vintage, 1990).
6. Laqueur identifies the very first example of anti-masturbation writing as the anonymous pamphlet *Onania*, which he dates between 1708 and 1716, favouring 1712 as a middle date within this range. He attributes authorship to John Marten, whose confirmed publications include *Treatise of Venereal Disease* (1708) and *Gonosologium Novum* (1709). He dismisses another previously proposed possibility, Balthasar Bekker, a resident of Amsterdam and minister of the Dutch Reformed Church who visited

England and France before he died in 1698. See Thomas Laqueur, *Solitary Sex: A Cultural History of Masturbation* (New York: Zone Books, 2003), 84. For various datings of *Onania* see Christopher Fox, 'The Myth of Narcissus in Swift's *Travels*', in *Reader Entrapment in Eighteenth-Century Literature*, ed. Carl R. Kropf (New York: AMS Press, 1987), 92–3; G. J. Barker-Benfield, *The Culture of Sensibility: Sex and Society in Eighteenth-Century Britain* (Chicago: University of Chicago Press, 1992), 329; Franz X. Eder, 'Discourse and Sexual Desire: German Language Discourse on Masturbation in the Late Eighteenth Century', *Journal of the History of Sexuality* 13, no. 4 (October 2004): 434; and Anne Elizabeth Carson, '"Exquisite Torture": The Autoeroticism of Pope's Eloisa', *Eighteenth-Century Studies* 40, no. 4 (Spring 2007): 618.
7. Laqueur, *Solitary*, 210.
8. Ibid., 210.
9. Ibid., 279.
10. Ibid., 226.
11. Ibid., 210.
12. Ibid., 308.
13. Ibid., 314, 316.
14. Ibid., 340.
15. Alexandre Wenger, 'Lire l'onanisme. Le discours médical sur la masturbation et la lecture féminine au xviiie siècle', *Clio* 22 (2005): 228. Wenger explains how the pathologising of masturbation was given impetus by the shift away from the model of '*homme-machine*' (man-machine), which envisions a strict dualistic separation between the mind and the body, towards vitalism, which sees human beings as more than the sum of their parts and the body as closely bound to the mind (with the character of women's minds directly determined by their purportedly weaker and more sensitive bodies). All translations from French are mine.
16. Samuel-Auguste Tissot, *De la santé des gens de lettres*, 1768 (Paris: Éditions de la Différence, 1991), 166.
17. Christoph Wilhelm Friedrich Hufeland, *La macrobiotique ou l'art de prolonger la vie de l'homme; par C.-F. Hufeland, Premier médecin et conseiller d'État du roi de Prusse*, 1796, trans. A. J. L. Jourdan (Paris: J. B. Baillière, 1838), 211, 210.
18. James Fordyce, *Sermons to Young Women*, 1766, 6th ed., 2 vols. (Dublin: Printed for James Williams, 1767), 2: 107.
19. Vicesimus Knox, *Essays, Moral and Literary*, 2 vols. (London: Printed for Edward and Charles Dilly, 1778), 1: 68.
20. Knox, *Essays*, 1: 70. Eve Kosofsky Sedgwick discusses in some detail the special connection that was made between sentimental fiction and masturbation. See Eve Kosofsky Sedgwick, 'Jane Austen and the Masturbating Girl', *Critical Inquiry* 17, no. 4 (Summer 1991): 820.
21. Thomas Beddoes, *Hygeia: Or Essays Moral and Medical on the Causes Affecting the Personal State of our Middling and Affluent Classes*, 3 vols. (Bristol: Printed by J. Mills for R. Phillips, 1802–3), 1.4: 40. This work is divided into essays with their own title and separate page numbering, so citations refer to volume number, essay number and page number within each essay. In 1797, Barbauld consulted with Beddoes at his practice in Hope

Square, Hotwells, Bristol, for unspecified health reasons, and, in 1799, she and her husband participated in experiments that he was conducting with nitrous oxide at his newly established Pneumatic Institution. See McCarthy, *Voice*, 403. Significantly, Beddoes identifies 'heaviness' and 'sleepiness' as an effect of masturbation. Beddoes, *Hygeia*, 1.4: 42. Beddoes credits Tissot directly among those who had persuasively established masturbation as a modern problem. Another to whom he significantly acknowledges himself indebted is Christian Gotthilf Salzmann, some of whose writing Mary Wollstonecraft (later Godwin) translated for Joseph Johnson and who later translated into German William Godwin's memoir of Wollstonecraft.

22. Beddoes, *Hygeia*, 1.4: 45.
23. Ibid., 1.4: 45. For Beddoes, the problem with novels extended beyond facilitating masturbation. Beddoes condemns this fiction for generally promoting consumption and luxury, disapproving of novels that celebrated fashion and frivolity even more than 'common love-stories'. Beddoes, *Hygeia*, 1.4: 78.
24. Ibid. Elsewhere, Beddoes cites cases in which 'books … containing a plain anatomical and physiological exposition … have preserved or restored those, about to be the victims of their untutored appetites'. Beddoes, *Hygeia*, 1.4: 71.
25. My source for this essay is Anna Letitia Barbauld, *Selected Poetry and Prose*, ed. William McCarthy and Elizabeth Kraft (Peterborough: Broadview Press, 2002), where the editors note its overlap with an essay Barbauld composed for her earlier edition of the *Correspondence of Richardson* (1804).
26. Barbauld, *Selected*, 401. Joseph Addison, 'No. 37', in *The Spectator*, ed. Donald F. Bond, 5 vols. (Oxford: Clarendon Press, 1965), 1: 158.
27. Ibid., 401.
28. Ibid. The readerly desire for an endless supply of novels elsewhere invited analogies that anticipate emergent understandings of the phenomenon of addiction. Barbauld's brother, John Aikin, a practising physician, notably likens novels to 'snuff and tobacco', and another female novel-critic, Clara Reeve, compares novels to a '*drug* in the *terms* of *trade*'. John Aikin, *Letters from a Father to a Son*, 2 vols. (London: Printed for J. Johnson, 1793–1800), 1: 83. Clara Reeve, *The Progress of Romance and the History of Charoba, Queen of Ægypt*, 2 vols. (Colchester and London: Printed for W. Keymer and G. G. J. and J. Robinson, 1785), 2: 38.
29. Barbauld, *Selected*, 401–2.
30. Laqueur, *Solitary*, 321–2. Barbauld misattributes this piece to David Garrick.
31. Barbauld, *Selected*, 414.
32. Ibid., 408.
33. Ibid., 386.
34. Ibid., 386.
35. Ibid., 390. In the introduction to Charlotte Lennox's *The Female Quixote* (1752) in volume twenty-four of the series Barbauld implies specific recognition of the impetus that the 'languishing love romances' of Scudéry and others had given to the romantic and sexual fantasies of their female readers. Anna Letitia Barbauld, ed., *The British Novelists*, 50 vols. (London: Printed

for F. C. and J. Rivington, 1810), 24: i.
36. Barbauld, *Selected*, 386.
37. Ibid., 390.
38. Elsewhere, Rousseau describes the perils of masturbation in *Émile, ou De l'éducation* (1762). Laqueur comments that it is 'moral foreboding about masturbation that haunts the sexual awakening of Emile ... and, by extension, that of all adolescents', reporting that after the publication of this novel Tissot sent Rousseau a copy of *L'Onanisme* 'in the spirit of a fellow worker in the vineyards of a great moral cause'. Laqueur, *Solitary*, 42.
39. Barbauld, *Selected*, 401. Addison, 'No. 37', 1: 155.
40. Within Laqueur's cultural history of masturbation, Addison comes up only briefly. Laqueur identifies Addison explicitly among the eighteenth-century champions of imagination as a creative 'faculty linked to novelty, change, and freedom', adding, 'Addison, of course, was not thinking of the pleasures of "yielding to filthy imagination" that *Onania* warned against when he wrote his essay [on the pleasures of imagination] more or less simultaneously with ... Marten's altogether less edifying tract'. Laqueur, *Solitary*, 318. In his view, '[i]t would probably never have occurred to ... [Addison] in so elevated a context'. Laqueur, *Solitary*, 318. Yet, readers of *Spectator* No. 37 might not be so sure.
41. Addison, 'No. 37', 1: 158.
42. Bradford K. Mudge, *The Whore's Story: Women, Pornography, and the British Novel, 1684–1830* (Oxford: Oxford University Press, 2000), 69. In this monograph, Mudge offers an extensive analysis of *Spectator* No. 37 within his history of an evolving British tradition of pornographic writing that he argues intertwines with a feminised culture of consumption of entertainments, including romances and novels. He identifies the landscape of Leonora's garden, including its 'Grotto', as conjuring the 'fantastic' and 'unreal' scenes of romance. Mudge, *Whore's*, 68. To this point it might be added that Leonora's 'Grotto' suggests a yonic image, aligning the garden as well as the library with female sexuality and privacy.
43. Rebecca Tierney-Hynes establishes how 'extensive' reading, associated here with Leonora, became conflated in the eighteenth century with 'absorptive, seductive, and unreflective reading', and 'intensive' with 'critical, distant reading'. Rebecca Tierney-Hynes, *Novel Minds: Philosophers and Romance Readers, 1680–1740* (New York: Springer, 2012), 4.
44. Addison, 'No. 37', 1: 153. An Orientalist anti-luxury argument that conflates the East with effeminacy and corruption in addition to luxury might be discerned in both Addison and Beddoes's figuration of 'the NILE of female unhealthiness'.
45. Barbauld, *Selected*, 399. Addison mentions *Arcadia* among Leonora's books, but without any indication of problematic usage.
46. For more on this point, see Catherine E. Moore, '"Ladies ... Taking the Pen in Hand": Mrs Barbauld's Criticism of Eighteenth-Century Women Novelists', in *Fetter'd or Free?: British Women Novelists 1670–1815*, ed. Mary Anne Schofield and Cecilia Macheski (Athens, OH: Ohio University Press, 1986), 383–97.
47. Barbauld, *Selected*, 414.
48. Ibid., 414.

49. Ibid., 396.
50. Barbauld's assessment of novels produced by writers of other nationalities is ambivalent on different grounds. In the case of German novels, Barbauld worries about the male role models provided, for example, by Johann Wolfgang von Goethe's Werther. She speculates that the Chinese novel she has read in translation will simply not appeal to English readers because of cultural differences in manners. Barbauld, *Selected*, 396–9.
51. Barbauld, *Selected*, 400. In downplaying objections to Manley, Barbauld is perhaps again following the precedent set by Addison. The mention of Leonora's possession of a key to *The New Atalantis* allows at least some possibility that her primary interest in it is not for its sexually explicit passages but as a source of political gossip and scandal. For her part, Ros Ballaster wonders whether Manley (and Behn, too) exploited the perceived '"lesser" transgression of representing and employing active female sexual desire' as a cover for their political interventions. Ros Ballaster, *Seductive Forms: Women's Amatory Fiction from 1684–1740* (Oxford: Clarendon Press, 1992), 116.
52. Barbauld, *Selected*, 400–1.
53. Ibid., 401.
54. Ibid., 403.
55. Ibid., 403.
56. Ibid., 425. The phrase 'indelicate pictures' indirectly recalls a passage in *A Vindication of the Rights of Woman* (1792) where Wollstonecraft denounces the 'dangerous pictures' created by the 'exalted fervid imaginations' of novel-writers. Barker-Benfield notably reads this passage as a warning against the masturbatory dangers of sentimental fiction. Mary Wollstonecraft, *A Vindication of the Rights of Woman*, 1792, ed. Sylvana Tomaselli (Cambridge: Cambridge University Press, 1995), 151. Barker-Benfield, *Culture*, 329.
57. Barbauld, *Selected*, 419.
58. The original source for this anecdote is Hannah More. See George Birkbeck Norman Hill, *Johnsonian Miscellanies*, 2 vols. (New York: Harper and Brothers, 1897), 2: 190.
59. Claudia L. Johnson, '"Let Me Make the Novels of a Country": Barbauld's *The British Novelists* (1810/1820)', *NOVEL: A Forum on Fiction* 34, no. 2 (Spring 2001): 175. Johnson quotes from Michael Sadleir, *XIX-Century Fiction: A Bibliographical Record*, 2 vols. (London: Constable, 1951), 2: 90.
60. Johnson, 'Let', 175. Other secondary sources to discuss *The British Novelists* include Katharine M. Rogers, 'Anna Barbauld's Criticism of Fiction – Johnsonian Mode, Female Vision', *Studies in Eighteenth-Century Culture* 21 (1992): 27–41. Rogers notably stresses that as a novel-critic Barbauld displays not a narrow but a 'broad and sophisticated' morality, 'raising her above the platitudes of her day' (32).
61. Barbauld, *Selected*, 386. Barbauld attributes this work to Scudéry, but it is actually by La Calprenède.
62. Barbauld, *Selected*, 410–11.
63. Ibid., 388–9.
64. Ibid., 392.

65. Ibid., 378, 377.
66. Ibid., 378. In his famous preface to *Joseph Andrews* (1742), Fielding characterises the novel as a species of fiction modeled on the epic and comedy rather than upon those 'voluminous Works commonly called *Romances*, namely *Clelia, Cleopatra, Astraea, Cassandra*, the *Grand Cyrus*, and innumerable others', coining the descriptive terms 'comic Romance' and 'comic Epic-Poem in prose' to further clarify the distinction. Henry Fielding, *Joseph Andrews*, ed. Martin C. Battestin (Middletown, CT: Wesleyan University Press, 1967), 4. In contrast to Fielding, Barbauld does not see a sharp distinction between romances and novels but considers them instead to occupy different points along the same literary continuum.
67. Barbauld, *Selected*, 377.
68. Ibid., 407–8.
69. Ibid., 407.
70. Ibid., 410.
71. Ibid., 378–9.
72. John Aikin and Anna Letitia Barbauld, *Miscellaneous Pieces in* Prose, 1773, 3rd ed. (London: Printed for J. Johnson, 1792), 39.
73. My source is R. H. Lonsdale, ed. *The Poems of Thomas Gray, William Collins, and Oliver Goldsmith* (London: Longmans, 1969). Poetry is cited by line number throughout this essay.
74. Beddoes, *Hygeia*, 1.4: 68.
75. Barbauld, *Selected*, 411–12.
76. Ibid., 378.
77. Ibid., 378.
78. To return briefly to *Spectator* No. 37, there is a possible hint that Leonora is making the same problematic usage of Thomas d'Urfey's poetry as of French romance in the reference to her copy as 'doubled down in several places', and the reader is left to wonder too at the presence of *The Fifteen Comforts of Matrimony* (1706) on Leonora's shelves, a work that openly discusses sex, although it is hardly erotic. As such, Barbauld might have some further precedent in Addison for identifying other kinds of literature as having potential masturbatory applications. Addison, 'No. 37', 1: 156.
79. My source for this poem and others cited below is Anna Letitia Barbauld, *The Poems of Anna Letitia Barbauld*, ed. William McCarthy and Elizabeth Kraft (Athens, GA: University of Georgia Press, 1994).
80. Of course, it was a paradox of anti-masturbation writing that referencing masturbation even to condemn it could inadvertently alert readers to possibilities and encourage them to indulge in it, Jean Baptiste Louis de Thesacq de Bienville (J. D. T. de Bienville), for example, recommending the reading of Tissot to counteract any impact his own writings might have that way. Jean Baptiste Louis de Thesacq de Bienville (J. D. T. de Bienville), *La nymphomanie, ou traité de la fureur utérine*, 1771 (Amsterdam: Marc-Michel Rey, 1777), 25.
81. Barbauld, 'Allegory', 215.
82. Hufeland explicitly warns, '*Ce vice honteux étouffe tout principe de vie, tarit la source de toute énergie, et ne laisse à sa suite que faiblesse, inertie, pâleur mortelle, dépérissement du corps et abattement de l'âme*' (this shameful vice snuffs out all principle of life, drains the source of

all energy, and leaves nothing in its wake but weakness, inertia, mortal pallor, wasting of the body and diminishment of the soul). Hufeland, *Macrobiotique*, 208.
83. Barbauld, 'Allegory', 220.
84. Richard C. Sha, 'Scientific Forms of Sexual Knowledge in Romanticism', *Romanticism on the Net* 23 (2001): n. p., https://doi.org/10.7202/005993ar.
85. Sedgwick, 'Jane', 833.
86. Ibid., 834.
87. Ibid., 'Jane', 819.
88. Another writer we might situate within a tradition of female Romantic writing open to an erotics of masturbation is Mary Robinson. Like Barbauld, Robinson plays with masturbatory tropes in her poetry, most typically involving female speakers yearning for absent male lovers, such as, for example, in 'Stanzas. Written after Successive Nights of Melancholy Dreams' (1793). 'Ode to Rapture' (1793) offers a striking variation on this trope featuring same-sex desire, as a female personification of Nature desperately longs to hold onto the image of '[t]he glowing Phantom' (34) of Rapture, likewise gendered feminine. Indeed, it may be possible to trace a direct line of descent from Barbauld to Robinson, who in her memoirs relates her personal experience of 'rapture' as an adolescent girl first reading Barbauld's poetry. See Mary Robinson, *Memoirs of the Late Mrs Robinson, Written by Herself*, 1801, 2 vols. (London: Printed for R. Phillips, 1803), 1: 102. My source for Robinson's poetry is Mary Robinson, *Selected Poems*, ed. Judith Pascoe (Peterborough: Broadview Press, 2000).

Chapter 7

Resistive Embodiment and Incestuous Desire in Mary Shelley's *Mathilda*

Crystal Veronie

Shortly after the death of her three-year-old son William in 1819, Mary Wollstonecraft Shelley wrote *Mathilda*, a narrative about the aftereffects of a father's incestuous desire for his daughter.[1] Sent to her father William Godwin for publication in 1820, 'Mathilda' remained unpublished and obscure until Elizabeth Nitchie brought the novel to press in 1859.[2] Since that time, *Mathilda* has served as a touchstone for scholars such as Anne K. Mellor, Terence Harpold and Frederick Burwick, who have all read the novel as a semi-autobiographical text that provides insights into the author's life, psychology and relationships with members of the Godwin-Shelley circle.[3] Over the past twenty-five years, however, non-biographical readings of *Mathilda* such as those by Charlene E. Bunnell, Diana Edelman-Young, Lauren Gillingham, Graham Allen and Rebecca Nesvet have gained favour and refocused scholarly attention on the literary merits of the work rather than on its biographical connections.[4] Taking cue from these scholars, I approach *Mathilda* as a literary text that charts the development of a new discourse on embodiment in late Romanticism. Centrally concerned with the pathologisation of women's bodies, *Mathilda* has much to reveal about nineteenth-century discussions of corporeality, embodiment and autonomy in women's writing during the years proximate to the emergence of gynaecology as a new field of medicine dominated by medical men. This essay offers a new reading of Mathilda's accounts of illness as strategies of 'resistive embodiment', arguing that Mathilda's descriptions of her mental and physical illnesses function as techniques of writing that foreground her bodymind as possessing the capacity to subvert or deflect empirical means of perception as an extension of patriarchal surveillance.[5]

As a critical term, 'resistive embodiment' offers itself to scholarly discussions about resistance to patriarchal control in women's writing. It centres embodiment in accounts of feminist thought and reminds us that resistance is always an embodied action. My development of this term and reading of *Mathilda* expand on the recent scholarship of Jared S. Richman and Jason S. Farr, which closely attends to the representation of bodies in eighteenth- and nineteenth-century fiction.[6] As Londa Schiebinger has observed, by the nineteenth century, the field of scientific and medical research largely excluded women, even though they were increasingly becoming the objects of that research.[7] In such a context, Mathilda's psychophysiological response to her father's sexual transgression matters. Passages detailing Mathilda's efforts to escape from her father's lascivious gaze demonstrate Shelley's engagement with new medical conceptions about the inner workings of living bodies.[8] Merging the visual, auditory and tactile with the imaginative, these new conceptions generated techniques of assessment such as auscultation, percussion and palpation to capture and chronicle data such as temperature measurements, categorise heart and lung sounds or facial features associated with mental disturbances; recognition of hereto unseen phenomena arose from the emergence of these new methods.[9] These aspects of Shelley's writing are particularly noteworthy in Mathilda's depictions of her flight from her father and her account of the various illnesses she develops, including her collapse after her father's suicide and her development of a 'rapid consumption' that claims her life (*M* 207).

'Resistive embodiment' manifests itself in different forms and moments in *Mathilda*, especially the moments following the confession of incestuous desire by the heroine's father. At this point, Mathilda takes leave of her father in a sudden 'terror', which she afterwards claims, 'I could not restrain' (*M* 174). In her flight, she manifestly subverts socio-historical associations between illness and passivity. In the scene that precipitates this unusual response, the heroine has already assumed the active role, having drawn her father out into a 'neighbouring wood of beech trees' at sunset, to uncover the secret to her father's strange behaviour and emotional distress (*M* 170). Prior to his disclosure, her father warns her that what she seeks is forbidden knowledge. He compares Mathilda's relentless 'curiosity' to a brutal vivisection that, if satisfied, would be tantamount to tearing his 'heart' from his 'breast ... to read its secrets in it as its life's blood was dropping from it"' (*M* 172). Nearly insensate with suspense, Mathilda dreads the possibility that her father conceals a secret hatred of her. For Mathilda, the worst outcome of his revelation would be the withdrawal of his paternal love – in the absence of which she declares herself, 'the most miserable worm that crawls' (*M* 172). In this state of utter dejection and 'transported by violent emotion', Mathilda assumes a posture reminiscent of the religious ecstatic: 'rising from his feet, at which I had thrown myself, I leant against a tree, wildly raising my eyes to heaven' (*M* 173). As her father confesses his incestuous desire for her, however, Mathilda is felled once more – she declares, 'I heard them and sunk on the ground, covering my face and almost dead with excess of sickness and fear: a cold perspiration covered my forehead and I shivered in every limb' (*M* 173). Mathilda alternates between despondency and psychophysiological illness, as conveyed by her languid and weeping form with eyes turned upward 'to heaven' and moments of absolute and sudden 'terror' (*M* 173–4). And, yet, in this state of mental and physical collapse, having succumbed to the shock of her father's confession, Mathilda insists that on some level beyond her wilful control, her bodymind retains the capacity to respond and remove her from her father's vicinity and the immediate physical danger of sexual assault. As she observes him stir from his faint, Mathilda reports a sudden surge of energy that 'with a terror I could not restrain – I sprung up and fled, with winged speed, along the paths of the wood and across the fields until nearly dead I reached our house … shut myself up in my own room' (*M* 174). In her description of that fortuitous escape, Mathilda employs a strategy of 'resistive embodiment' that insists that her bodymind retains the agency to act on her behalf, even if that defence is executed in a state beyond her willed control.

In this curious way, Mathilda depicts her body as possessing a transformative power of its own that works to protect her emerging sense of autonomy. In other words, her accounts of the state of her own body at specific moments serve to establish that an intuitive relationship exists between the body and the mind. Shelley's exploration of the intricacies of the heroine's bodymind connection in *Mathilda* bears the trace of contemporary nineteenth-century medico-scientific interests in the physiological underpinnings of sympathy that Alan Richardson proposes Percy Shelley explores in *Laon and Cythna*, a poem that Richardson recognises as 'implicitly incestuous' even if it is not 'explicitly sexual'.[10] Moreover, Richardson resituates Romantic concerns about sibling incest within 'the larger culture of sensibility' that arose in the mid-eighteenth century and spanned well beyond the Romantic period.[11] As a narrative that engages closely with a woman's psychophysiological response to the threat of paternal-filial incest, Mathilda deserves closer attention as a novel that engages with nineteenth-century medico-scientific discourse on the relationship between the body and mind. Indirectly, Shelley seems to be suggesting that Mathilda's body, mind and 'sociopolitical' concerns around patriarchal power can never really be separated into distinct categories.[12] Rather, Mathilda's symptoms invite readers to ponder the social and domestic politics that impinge on a woman's sexual development, as well as the confluence between somatic and mental expressions of pain and illness that result when a woman's natural development of autonomy is challenged.

As a conceptual model, resistive embodiment inspires new insights into Mathilda's relationship with her bodymind and her growing recognition of her autonomy, suggesting her resultant illnesses as a kind of resistance to patriarchal control and surveillance. Despite her escape from the immediate threat of sexual assault, Mathilda experiences changes in her mental constitution that imply that her father's verbal revelation fundamentally alters their relationship, her bodymind and her identity. Her father's words traumatise her mentally and physically in ways that emphasise the 'enmeshment' of her body and mind.[13] From this time on, Mathilda perceives herself as 'mark[ed]' by her father's socially taboo desire (*M* 203). Mathilda's psychophysiological response to his confession of lust for her, combined with her own conflicted feelings, fundamentally alter how she perceives herself. Thus, Mathilda's symptoms of melancholy and hysteria, as well as her obsessive and morbid fixation on reconciliation with her father after death, correspond to or proceed from her internalisation of her father's sexual transgression.

Until now, scholars have focused substantially on what *Mathilda* reveals about Mary Shelley's life, as if the novel constitutes a hybrid of autobiography and fiction or 'autobiografiction' in Stephen Reynolds' formulation.[14] Read thus, the novel seems to answer the burning question of readers regarding incestuous desire left unanswered by William Godwin and Mary Shelley's correspondence. Certainly, Mary Wollstonecraft's 'The Cave of Fancy' and Mary Shelley's own experiences with loss inform Mathilda's narrative.[15] However, there are different potential insights to be generated from considering *Mathilda*, alternatively, as 'fictionalised pathography' – allowing readers to recognise the text as a blending the generic conventions of pathography with fiction.[16] Anne Hunsaker Hawkins identifies pathography as 'a sub-genre of autobiography' wherein authors relate experiences of illness or disability, which, she observes, found significant popularity after the turn of the twentieth century.[17] Emily B. Stanback's analysis of Samuel Taylor Coleridge's journals and letters as 'epistolary pathographies' has helped establish the generic conventions for pathography in the late eighteenth and early nineteenth centuries.[18] Psychoanalytic-inspired approaches might provide further support for reading *Mathilda* as a pathography, as we see with Hawkins, for example, asserting that pathography arises from a person's 'need to come to terms with a traumatic experience' that 'often involves the need to project it outwards – to talk or write about it'.[19] Considering *Mathilda* as a fictionalised pathography allows us to appreciate, too, its literary similarities to other fictional and non-fictional accounts of trauma that have been recorded in letters, essays, diaries and so forth.

In this context, a useful reference point is Fanny Burney's 1811 Mastectomy Letter to her sister, Esther, where the author uses writing as a therapeutic intervention to cope with the traumatic experience of surgery.[20] Here, Burney builds anticipation through the multiple exchanges between herself and the medical professionals involved, particularly her surgeon, 'Dr Larry'.[21] She details the preparations for the fateful encounter, executed without the benefit of anaesthesia. Despite her active involvement in her treatment plan, Burney describes her response to the preparations immediately before the commencement of surgery as alternating between defiance and passivity. Kathleen Béres Rogers regards the absence of medical restraints noted in Burney's account, a standard feature of surgery at that time, as evidence that Burney 'writes her agency into her account to Esther'.[22] Burney appears to extend her agency to the level of her flesh, writing her material body into her narrative as a fellow resistor in recording the detail about how 'the flesh resisted in a manner so forcible as to oppose & tire the hand of the operator'.[23] Burney's small acts of resistance to the surgeon and physicians' dictates, especially within her overall consent to the procedure, signals an insecurity about the medical gaze and penetration of the body, framed as an assault on one's autonomy. Burney insists that the experience was so traumatic that 'not for days, not for Weeks, but for Months I could not speak of this terrible business without nearly again going through it!'[24] Her words call attention to the inter-relationship between speaking and writing and memory, especially in regards to embodied memories of a painful or traumatic nature and the need for a person to narrate the event(s) as a way of regaining control of their life through the process of telling or writing.

Much of *Mathilda* concerns the aftereffects of the near sexual assault of the heroine by her father.[25] Thus, *Mathilda* recasts the topic of paternal-filial incest with a focus more on the repercussions of transgressive desire, as opposed to the physical act of sexual violence, for the female victim. In appreciating the importance of this particular focus, it is helpful to acknowledge that incest was a frequently explored topic in Romantic literature and one that was repeatedly investigated by others within Mary Shelley's own circle. As mentioned earlier, Percy Shelley published his poem about revolutionary sibling-lovers, *Laon and Cythna*, in 1817, around the same time that Lord Byron circulated his closet drama about sibling incest, *Manfred: A Dramatic Poem*.[26] Moreover, in the months leading up to the composition *Mathilda*, Shelley and her husband collaborated on his father-daughter incest play

The Cenci (1819). Shelley translated works for her husband, and she took an active role in helping her husband write and promote his play.[27] Unlike *Laon and Cythna*, *The Cenci* characterises incest as a form of patriarchal tyranny, with its most serious trespass as the father's sexual violation of his daughter. As in most literary depictions of incestuous relationships, Beatrice and her father die; contrarily, Mathilda survives her father's advances and his death by three years. Mathilda's fantasies of a posthumous reunion with her father prove difficult to reconcile with his history of incestuous abuse.[28] In *Mathilda*, Shelley explores the heroine's devotion to her father as an internalised acceptance of patriarchal power that is irreconcilable with her autonomy. Mathilda's devotion to her father both before and after his advance echoes the assertions about the similarity between women in a patriarchal society and domesticated animals that Sharon Ruston has identified as a recurring trope in Wollstonecraft's *A Vindication of the Rights of Woman* (1792).[29] In other words, the novel conveys that to survive the oppressive tyranny of patriarchy, women must overcome the internalisation of patriarchal values that has trained them to behave passively.

Embodied Contexts

Mathilda is concerned with domestic politics and those relationships of power that most concern women. Shelley examines paternal-filial power relationships in her portrayal of the heroine's illnesses. A brief study of the sociohistorical perspective of changes occurring in science and medicine in the later decades of the eighteenth and initial decades of the nineteenth centuries allows us to situate *Mathilda* within the sociocultural perspectives that gave rise to Shelley's novel. When Shelley wrote *Mathilda*, literary and aesthetic discourse had not yet separated from scientific and medical discourse, as it would later in the nineteenth century. Thus, it is imperative that literary discussions of incest be viewed in the context of specific changes occurring in science and medicine during the decades leading up to *Mathilda*. At the same time that Romantic writers explored incest as a form of transgressive sexuality, women were increasingly becoming the subjects of medical studies, which sought to locate, as Schiebinger explains, sex differences in 'every bone, muscle, nerve, and vein'.[30] Ornella Moscucci, Roberta McGrath and Helen King have argued that the discourse that led to the institutional development of gynaecology as a distinct branch of women's healthcare rests on the pathologisation of women's bodies that began around 1820 and ultimately resulted in the recategorisation of genders into what Schiebinger calls 'distinct telos – physical and intellectual strength for the man, motherhood for the woman'.[31] While empirical medicine radically altered the perception of the sexes, it did not usurp power in the political landscape for women.[32]

Romantic notions of desire differed significantly from later Victorian and modern ideas of desire and sexuality. Mario Praz argues that the aesthetics of 'Horror and Terror' influenced Romantic writers 'to such an extent' that 'Beauty and Death' 'became fused into a sort of two-faced herm, filled with corruption and melancholy and fatal in its beauty – a beauty of which, the more bitter the taste, the more abundant the enjoyment'.[33] Rebecca Nesvet's recognition of 'Mary Shelley's participation in [the Marquis de] Sade's network of literary influence' resituates Shelley within key nineteenth-century conversations on the interplay between desire, sexuality and power.[34] Indeed, Mathilda's descriptions of Woodville's fiancée's dying body and that of her own body point towards a Romantic aesthetics consistent with Praz, in which representations of dying women and female corpses register as both terrible and beautiful.[35] Richard C. Sha traces crosscurrents between Romantic aesthetics and sexuality and finds Romantic notions of perversion to relate to the connection of nonproductivity with indifference and discerning tastes.[36] In *Sexual Enjoyment in British Romanticism* (2015), David Sigler proposes that aesthetics played an important role in advancing theories of sexual differentiation.[37] In *Mathilda*, Shelley calls attention to the crosscurrents between the aestheticisation (and fetishisation) of dying and dead women and the pathologisation of women's bodies by medical men. By the time that she tells her story, Mathilda may be dying of consumption, but she retains control of her narrative voice; her authoritative account presses back on the literary convention of dying women silenced by their illnesses or the morbid state of their disease, such as Wollstonecraft's inert and nearly silent form in Godwin's *Memoirs of the Author of* A Vindication of the Rights of Woman (1798).[38]

Gestures to her failing body – her 'wasting form' – punctuate the final pages of Mathilda's story (*M* 209). Yet, Mathilda denies readers the satisfaction of a comprehensive view of her body. She justifies withholding the details of 'the final decay of nature' by telling Woodville that 'death is a too terrible object for the living' (*M* 208, 209). Nor does she seek sympathy. Although she addresses her story to Woodville, she declares at the end of her life that she is 'glad Woodville is not with ... [her] for perhaps he would grieve' (*M* 208). Rather than a prominent image of the beautiful dying woman so reified by Romantic male writers, Mathilda offers only intermittent gestures to her ill and dying body – the effect being that her narrative becomes a collage or assemblage of various parts and shadowy forms strung out across the temporal space of three years. The silences and absences of Mathilda's body in her narrative work discursively, effectively moving the narrative forward in ways that subtly shield Mathilda's autonomy from invasive scrutiny and objectivisation. In this way, Shelley invites readers to use their own imaginations to fill in the gaps. Thus, *Mathilda* expands on and recalibrates Romantic notions of the fragment concerning women's perspectives on sexuality, embodiment, illness and death.[39]

As a story about a woman broken by sexual transgression, *Mathilda* offers a mosaic of corporeal fragments that reassemble the heroine into a new and more considered representation of a survivor of sexual assault. Considering that, as Stanback posits, disabled subjects such as beggars and madwomen and those who have experiences with embodiment, such as in the Nitrous Oxide trials, inspired the poetry and aesthetic theories of writers central to the British Romantic movement, it should not be a surprise that Shelley's novel on incest explores sexual transgression as both a destructive and generative force.[40] The destruction of Mathilda's innocence and her expectations for her life transform her from a lonely and creative girl of sixteen into a complex woman with authoritative experiences of sexual trauma, parental loss and chronic illness. Further, this transformation shares an affinity with what Farr identifies as 'flexible renderings of sexuality through representations of impairment'.[41] Farr finds that 'Deformity and other forms of bodily difference – including deafness, chronic disease, and chronic illness – serve as vital tools for British novelists, who imagine physical variability and queer desire as interrelated, consequential literary devices'.[42] Similarly, Mathilda's various illnesses – hysteria, melancholy, consumption – factor into her sexual maturation. Techniques of writing that redirect readers to Mathilda's body imply that her sense of who she is in relation to the world around her emerges in relation to and through her non-normative embodiment. Shelley employs resistive embodiment to explore the problematical relationship between filial and heterosexual desire that leaves women sexually exploited in ways that materially relate to their health and sexual development.

Resistive Embodiment and Incestuous Guilt

In her somatic descriptions of her emotions, Mathilda employs her body to express her experiences of psychological pain. Just before her father's confession, Mathilda confesses her own fear that her father will abandon her. At the moment of her father's confession, Mathilda faces a sudden shift in her understanding of her father's expectations, throwing her into 'despair' (*M* 173). She describes this emotion as a violent 'phantom' that, once manifested, becomes a constant companion to her, relating,

> After the first moments of speechless agony I felt her fangs on my heart: I tore my hair; I raved aloud; at one moment in pity for his sufferings I would have clasped my father in my arms; and then starting back with horror I spurned him with my foot: I felt as if stung by a serpent, and if scourged by a whip of scorpions which drove me – Ah! Whither – Whither? (*M* 173)

Mathilda labels despair as the emotional response to being recategorised from beloved daughter to object of desire. Mathilda views this sudden shift in the relationship with her father as a threat of violence of the sexual and psychological kind. Despite fear of penetration, Mathilda is driven by internalised patriarchal values to accept her father's behaviour and to find 'pity for his sufferings' (*M* 173); however, her sense of duty is insufficient to nullify the perceived violence. Her somatic reaction to the threat of sexual violence instigates a sensation that she likens to a 'serpent' or 'whip of scorpions'.[43] In this way, Mathilda communicates her resistance to her father's incestuous desire as a force that materialises through her body.

The extreme degree of Mathilda's pendulous emotions causes her physical and mental collapse. Mathilda describes that moment as life-threatening, as she 'sunk on the ground, covering … [her] face and almost dead with excess of sickness and fear' (*M* 173). Surprisingly, she is soon joined on the ground by her father. As she recalls, 'He sunk to the earth fainting, while I, nearly as lifeless, gazed on him in despair' (*M* 173).[44] Indeed, her fear of his devilish visage just seconds before, which her father himself describes as the 'mien of the fallen archangel', evaporates, and 'violent emotion' melts into compassion (*M* 173). Mathilda shifts from fear of penetration to fear for her father's imminent death, as evidenced by her prayer for deliverance: 'And then I wept aloud, and raised my eyes to heaven to entreat for a respite to my despair and an alleviation for his unnatural suffering' (*M* 173). While it is tempting to read the father's sudden collapse as an act that feminises him, as a subversion of his masculine sexual potency, Sha explains that several late eighteenth-century medical texts deny any difference in male and female nervous diseases or their treatment.[45] Prior to her father's fall, Mathilda experiences a series of psychophysiological reactions that include weakness, 'convulsion', 'cold perspiration' and madness – 'I tore my hair; I raved aloud' (*M* 173) – and these reactions return in the interim between her recognition of the signs that her father will 'revive' and her sudden flight (*M* 174). Her bodymind responds instantly to her father's signs of life, 'with winged speed' (*M* 174). At the level of character, Mathilda's sudden move into action evokes, again, the strategy of resistive embodiment whereby her body swiftly overrules her compassion for her father's fallen state. Figured as agential and empowered, her bodymind acts to ensure her self-preservation, even without conscious intent. Reading Mathilda's action at this moment as an act of resistive embodiment allows us to understand, in turn, that her bodymind responds in a way that overrules filial obedience to paternal authority.

There are additional significant implications in recognising the strategy of resistive embodiment at play, in countering readers' presumptions of Mathilda's complicity or active engagement in a seduction of her father. Shelley writes resistance to Mathilda's father's incestuous desire into the heroine's very flesh. The timely action of Mathilda's bodymind results in her escape from the threat of sexual assault, despite her insistence that this action occurs outside of her conscious control. Ruston explores Wollstonecraft's knowledge of and involvement in discussions about instinct, domestication and reason in animals that were ongoing in natural history when Wollstonecraft wrote the *Vindication*.[46] While Mathilda recalls her escape as outside of her conscious control, I suspect that in this instance, Shelley interrogates contemporary scientific debates on instinct, reason and the soul that had evolved from Enlightenment-period conversations on vitality, such as Robert Whytt's proposal that the soul was 'sentient at a non-conscious level'.[47] Further, Shelley experiments with the nuances of difference between instinctual actions and those that occur outside of conscious thought as a reaction to experiences of extreme stress. While today it is thought problematic to suggest that the passivity or action of the body implies the intentions of the woman under question, Shelley appears to be processing Mathilda's flight as a possible response to extreme stress. She describes the narrator's bodymind in ways that imply that a hereto undiscovered connection exists between the body and mind. Therefore, for Shelley, bodyminds can act unconsciously in ways that promote self-preservation.[48]

In his drive to satisfy his own deviant desires, Mathilda's father denies her autonomy. Mathilda attributes her father's desire to some quality in herself that had 'inspired' his abuse, and she blames herself for her father's sexual transgression (*M* 203).[49] She claims that she has been 'polluted by the unnatural love ... [she] had inspired, and that ... [she] was a creature cursed and set apart by nature' (*M* 203).[50] Considering her age, Mathilda's belief that she carries a trace of her father's crime – that his 'infamy and guilt was mingled with [her] portion' (*M* 196) – likely stems from her immature state of development.[51] Mathilda's reaction to her father's confession of love transforms her relationship with herself.

Thus, her internalisation of her father's guilt can be better understood as a failure in their filial relationship with similarities to what Luce Irigaray refers to as a 'perver[sion]' in the formation of the 'between-two'.[52] According to Irigaray, the failure occurs 'because it [the relation] is fabricated by only one subject'.[53] Indeed, Mathilda's father's confession of incestuous love reduces her to an object and denies her right to autonomy, to 'becoming' her own fully-realised person.[54] When Mathilda describes herself as 'mark[ed]' by her internalised guilt (M 203), it is because she conflates her father's objectivisation of her with cultural conceptions of women's pathology. Felicity Nussbaum explains that eighteenth-century British notions of femininity located the source of feminine 'defect' in the 'womb, hidden and interior, rather than the more visible female organs'.[55] Through Mathilda's persistent and unsubstantiated sense of guilt, Shelley critiques the pathologisation of women's bodies, seeing such discourse as a form of patriarchal oppression.[56] It exerts control over women by manipulating how they understand themselves and uses science and medical theories about women's bodies to reinforce social expectations that render women passive.

Fictionalised Pathography and Resistive Embodiment

Reading *Mathilda* as a fictionalised pathography changes the way that we view Mathilda's guilt. Before she receives her father's letter, Mathilda fantasises that time and isolation will expiate the stain of her father's transgressive desire. She imagines that she will flee to

> the Continent and become a nun; not for religion's sake, for I was not a Catholic, but that I might for ever be shut out from the world. Where I should find solitude where I might weep, and the voices of life might never reach me. (M 175)

Mathilda even daydreams that she sentences her father to 'spend another sixteen years of desolate wandering', after which he might return to her 'with sinless emotion' (M 175). In her efforts to wipe away her father's crime, Mathilda grasps at ways that she can avoid the inevitable loss of paternal love, which is the only kind of love she has known. Further, this moment of wish-fulfilment appears mediated to fit within the paradigm that she later embraces. Indeed, it could be considered an origin for Mathilda's belief that her illnesses function beneficially to hasten her towards a spiritual reconciliation with her father after death.

Mathilda's narrative portrays a type of denial frequently found in pathography. She attempts to bargain for more time, even if the terms of that negotiation bear little resemblance to reality. Hawkins explains that the process of writing a pathography is one of mythmaking, and it can be both disabling and enabling:

> Pathography can be seen as a re-formulation of the experience of illness, as the artistic production and continuation of the instinctive psychological act of formulation: it gathers together the separate meanings, the moments of illumination and understanding, the cycles of hope and despair, and weaves them into a whole fabric, one wherein a temporal sequence of events takes on narrative form.[57]

Hawkins identifies how the process of narrativising experiences of illness constitutes acts of meaning-making.[58] Thus, Mathilda not only narrates her experiences of illnesses and their aftermath but also reframes her entire life story based on the mythos that she has created about her illnesses, their cause and the rewards of her suffering.

In the second type of resistive embodiment in *Mathilda*, the heroine's ill bodymind provides her with unseen advantages and opportunities for reflection and insight.[59] In contrast to depictions of illness that represent increasing passivity, Mathilda's illnesses give occasion to her agency. In her life story that she has addressed to Woodville, Mathilda attributes specific benefits to her illnesses that assist her in gaining a broader perspective on her life and spirituality. For example, after her father's suicide, Mathilda experiences an illness initially marked by 'convulsions and faintings', but which, after a period of weeks, gives way to a 'convalescence' (*M* 184–5). During this time of weakness and confinement to a sickroom, Mathilda constructs an elaborate deceit to mitigate the moral dilemma in which she finds herself. Since staying amongst familiars would necessitate her concealment of the exchanges that led to her father's suicide, Mathilda determines to escape the life she has hereto known by 'feign[ing]' her death and 'retreat[ing]' into a solitary life (*M* 186–7). Therefore, Mathilda's ill bodymind can be read as subversive in that its apparent passivity shields Mathilda's inner machinations from becoming known. The weakness of her body actually provides the opportunity for Mathilda to plan her escape. In this way, Mathilda insinuates that her body acts as a co-conspirator in her escape from her family.

It is not through recovery and health that Mathilda finds autonomy; rather, her illnesses facilitate the space and opportunity for self-reflection and individuation. In this way, strategies of resistive embodiment can be understood as productive methods that evolve through Mathilda's ill bodymind. While solitude on the heath provides Mathilda with a sanctuary, she yet laments, 'Often amid apparent calm I was visited by despair and melancholy' (*M* 189). Mathilda associates her 'melancholy' with her father's transgressive desire and suicide (*M* 190). In her failure to find sympathy with Woodville, a poet who befriends her on the heath, Mathilda compares herself to 'blighted fruit', unable to 'revive' under the 'radiance' of the 'sun' (*M* 190). More and more, she identifies herself in terms associated with chronic illness. Her symptoms converge on madness and result in her redramatisation of the fateful encounter she had with her father (*M* 200). In challenging Woodville to co-suicide by a 'Laudanum' overdose, Mathilda reverses the masculine-feminine roles played out in her encounter with her father (*M* 200). Woodville's attempt to spare Mathilda the 'cursed drink' and relieve her despair with comforting words fails to recover her mental wellbeing. Mathilda asserts that his comforting words only provide a 'momentary relief' (*M* 203). After Woodville's departure, she gains a sense of who she is in relation to the world. In a waking reverie on her return to the cottage, she imagines a sort of 'fairy scene', her reunion with her father and the dissolution of the 'mark of misery' on her 'brow' (*M* 205).[60] She gains the distance that she needs to reimagine herself and reconcile with her father on her own terms by virtue of her madness. Her account of her mental illness argues that her ill mind plays a pivotal role in her recognition of her own agency.

In addition to her mental decline, Mathilda's descent into a 'rapid consumption' can be read as returning to the strategy of resistive embodiment in that this physical degeneration provides a permissive opening for her to take back control over her life through storytelling (*M* 207). Mathilda has remained silent due to fears that her story is one of 'sacred horror' that makes it 'unfit for utterance' (*M* 151); however, her impending death releases her obligation to silence. Her 'sunken cheek', her 'hectic fever' and her 'wasting form' locate her at the brink of consumptive death (*M* 207, 209).[61] Clark Lawlor explains that Romantic literary depictions of consumption varied greatly along gendered lines. While representations of male consumptives associated their extreme sensitivity with poetic genius, those of female consumptives often implied them as self-indulgent, overconsuming and 'ornamental' – in other words, women dying of consumption in Romantic literature tend to appear 'fashionable'.[62] Mathilda's narrative negates this binary. Her consumption occurs despite her activity outdoors and ascetic lifestyle. In her consumptive state, Mathilda rewrites her own narrative as a last agential act, which allows her to renegotiate the events and details of her life to produce an account that relates both her individuation and her reconciliation with her father. In doing so, she reframes her inability to find sympathy with Woodville as fortuitous. She insists that her three years of mental and physical suffering have prepared her to let go of earthly desires and manifest the spiritual reunion she had long desired with her father (*M* 191). Indeed, her consumption promises her an 'innocent death', which Mathilda proclaims, 'will be sweeter even than that which the opium promised' (*M* 207). In this way, Mathilda's representation of her final illness anticipates Victorian tropes of 'fallen women' redeemed by consumptive deaths.[63] Because she views the degeneration of her body as a necessary step towards autonomy, Mathilda embraces 'the progressive decay of ... [her] strength' and welcomes death as generative, asserting, 'no maiden ever took more pleasure in the contemplation of her bridal attire than I in fancying my limbs already enwrapped in their shroud: is it not my marriage dress?' (*M* 208). This embrace of degeneration, decay and death critiques social expectations that represent marriage and motherhood as the pinnacle and fecundity of a woman's life. For Mathilda, death opens a productive new opportunity to achieve the autonomy denied to her in her living relationship with her father.

Mathilda explores a morbid generativity whereby the disabling effects usually associated with illness actually enable the titular character to achieve a kind of self-actualisation.[64] While Mathilda finds neither recovery of her bodymind nor the promise of normative sexuality with Woodville, she can regain a sense of control over her own narrative by telling her story. *Mathilda* interrogates the interrelationship between the mind and the body in ways that challenge contemporary understandings of instinctual behaviour, psychophysiological responses to stress and psychosomatic symptoms of illness. In its representation of Mathilda's consumption, the novel engages with Romantic notions of the disease, its 'hectic fever' and the wasting appearance of its victims.[65] In some respects, Mathilda even participates in the Romantic aesthetics of beauty associated with women dying of consumption, especially in her spiritualising of death.[66] Mathilda's desire for reconciliation requires the father's restoration to the ideal of devoted parent. Thus, in consumptive death, Mathilda's body, previously sexualised by her father, becomes sanctified.

Understood as part of an evolving discourse on embodiment in Mary Shelley's late Romantic writing, the concept of resistive embodiment makes possible new readings of Shelley's fiction. *Mathilda* provides a woman's perspective of paternal-filial incest that undermines notions of the heroine as a passive victim and challenges us to reconsider how we think about transgressive sexuality in the writing of Romantic women writers. Mathilda's illnesses subvert cultural depictions of women as ill, passive or pathological, reject notions of the invisible feminine 'defect' and expose uneven domestic relations that inhibit women's achievement of selfhood and autonomy and their sexual development as a facet of that sense of self.[67] By reading *Mathilda* as a fictionalised pathography, we can recognise denial in Mathilda's bargaining for more time with her father and in the mythos that she writes about spiritual reconciliation with him in the afterlife. Further, we gain an expanded understanding of the way that literary form matters in Shelley's writing, in the writing of Romantic women writers more generally and, especially, as it relates to the development of Romantic aesthetics informed by disability, sexual differentiation and shifting conceptions of how female sexuality, agency and selfhood relate.

Notes

1. For an explanation of the variation of spelling of 'Mathilda' in publications, see Janet Todd, Introduction to *Mary; Maria; Matilda* (New York: Penguin Books, 2004), xxvii.
2. Elizabeth Nitchie and Mary Wollstonecraft Shelley, 'Mathilda', *Studies in Philology* 56, no. 3 (October 1959): i+iii+v+vii–xv+1–104.
3. Anne K. Mellor, *Mary Shelley: Her Life, Her Fiction, Her Monsters* (New York: Routledge, 1989). Terrence Harpold, '"Did You Get Mathilda from Papa?": Seduction Fantasy and the Circulation of Mary Shelley's "Mathilda"', *Studies in Romanticism* 28, no. 1 (Spring 1989): 49–67. Frederick Burwick, 'Incest on the Romantic Stage: Baillie, Byron, and the Shelleys', in *Decadent Romanticism: 1780–1914*, ed. Kostas Boyiopoulos and Mark Sandy (Farnham: Ashgate, 2015), 27–41. This list is not meant to be exhaustive.
4. Charlene E. Bunnell, '"Mathilda": Mary Shelley's Romantic Tragedy', *Keats-Shelley Journal* 46 (1997): 75–96. Diana Edelman-Young, '"Kingdom of Shadows": Intimations of Desire in Mary Shelley's "Mathilda"', *Keats-Shelley Journal* 51 (2002): 116–44. Lauren Gillingham, 'Romancing Experience: The Seduction of Mary Shelley's "Matilda"', *Studies in Romanticism* 42, no. 2 (Summer 2003): 251–69. Graham Allen, 'Matilda', in Graham Allen and Mary Shelley, *Critical Issues: Mary Shelley* (Basingstoke: Palgrave Macmillan, 2008), 41–63. Rebecca Nesvet, 'Mary Shelley and Sade's Global Network,' in *Women's Literary Networks and Romanticism: 'A Tribe of Authoresses'*, ed. by Andrew O. Winckles and Angela Rehbein (Liverpool: Liverpool University Press, 2017), 245–73.
5. This chapter draws on ideas that I discuss in my article, 'Maternal-Child Bonds and Resistive Embodiment in Sara Coleridge's Writing', *Essays in Romanticism* 29, no. 2 (November 2022): 169–85. In working with the concept of 'bodymind', I am indebted to twenty-first century disability scholar Margaret Price. Price coins the term 'bodymind' to stress the interconnection between the body and the mind, in contrast to Cartesian conceptions of them as two 'separate conceptual and linguistic territories' (building on longstanding critiques of the Cartesian perspective). Margaret Price, *Mad at School: Rhetorics of Mental Disability and Academic Life* (Ann Arbor: University of Michigan Press, 2011), 240.

6. Jared S. Richman considers the Creature's speech as a significant element of his non-normative embodiment. Richman, 'Monstrous Elocution: Disability and Passing in *Frankenstein*', *Essays in Romanticism* 25, no. 2 (2018): 187–208. Jason S. Farr considers practices of staring and offers new interpretations of Frances Burney's *Camilla* (1796) and Maria Edgeworth's *Belinda* (1801). Jason S. Farr, *Novel Bodies: Disability and Sexuality in Eighteenth-Century British Literature* (Lewisburg: Bucknell University Press, 2019), 131–63.
7. Londa Schiebinger, *Nature's Body* (Boston: Beacon Press, 1993), 204. 'Women were barred from medicine, largely because a woman doctor was considered to be a contradiction in cultural terms when the relationship between doctor and patient was believed to be the gendered one of gazer and object of the gaze'. Emma Liggins, 'The Medical Gaze and the Female Corpse: Looking at Bodies in Mary Shelley's *Frankenstein*', *Studies in the Novel* 32, no. 2 (Summer 2000): 130.
8. Michel Foucault proposes that the new medical perception that emerged at the turn of the nineteenth century arrived as an alteration in the 'structure' of 'knowledge', 'revealing through gaze and language what had previously been below and beyond their domain'. Thus, 'A new alliance [was] forged between words and things, enabling one to see and to say'. Foucault, *The Birth of the Clinic: An Archaeology of Medical Perception*, translated by A. M. Sheridan Smith (New York: Vintage Books, 1994), xii.
9. Erasmus Darwin creates taxonomic categories of fevers based on differentiating characteristics. Darwin, *Zoonomia; or, The Laws of Organic Life*, vol. I (New York: T. &. J. Swords, 1796). Jean-Nicolas Corsivart categorises heart sounds. Corsivart, *Essays on the Organic Diseases of the Heart and Great Vessels*, translated by Jacob Gates (Boston: Bradford & Read, 1812). Charles Bell chronicles and categorises facial expressions as indicative of mental illness. Bell, *Essays on the Anatomy of Expression in Painting* (London: Longman, Hurst, Rees, and Orme, 1806).
10. Richardson compares the Romantic fascination with sibling incest with eighteenth-century proto-psychological discussions about 'shared childhood associations', such as David Hartley's *Observations on Man, His Frame, His Duty, His Expectations* (1749). Alan Richardson, 'The Dangers of Sympathy: Sibling Incest in English Romantic Poetry', *Studies in English Literature, 1500–1900* 25, no. 4 (Autumn 1985): 740.
11. See Alan Richardson, 'Romanticism and the Body', *Literature Compass* 1 (2004): 3–4.
12. Price, *Mad at School*, 240.
13. See Sami Schalk's articulation of Price's 'bodymind'. Schalk, *Bodyminds Reimagined: (Dis)ability, Race, and Gender in Black Women's Speculative Fiction* (Duke University Press, 2018), 5.
14. Max Saunders devotes a chapter to Stephen Reynold's 1906 essay, titled 'Autobiografiction'. Saunders, 'Autobiografiction: Stephen Reynolds and A. C. Benson', in *Self Impression: Life-Writing, Autobiografiction, and the Forms of Modern Literature* (Oxford: Oxford University Press, 2010), 165–207.
15. Todd, *Mary*, xviii.
16. This is my term. I am theorising 'fictionalised pathography' as an extension of Emily B. Stanback's work on 'epistolary pathographies'. Stanback,

'Between the Author "Disabled" and the Coleridgean Imagination: STC's Epistolary Pathographies', in *The Wordsworth-Coleridge Circle and the Aesthetics of Disability* (London: Palgrave Macmillan, 2017), 187. Also see Stanback's 'pathographical epitaphs' in the collaborative project she co-directs with Polly Atkin, *The Gravestone Project*: www.thegravestoneproject.com/memorial-20-70. Arden A. Hegele proposed something similar with the term 'fictional pathography' in 'Monstrous Autobiography: The Case of *Frankenstein*', a talk that she gave on 30 November 2015, at the Fondation des États-Unis, Cité internationale universitaire de Paris. Hegele discusses *Frankenstein* (1818) as a 'pseudo-medical case history' in chapter 4 of her book, *Romantic Autopsy: Literary and Medical Reading* (Oxford: Oxford University Press, 2022).

17. Anne Hunsaker Hawkins, *Reconstructing Illness: Studies in Pathography*, 2nd ed. (West Lafayette: Purdue University Press, 1999), 3. See also Jeffrey K. Aronson, 'Autopathography: The Patient's Tale', *BMJ* 321, December 23–30 (2020): 1599–1602.
18. Stanback, *Aesthetics of Disability*, 187.
19. Hawkins, *Reconstructing Illness*, 3.
20. Fanny Burney, 'Letter to Esther Burney, 22 March-June 1812', *Fanny Burney: Selected Letters and Journals*, ed. Joyce Hemlow (Oxford: Clarendon Press, 1986), 127–41. For an alternative reading, see Melina Moore, 'Mary Shelley's "Mathilda" and the Struggle for Female Narrative Subjectivity', *Rocky Mountain Review* 65, no. 2 (2011): 209.
21. Burney spells her surgeon's name 'Larrey' and 'Larry' at different points in her mastectomy letter. Burney, 'Letter', 139.
22. Kathleen Béres Rogers, 'Public Intimacies: Frances Burney's and Jane Cave Winscom's Accounts of Illness', *Romanticism and Victorianism on the Net*, no. 62 (October 2012): n. p., http://doi.org/10.7202/1026006ar.
23. Burney, 'Letter', 139.
24. Ibid., 139.
25. 'However, the language in which Mathilda accuses her father implies rape. He undergoes "a change that to remember made" her "shudder and then filled [her] with the deepest grief". That process – terror, followed by grief – sounds like the rape survivor's cognitive process.' Rebecca Nesvet, 'Mary Shelley and Sade's Global Network', in *Women's Literary Networks and Romanticism: 'A Tribe of Authoresses'*, ed. Andrew O. Winckles and Angela Rehbein (Liverpool: Liverpool University Press, 2017), 265.
26. Percy Shelley's Laon and Cythna share love and revolutionary ideals. Alan Richardson, 'Romantic Incest: Literary Representation and the Biology of the Mind', in *The Neural Sublime: Cognitive Theories and Romantic Texts* (Baltimore: Johns Hopkins University Press, 2010), 97–115.
27. Nesvet, 'Mary Shelley and Sade's Global Network', 261.
28. See Pamela Clemit, 'From *The Fields of Fancy* to *Mathilda*: Mary Shelley's Changing Conception of her Novella', in *Mary Shelley in Her Times*, ed. Betty T. Bennett and Stuart Curran (Baltimore: Johns Hopkins University Press, 2000), 68.
29. Sharon Ruston, *Creating Romanticism: Case Studies in Literature, Science and Medicine of the 1790s* (New York: Palgrave Macmillan, 2013), 46–7.

30. Londa Schiebinger, 'Skeletons in the Closet: The First Illustrations of the Female Skeleton in Eighteenth-Century Anatomy', in *The Making of the Modern Body: Sexuality and Society in the Nineteenth Century*, ed. Catherine Gallagher and Thomas Laqueur (Berkeley: University of California Press, 1987), 42–82. See also Thomas Laqueur, *Making Sex: Body and Gender from the Greeks to Freud* (Cambridge, MA: Harvard University Press, 1990), 162.
31. See Helen King, *Midwifery, Obstetrics, and the Rise of Gynaecology: The Uses of a Sixteenth-Century Compendium* (Farnham: Ashgate, 2007), Ornella Moscucci, *The Science of Woman: Gynaecology and Gender in England, 1800–1929* (Cambridge: Cambridge University Press, 1990), 13; Roberta McGrath, *Seeing Her Sex: Medical Archives and the Female Body* (New York: Manchester University Press, 2002), 34; Schiebinger, *The Mind Has No Sex?* (Cambridge, MA: Harvard University Press, 1989), 190–1.
32. Schiebinger explains that 'difference was arranged hierarchically' and thus, 'the age-old dominance of men over women remained in force (in spite of opposition to the fundamental premise of the revolution – that sex pervades the body'. Schiebinger, *The Mind Has No Sex?*, 191. 'Emphasizing the incommensurablity of male and female bodies entailed foregrounding the role of the reproductive system, so that this difference was seen as more important than any similarities between men and women'; Mary Poovey, *Uneven Developments: The Ideological Work of Gender in Mid-Victorian England* (Chicago: University of Chicago Press, 1988), 6.
33. See Mario Praz, *The Romantic Agony*, trans. Angus Davidson (London: Oxford University Press, 1933), 31.
34. Nesvet challenges Praz's assumption that 'Mary Shelley appropriated [Percy Shelley and Lord Byron] those men's knowledge of Sade's text, having none of her own'. Nesvet, 'Mary Shelley and Sade's Global Network', 246–7.
35. 'In the nineteenth century, practices which involved looking at dead bodies were classified as potentially perverse'. Liggins, 'The Medical Gaze and the Female Corpse: Looking at Bodies in Mary Shelley's *Frankenstein*', 129.
36. See Richard C. Sha, *Perverse Romanticism: Aesthetics and Sexuality in Britain, 1750–1832* (Baltimore: Johns Hopkins University Press, 2009).
37. See David Sigler, *Sexual Enjoyment in British Romanticism: Gender and Psychoanalysis, 1753–1835* (Montreal: McGill-Queen's University Press, 2015), 41.
38. Godwin praises, at length, the attentions of Wollstonecraft's doctor, Mr Carlyle, regarding her end-of-life care, but he only once quotes his wife in her final days: her request that the nurse not be encouraged to 'reason' with her. William Godwin, *Memoirs of the Author of* A Vindication of the Rights of Woman (London: Printed for J. Johnson, 1798), 196.
39. See Marjorie Levinson, *The Romantic Fragment Poem: A Critique of a Form* (Chapel Hill: University of North Carolina Press, 1986).
40. Stanback, 'Pneumatic Self-Experimentation and the Aesthetics of Deviant Embodiment' in *The Wordsworth-Coleridge Circle and the Aesthetics of Disability* (London: Palgrave Macmillan, 2017), 97–139.
41. See Farr, *Novel Bodies*, 13.
42. Farr, *Novel Bodies*, 8.
43. Kathleen Béres Rogers explores the pathological implications of the word 'enthusiasm' in Mary Shelley's first novel. Béres Rogers, *Creating Romantic*

Obsession: Scorpions in the Mind (New York: Palgrave Macmillan, 2019), 55–89.

44. Mathilda and her father's near-simultaneous falls allude to the fall of Adam and Eve: 'now, I must ever lament, those few short months of Paradisaical bliss; I disobeyed no command, I ate no apple, and yet I was ruthlessly driven from it' (*M* 162).

45. Sha references George Cheyne's *English Malady* (1784), John Hill's *The Construction of the Nerves, and Causes of Nervous Disorders* (1758), and Samuel Tissot's *Three Essays* (1773). Sha, *Perverse Romanticism*, 84–5.

46. Ruston examines Wollstonecraft's reviews of writing on natural history for the *Analytical Review* between 1788 and 1792, including works by Thomas Bewick, Ralph Beilby, William Smellie, John Rotherham and Comte de Buffon. Ruston traces Wollstonecraft's response in the *Vindication* to these natural history philosophers, especially Smellie. For Wollstonecraft, 'Instinct means, therefore, a mechanical, natural, or an unthinking response to the world'. Ruston, *Creating Romanticism*, 50–1.

47. Roy Porter puts Robert Whytt's *On the Vital and Other Involuntary Motions of Animals* (1751) in conversation with vitalist theories proposed by Albrecht von Haller, John Hunter, Luigi Galvani, Alessandro Volta, Erasmus Darwin and others. I mention Robert Whytt's *On the Vital and Other Involuntary Motions of Animals* (1751) to highlight that broad differentiations existed in scientific discussions about the role of the soul and its existence in relation to unconscious movements or actions of bodies. Roy Porter, *The Greatest Benefit to Mankind: A Medical History of Humanity* (New York: Norton, 1997), 250–3.

48. Later in the nineteenth century, scientific experiments on animals would reveal the role of the adrenal glands and other organs of what is now called the endocrine system. The connection between extreme stress and shock would not be fully articulated, however, until American physiologist Walter Bradford Cannon published his findings on physiological responses to stress. Cannon, *Bodily Changes in Pain, Hunger, Fear and Rage: An Account of Recent Researches into the Function of Emotional Excitement* (New York: D. Appleton, 1915).

49. Clemit identifies Mathilda as 'both guilt-ridden and innocent, both sexual transgressor and sexually pure'. Clemit, 'From *The Fields of Fancy* to *Mathilda*', 71.

50. See Julia Shaffer's proposal that Mathilda's desire for her father is of the kind described by Jane Gallop as a 'veiled seduction in the form of the law', whereby blame for desire shifts from the father to the daughter. Julia Shaffer, 'Familial Love, Incest, and Female Desire in Late Eighteenth- and Early Nineteenth-Century British Women's Novels', *Criticism* 41, no. 1 (Winter 1999): 85. Jane Gallop, *The Daughter's Seduction: Feminism and Psychoanalysis* (Ithaca: Cornell University Press, 1982), 70–1, 76.

51. See also Tilottama Rajan, 'A Peculiar Community: Mary Shelley, Godwin, and the Abyss of Emotion', in *Romanticism and the Emotions*, ed. Joel Faflak and Richard C. Sha (Cambridge: Cambridge University Press, 2014), 147–70.

52. Luce Irigaray, *The Way of Love*, trans. Heidi Bostic and Stephen Pluháček (New York: Continuum, 2002), 109.

53. 'Not accepting and respecting this permanent duality between the two human subjects, the feminine one and the masculine one, amounts to preventing one of the two – historically the feminine – from attaining its own Being, and thus from taking charge of the becoming of what it already is and of the world to which it belongs, including as made up of other humans, similar or different'. Irigaray, *The Way*, 110.
54. Ibid., 110.
55. Despite the prevailing shift from Galenic medicine to empirical medicine, the pathology of women's diseases was still regarded to rest with disturbances caused by women's internal reproductive organs. Felicity Nussbaum, 'Dumb Virgins, Blind Ladies, and Eunuchs: Fictions of Defect', in *'Defects': Engendering the Modern Body*, ed. Helen Deutsch and Felicity Nussbaum (Ann Arbor: University of Michigan Press, 2000), 31.
56. For an alternative reading, see Jenny DiPlacidi, *Gothic Incest: Gender, Sexuality and Transgression* (Manchester: Manchester University Press, 2020), 69.
57. Hawkins attributes her understanding of formulation to Robert J. Lifton's concept of 'formulation' as an act of psychological renovation in *Death in Life: Survivors of Hiroshima* (New York: Birch Lane Press, 1993). Hawkins, *Reconstructing Illness*, 24.
58. Ibid., 24.
59. Susan Wendell, *The Rejected Body: Feminist Philosophical Reflections on Disability* (New York: Routledge, 1996), 68–9.
60. Béres Rogers's explores late eighteenth-century understandings of somnambulism as pathological. See her discussion of Erasmus Darwin's *Zoonomia* (1794) and the 'reverie'. Béres Rogers, *Creating Romantic Obsession*, 23–4.
61. 'As the disease progresses, the patient becomes emaciated, and even skeletal, with the lips drawn back to reveal teeth; eye sockets are hollowed and bones stick out from the flesh. The "hectic fever" worsens, characteristically strongest towards the evening, giving the patient's skin a vivid "hectic flush" which strongly contrasts with the otherwise whitened and drained appearance'. Clark Lawlor, *Consumption and Literature: The Making of the Romantic Disease* (Hampshire: Palgrave Macmillan, 2006), 5.
62. Lawlor reports that medical discourse contributed to popular Romantic conceptions of the different presentations of consumption in men and women: 'consumptive males were to be more creative, intelligent, poetic: the shapers of representations; women became those beautiful images'. Lawlor, 44. Additionally, feminine consumption became associated with sedentary and over-indulgent lifestyles. Lawlor, *Consumption*, 158–9.
63. Lawlor, *Consumption*, 167.
64. For an alternate reading of Mathilda's illnesses in relation to transgressive desire, see Judith Barbour, '"The meaning of the tree": The Tale of Mirra in Mary Shelley's *Mathilda*' in *Iconoclastic Departures: Mary Shelley after Frankenstein*, ed. Syndy M. Conger, Frederick S. Frank and Gregory O'Dea (London: Associated University Presses, 1997), 102.
65. Lawlor, *Consumption*, 5.
66. Ibid., 162.
67. Nussbaum, 'Dumb Virgins', 34.

Chapter 8

'Our Dire Transgression': Mary Diana Dods in the Biblical Sense

Colin Carman

'Enter into the joy of your master.'[1]

The writing of Mary Diana 'Doddy' Dods (c. 1790–1830) has long been overshadowed by their queer public life. Dods, a Scot, was known as one of two illegitimate children born to the fifteenth Earl of Morton, George Douglas. By 1827, Dods began to assert that they were male through the adoption of masculine attire and the name 'Walter Sholto Douglas', a name derived from their paternal lineage. Dods was known for wearing a tailored jacket and short curly hair. Dods's life partner was Isabella Robinson, later 'Mrs Sholto Douglas', the daughter of a housing developer. For Dods, the name 'Mr Sholto Douglas' was not a playful disguise but a fully realised selfhood. The scheme involved both an affirmation of Dods's transgender identity and calling of sexual identity itself into question. Geraldine Friedman identifies in Dods a radical instantiation of non-identity that subverts the 'genetic relationship usually assumed between gender masquerade and presumably "true" gender'.[2] 'Dods requires a different kind of biography', explains Friedman, given that they enacted a 'series of transgender careers so successful that they remained undiscovered for over 150 years'.[3] Yet, Dods's writing warrants equally close attention in and of itself, including for its own experiment in the subversion of established gender categories. Under the name David Lyndsay, Dods published their own retellings of the Bible's most dramatic stories, such as of Eden, Exodus and Christ before his crucifixion, queering the narratives in the process. These biblical retellings appeared in the conservative *Blackwood's Edinburgh Magazine* and made Lyndsay one of editor William Blackwood's favourite contributors. *Blackwood's*, fascinatingly, would become the primary outlet for Dods's challenges to the 'naturalness' of heterosexual desire. At the intersections of multiple forms of self-labelling – Scottish and English, husband and wife – Dods's multiple identities are the lived enactments of an anti-essentialism, a fundamental resistance to any form of constraint, whether it be literary or lifestyle-oriented. They are also a fascinating professional writer, and an important part of the history of transgender writing.

To begin, a brief recapitulation of the Dods personae may help us to better interpret two works, 'The First Murder' and 'The Plague of Darkness', and Dods's preoccupation with desire and sexualised states of shame. Dods was known, in their time, by at least four sobriquets: 'Dods' and 'Douglas' (in person, or rather, persons), 'Doddy' (as an affectionate nickname) and 'Lyndsay' (on the pages of *Blackwood's*). In their private life, Dods made their identity even more undecipherable through the use of initials. Dods used 'D' and 'MD Dods' as their autograph, while engaging in gender experimentation within London's elite literary culture. Betty Bennett has, in her biography of Dods, sorted out Dods's multiple pseudonyms, determining that the handwriting in letters signed 'David Lyndsay' and those signed 'D' and 'MD Dods' is identical. These are the relevant proper nouns. In addition, we must reflect on what to do with the confusion of pronouns. What connects Dods to contemporary debates lies in asserting agency over their gender identity rather than in passively accepting the fixed/binary gender binaries imposed by heteronormative culture. The fact that Dods signs with gender-neutral abbreviations is noteworthy, as an enactment of re-gendering which prefigures what linguist Dennis Baron calls 'today's sudden interest in personal pronouns'.[4] Dods's case may suggest that the transgender pursuit of appropriate pronouns is far from sudden, given its several-centuries-long history.

In what follows, I consider Dods's legacy as a friend of novelist Mary Shelley, as a way of indicating how a history of women's writing in Romanticism can be seen to be shaped by intimacy and interaction with Dods as a dramatist and queer public figure. The contact with Shelley is not the full extent of Dods's interactions with canonical Romantic writing – Dods, for instance, sent a draft of 'The First Murder' to Lord Byron prior to the text's publication. Yet, Shelley was particularly a fan of Dods and of David Lyndsay, a name she would sometimes misspell as 'David Lindsey'. While residing in Italy, Shelley wrote Thomas Medwin to report the following: 'by strange coincidence, the author (one David Lindsey) [*sic*] has chosen three subjects treated by Lord Byron; Cain, the Deluge and Sardanapalus ... This is all the literary news I have for you'.[5] Shelley served not simply as a friend but as Dods's ally and literary advocate. Dods met Shelley between 1822 and 1824, at the house of Dr William Kitchiner in Kentish Town, roughly a mile north of London. To gain Shelley's trust, Dods had to prove that *Blackwood's* was not as hostile to Percy Shelley's brand of radical politics as his widow believed.

Shelley's friendship with and advocacy for Dods stands in stark contrast to others in their social circle. Consider Eliza Rennie, author of *Traits of Character*, who recalled the astonishing sight of 'Miss Dods': 'Certainly Nature, in any of its wildest vagaries never fashioned anything more grotesque-looking than was this Miss Dods. She was a woman apparently between thirty and forty years of age', writes Rennie, and 'she wore no cap, and you almost fancied, on first looking at her, that some one of the masculine gender had indulged in the masquerade freak of feminine habiliments and that 'Miss Dods' was an alias for Mr. — '.[6] So 'grotesque' was Dods's visage to Rennie that the latter confesses she had to stop herself, in the polite setting of Kitchiner's salon, from laughing out loud. Half-fascinated and half-horrified by the sight of a trans person, Rennie aggressively gender-polices Dods, emphatically asserting Dods's status as a 'Miss'.

By contrast, Shelley's relationship with Dods was founded on friendly acceptance. Charlotte Gordon notes that Dods fell 'immediately in love with Shelley, deluging her with letters describing the anguish she felt on the days they did not meet', while Shelley saw her involvement with Dods in more platonic terms.[7] Shelley quickly formed a close friendship with Dods and began to champion Dods's writing. In 1825, David Lyndsay bragged to Blackwood that Shelley was now their intimate friend: '[a] fine Creature and a million times too good for the party to which she is so unlucky to belong'.[8] Here, Lyndsay not only assumes the role of Shelley's protective confidante, but also uses the equivocal term 'Creature' in an allusive manner that recalls the pitiable monster in *Frankenstein* (1818).

Shelley's esteem for 'Doddy & Isabel' (or, the 'Douglasses', as she described the couple in a letter to Williams) demonstrates how the author of *Frankenstein* could, in real life, sympathise with social outcasts shunned, by some, for their unusual appearance.[9] Shelley journaled in September of 1827 about Robinson as 'my lovely friend' and claimed, defensively, that a widowed woman such as herself had only friendship to keep her alive:

> It is my destiny, it would seem to form rather the ties of friendship than love – the grand evil that results from this is – that while the power of mutual Love is in itself a mighty destiny – friendship though true, yields to the adverse gale – and the vessels are divided far which ought never to part company.[10]

Shelley had introduced the couple herself in the attempt to play matchmaker, audaciously ahead of her time as a queer cupid and ally. Fearful secrecy was the order of the day, given that queer people had no choice but to hide in nineteenth-century Britain, for fear of blackmail, pillorying and hanging.

'In the early winter of 1825, Mary Shelley began what would grow into a very close friendship with Isabella Robinson and Mary Diana Dods', writes Bennett, 'and during the next two and a half years, one of these women arranged false passports for her two confidantes, the second became an unwed mother, and the third became a man'.[11] In the words of another Shelley-family biographer Emily Sunstein, 'Mary, Doddy, and Isabel concocted, and were to bring off, an incredible coup' insofar as they engineered a plan to rescue Robinson from her socially inferior status as an unwed mother, to marry a gender variant Scottish author, and to provide a safe and stable domicile for Adeline (Robinson's illegitimate daughter from a prior relationship).[12]

The Shelley-Dods-Robinson triangle would frequently communicate in code. One letter from Shelley contains a lacuna that precludes the reader from knowing what word she and Jane Williams used to denote their genitals. In the same letter, replete with use of aliases and a foreign language, Shelley refers to 'D.' for Doddy and 'Isa' for 'Isabel', expressing her relief that Doddy is donning men's pants: 'I am glad for Isabel's sake that D. now seriously thinks of *les culottes* [breeches]'.[13] By 1826, Shelley was acting on Dods's behalf, even making excuses for them; she wrote Alaric Watts, editor of *The Literary Souvenir*, to explain that Lyndsay's absence from England had occasioned 'delay' but that their works were worth the wait.[14] Again, in late October, Shelley wrote to Colburn to persuade the publisher that Mr Lyndsay's writing 'is indeed a production of genius', urging some kind of 'negotiation with my friend'.[15] One year later, Shelley saw to it that her friend Dods could wed Isabel Douglas, leave England, and assume the roles of husband and wife. Still, the couple would need passports if Dods wished to work in France, and to that end, Shelley leaned on her friend John Howard Payne (an American actor and songwriter) to play along and cooperate in the plot; she even asked Payne to find two friends to impersonate Dods and Douglas since they were allegedly too 'ill' to travel to London to procure the passports themselves.[16] Payne came in handy: a pair of his actor friends posed as Mr and Mrs Douglas and went as far as to use handwriting sent to Payne by Shelley so that the couple's signatures could be forged. Dods's determined self-invention and numerous re-genderings took place against a backdrop of political and social upheaval. By 1832, Mary Shelley learned that Walter Sholto Douglas had died and that their widow, Isabella Robinson Douglas, had remarried to a British minister who had retired to Italy. Dods had always been the cynosure in the Shelley-Dods-Robinson triangle and, without Dods, Shelley fell out of touch with Robinson and even came to wonder what she saw in Robinson in the first place.

In terms of women's writing in Romantic-era England, Dods's status as a trans and genderfluid writer not only changes the parameters of the category of the so-called 'woman writer' but expands it. Dods was not simply performing masculinity but crossing gender norms while scrambling many of the stylistic norms that make prose fiction cohere on the most superficial of levels. Let me begin with 'The First Murder: The Rejection of the Offering' (1821), the first of their publications in *Blackwood's*. Dods's drama explores what is collectively remembered as the original regime of heterosexual bliss, offered to the first human family by God but rejected shortly thereafter. Dods's use of the collective 'our' in Eve's confessional 'our dire transgression' is of particular interest because it implies that we, as descendants of the first family, desire in ways that are innately defiant, performative, even mournful. Dods's 'The Plague of Darkness' (1821) considers how the ancient Israelites liberate themselves from bondage. Growing up, in this case, demands a denial of patriarchal rule in order to claim new forms of identity and self-determination. Dods's revisions of the Old Testament merit closer attention in terms of their erotic themes and stylistic fluidities. Both stories oscillate between prose fiction and verse drama. The two stories are thematically congruent, plunging the reader into the supposed first instances of sin, transgression, fratricide, along with the affective fallout of such acts, namely, self-punishment and shame.

Dods's lyric-drama centres on the first family's descent into murder and incest. 'The First Murder' is the clearest proof that Dods wished to poeticise the ways in which heterosexual happiness faces a stunning collapse. That paradisiacal locus of Eden – from the Hebrew word for 'delight' – is always already lost to Adam and Eve and to all of the others who have no choice but to desire and form the family unit in a postlapsarian place of 'sin'. It is a word that, incidentally, makes its first appearance in God's speech to Cain soon after his mother's fall: 'And if you do not do well, sin is lurking at the door; its desire is for you, but you must master it'.[17] The implication is that short-lived happiness in the garden of Eden cannot be cleaved from the couple's disgraced exile. In 'The First Murder', shame is explicitly linked to the experience of erotic enjoyment. What is human desire without shame, asks Dods, and why does the will to transgress always lurk at the door to desire. According to Dods, after the mythical fratricide, Eve took sides, for 'Eve, in this first polemical contest, had taken the part of Cain; Adam, that of Abel'. The first father, Adam, is animated by a deep-seated 'anger' towards that 'froward child', whereas Eve is defined by her apologetic sympathy, or those 'endeavors to excuse and palliate the offense of their son'.[18] Eve defies God the father and, in doing so, Adam the first father and, from there, down they go into a traumatising tailspin. The tragic fates of Cain and Abel parallel the punishment experienced by their parents.

Dods is less interested in Adam's aggression towards his sons than in Eve ('our grand ancestress') and her siding with humankind's first murderer (also her firstborn) by refusing to reject Cain.[19] Whereas the fall of Adam and Eve is meant to account for the existence of shame, the following tale further dramatises the family romance but in terms of how the deadly rivalry between brothers only intensifies the violence in Adam and Eve's bloodline. The implication of Dods's biblical borrowings is that erotic desire is constituted not by an original sin but by and through a wide range of performances. In contrast to an effusive Eve, God is neither seen nor heard in Dods's retelling. In fact, Dods silences the holy father in 'The First Murder', even if his function as the first lawmaker suffuses the scene. From a Freudian perspective, there is a fine line between the prohibitions instituted by God the Father and the father of the primal horde who, before his sons kill and devour him, was granted absolute access to whatever and whomever he pleased. In effect, God lost the right to unlimited *jouissance*.[20] The origin of desire – particularly Eve's – tragically coincides with the restrictions placed upon her desire not simply to unite with Adam but to know good versus evil. This intertwining of desire and the law is best expressed by Eve herself who, in keeping with the phallocentrism of Genesis, takes the blame for what she calls 'that parent sin', even if, in Dods's reinterpretation, Eve is not an abject sinner but a mythic transgressor with her own 'audacious spirit'. Dods's prose prologue to 'The First Murder' begins with the caveat that the story of 'Adam and his family' is the most sublime of all works, striking readers with 'amazement and fear' due to its aforesaid audacity and the 'blasphemous intrepidity' of its players.[21] In this way, Dods's dramatic scenes unfold in the confrontational space between unlimited desire and the only way that God knows how to strike back: through his punishment of the first parents and the restoration of the law.[22]

Dods's Eden is a fractious place where heterosexual enjoyment is, at best, a mixed feeling, a (brief) state of being outside, uncovered and shameless but already coloured by what is to come: a postlapsarian state of sinfulness marked by the first incidents of homicide (Cain–Abel), polyphony (Babel), incest (Nephilim–humankind, Noah–Ham) and homosexuality (Sodom). All of the aforesaid stories are about the failure of normative sexuality to flourish and the inability of humans to suppress the evil in their hearts. Dods's largely Christian readership in 1820s England was already accustomed to reading backwards, in keeping with the exegetical practice known as typology: everything in the Christian scriptures is shadowed forth by the first murder, the first exodus, the first resettlement of the promised land. In this way, Dods anticipates what Jacques Lacan locates as the 'dawn of history', or the point of origin where the law of the father and language itself are delivered, allegorically speaking, as conjoined twins. Lacan points to the Bible as the best exemplar of what he calls 'traditional laws' seeking to outlaw the 'confusion of generations', by which he means incest, or that first transgression that shatters the putative power of the law, logos, even the symbolic field itself.[23]

In calling 'The First Murder' a 'dreadful performance', Dods may be referring to the tragedy at the heart of desire itself, and in the case of the first couple in the Judeo-Christian tradition, Adam and his family are doomed from the start.[24] Ashamed of herself, Eve sympathises with Cain because she knows what it feels like to be objectified, and to stand before a disapproving father and feel ashamed. The 'brightest members of the hierarchy of heaven', writes Dods, are haunted by the 'darkest demons in the abyss of perdition'.[25] Such a concern brings Dods into dialogue with contemporary queer theory. Jane Ward has recently located the tragedy at the heart of heterosexuality, describing that central heartache, that thirst for complementarity (or, put more idiomatically, the *you-complete-me* delusion), in this way:

> Straight culture seems to rely on a blind acceptance that women and men do not need to hold the other gender in high esteem as much as they need to *need* each other and to learn to compromise and suppress their disappointment in the service of this need.[26]

Yet, this need for one's 'missing half', or the puzzle-piece that will provide one with a feeling of ecstatic unification, leads only to frustration. The fantasy of complementarity (preordained by the Manichean dichotomies at the opening of Genesis: light versus dark, waters versus dry land, humankind versus animals) falls into a dark abyss. Dods's Eve laments that a 'green and goodly world' has disintegrated into 'mildew and perpetual blight'.[27] What 'The Plague of Darkness' proves is that there is an even greater danger awaiting humankind.

Dods's queer enactments of gender expression figure forth classical psychoanalysis in ways that necessitate closer attention.[28] Dods not only anticipates but also shares what Freud identifies as the central importance of all origin stories. Freud notes in *Totem and Taboo* (1913) that myths mark 'the beginning of so many things – of social organization, of moral restrictions and of religion'.[29] What Dods's retellings teach us is that the birth of pleasure depends upon some earlier act of subversion and the demand for self-punishment. Both 'The First Murder' and 'The Plague of Darkness' (melo)dramatise a sort of master–slave dialectic that, according to Lacan, could be a template for desire. Dods's undoing of sexual difference should already be obvious; the designations of 'he'/'she'/'they' were a masquerade well before Lacan stressed the fact that sexual difference is always subject to misrecognition (*méconnaissance*).[30] Eve bears the mark of anxiety, or what Dods calls 'maternal anxiety ... for it would seem that from his birth Cain had been a wayward and untractable child', and for this fault, 'our grand ancestress' takes all the blame.[31] All waywardness and perdition, it seems, flow from her womb. Driven by her own instinct to protect Cain – 'unconscious of the crime he had committed ... [and] anxious to sooth and console him' – Eve becomes a mouthpiece for all forms of fallenness, or what she describes to Adam as 'all that now or may hereafter date / Their woes or sorrows from our dire transgression'. That she shifts the blame to Adam (through the collective 'our') is proof that the cause of Eve's desire is opaque, lost to herself.[32] It follows, then, that a transgressor like Eve cannot master what she cannot even locate. Apart from Dods's oedipalisation of the Adam-Eve-Cain narrative, their multiple temporalities (dually 'now' and 'may hereafter') and Eve's presumed guilt for all of humankind's 'woes' only reinforce the degree to which the desiring subject is split and self-estranged.

In terms of its genre, 'The First Murder' lacks cohesiveness as a self-professed 'sacred drama'; this work is genre-fluid and more of a queer pastiche than a straightforward adaptation. Dods induces a kind of whiplash in their reader by shuttling from prose to verse to dialogue, then back again. The great verse dramas of the Romantic age begin with a prose preface wherein authors sometimes justify their purpose – think of Percy Bysshe Shelley's Preface to his *Prometheus Unbound* – but 'The First Murder' hops around so wildly that Dods, rather than justifying, seems to apologise through their use of the same repeated phrasing. Prior to the verse-speech delivered by the angel of Abel, they note that the scene 'is again changed' and, shortly after, 'the scene is then again changed'.[33] The dance of styles in what Dods calls an extended 'performance' parallels not just the author's own gender fluidity but, less obviously, their self-conscious non-attachment to a single, overarching genre.

If 'The First Murder' allows Dods to revisit and revise the very ancestral scene in which human subjects are gendered and, therefore, classified according to the binary logic of heteronormativity, 'The Plague of Darkness' marks Dods's effort to eroticise the kinds of power relations that arise from the first family's legacy of transgressing and desiring in 'unnatural' ways. In this way, 'The Plague of Darkness' is an instructive companion piece to 'The First Murder', serving as another tale of self-exile and the seesawing states of mastery and subjection. When nineteenth-century writers with an eye on political reform wished to rally their readers around the ideal of female independence, they often evoked the Book of Exodus, which depicts the ancient Israelites and their liberation from Egyptian bondage. It was a powerful allusion and used by writers to create a sense of continuity between the oppressed people in their own time and the ancient Israelites in their subjugation under Ramses II (1304–1237 BCE), the same tyrant sardonically commemorated by Percy Shelley in his sonnet 'Ozymandias' as 'King of Kings', armed with a 'sneer of cold command'.[34] In abolitionist literature of the nineteenth-century United States, the Pharaoh of Egypt was a standard substitute for the white slave-master.[35] Dods, anticipating this discourse, may be exploring the perverse wish to be bound. Nowhere is such a desire more obviously expressed than in 'The Mount of Olives', Dods's brief poetic retelling of the place where Jesus, prior to his martyrdom, enters a final phase of inner turmoil and self-doubt. The Chorus concludes that Christ was the 'Lamb who died to save, / Who broke the bondage of the grave; / Who died and lives again'.[36] Caleb, one of two spies sent by Moses to scout out the land of Canaan, is the first to speak in Dods's 'The Plague of Darkness', and he similarly combines what would seem to be the crushing weight of Pharaoh's tyranny with the possibility of resurrection; he tells Moses, 'The scorpion-whip doth lash them to new life'.[37] Living under the lash, in an ironic way, can generate new modes of life.

At its core, Dods's version of the Exodus tale is Genesis (or, 'origin') told in reverse: a promised land (Canaan/Eden) is regained after an original sin, for humankind cannot *not* go on sinning according to the logic of the forbidden, *pace* Freud (who writes, 'there is no need to prohibit something that no one desires to do, and a thing that is forbidden with the greatest emphasis must be a thing that is desired').[38] The newly liberated Israelites, for example, find themselves lost inside what Exodus terms the 'wilderness of Sin'.[39] Even after the flood, or what Jacques Derrida, in 'Literature in Secret', calls the 'sacrificial holocaust offered by Noah', man's desire to commit 'evil' deeds is never fully expunged.[40] Gazing on his firstborns, God wishes to partake in the enjoyment that he created for every living thing on earth *but* himself. 'Jahweh' feels, according to Derrida, the original fear of missing out and by 'circumscribing his grace in such a terrible way, he punishes and destroys every other life on earth [for] the evil within them, namely their desire, whereas it was he who committed the sin of putting it in them'.[41] Hence God's jealousy of his creation's access to *jouissance*, an enjoyment denied to him, manifests itself through a murderous megalomania.

The earth has to undergo a genocidal deluge though sin survives in the form of voyeurism, even same-sex incest: 'And Ham, the father of Canaan, saw the nakedness of his father, and told his brothers outside'.[42] There is no judgment on Noah's inebriations – fathers usually get away scot-free – but Ham bears the mark of his ancestor, Cain, and ushers in yet another era of fragmentation and diaspora in the form of Babel. In short, the shame cycle continues. 'As always, desire is what engenders fault', observes Derrida.[43] That fraternal bonds are not only solidified but strengthened through fratricide was not lost on Freud who, in *Totem and Taboo*, seized upon the drama of fratricide to account for the etiology of repression. 'The Plague of Darkness' again dramatises the inextricability of 'unnatural' desire and the law. Here, too, Dods bestows a mysterious interiority upon characters seen as one-dimensionally 'evil' in the Judeo-Christian tradition.

Performing the role of the godhead, Pharoah knows that he must define his subjects in terms of phallic lack, and thus, he excoriates the Israelites as 'coward sons, / Of an effeminate land!'[44] He alone possesses the paternal throne and, later in the speech, he reveals the paranoid logic that underpins his unstable mastery: 'Ye coward slaves! ... learn to bear what Egypt's master bears / Serene and unrepining'.[45] For Pharoah to maintain his image as the strongman leader, he must fool his self-punishing sons into a state of servitude; they must enter into the joy of his Gothicised sadism. In turn, they must come to see their own subjugation (framed in gendered terms as 'effeminacy') not as abject but as totally natural. In 'The Plague of Darkness', Dods shows a softer side to Rampsinitis and declares, 'My throne will seem the awful seat of death, / And I the crowned spectre sitting there / Encircled by the dead'.[46] Uneasy lies the head that wears the crown, yes, but there is something more perverse at work in this power play: central to the Egyptian master's self-understanding is the idea that his power over his sons (and daughters) is tenuous at best, less a monolithic and objective quality than something he is performing through dress, speech and movement. Clearly, the man he imagines himself to be is not the sovereign desired by Moses and his people. It is Rampsinitis who speaks directly to this perversity when he asks Moses, 'Why, thus, perverse, provoke the wrath of Pharoah?'[47] Inevitably, Pharoah's loose grip on power hastens a downfall as speedy and sudden as the first family's fall in 'The First Murder'. Both are scenes of transgression that lead to a descent into diaspora and chaos, which are significant because what Dods is dramatising in their biblical retellings is the breakdown of patriarchal power, both imagined (Eden) and historical (Egypt). If their intention was not to rescue Eve from opprobrium, Dods wanted to poeticise the complexities of Eve's desires as the first daughter, first wife and first mother on earth. Derrida bears repeating, 'as always, desire is what engenders fault', and, at the centre of man's culpability stands the scapegoated Eve and the first fault that inaugurates the 'logic of repentance and forgiveness' itself.[48]

The extraordinary life of Mary Diana Dods and their writings are deeply entwined. Dods, whose year of death is still undetermined, remains a deeply obscure figure, a situation which is unsurprising in light of their various aliases and masquerades. Dods's interest in biblical history may look, on the surface, incongruent with their defiant forms of social masquerade. Yet, Dods was acutely keen to what was popular in an era transitioning from the radicalism of Byron and the Shelleys to the propriety of the Victorians. They would dwell in the spaces where desire and the law of the father find themselves at odds and where, inevitably, Edenic states of harmony and happiness are degraded into states of disease, diaspora and sexualised shame. They remain one of the queerest contributors to Romanticism and an ambiguous figure in its history of transgressive writing, and their queerish retellings of the Bible make them worthy of more sustained of scholarly attention from Romanticists and an important contributor to the 'dire' literary history of sexual transgression.[49]

Notes

1. Matthew 25:21.
2. Geraldine Friedman, 'Pseudonymity, Passing, and Queer Biography: The Case of Mary Diana Dods', *Romanticism on the Net* 23 (2001): n. p., https://doi.org/10.7202/005985ar.
3. Ibid.
4. Dennis Baron, *What's Your Pronoun?: Beyond He and She* (New York: Liveright, 2020), 4. Further justification for the usage of plural pronouns can be found with Rachel Mesch, who writes, 'Trans includes those who identify as nonbinary, genderqueer, pangender, and gender fluid'. Mesch, *Before Trans: Three Gender Stories from Nineteenth-Century France* (Stanford: Stanford University Press, 2020), 8. While championing the use of the plural pronoun, Mesch makes clear the inaccuracy of superimposing such above-cited modern monikers onto nineteenth-century European culture.
5. Shelley, Letter I, *Letters*, 232.
6. Betty T. Bennett, *The Letters of Mary Wollstonecraft Shelley*, vol. I (Baltimore: Johns Hopkins University Press, 1980), 533.
7. Charlotte Gordon, *Romantic Outlaws: The Extraordinary Lives of Mary Wollstonecraft and Mary Shelley* (New York: Random House, 2015), 476.
8. Bennett, *The Letters of MWS*, 533.
9. Ibid., 556.

10. Mary Wollstonecraft Shelley, *Mary Shelley's Journal*, ed. Fredrick L. Jones (Norman: University of Oklahoma Press, 1947), 199.
11. Betty T. Bennett, *Mary Diana Dods, A Gentleman and A Scholar: The Astonishing Revelation of a Daring 170-Year-Old Deception* (New York: William Morrow and Co., 1991), 18.
12. Emily W. Sunstein, *Mary Shelley: Romance and Reality* (Baltimore: Johns Hopkins University Press, 1989), 280.
13. Shelley, Letters I, *Letters*, 572.
14. Shelley, Letters II, *Letters*, 532.
15. Ibid., 534–5.
16. Miranda Seymour, *Mary Shelley* (New York: Grove Press, 2000), 384–5.
17. Genesis 4:7.
18. Mary Diana Dods, 'The First Murder; or, the Rejection of the Offering', *Blackwood's Edinburgh Magazine* (1821), 322.
19. Ibid., 321.
20. In his meta-psychological study, *Totem and Taboo*, Freud contends that the primal father's descendants killed and consumed him in order to achieve an identification with him. This marks a step towards civilisation and, paradoxically, progress through parricide. For more on taboo, see Joan Wallach Scott, in which she traces, like Dods and Freud, the supposed 'naturalness' of the patriarchy to the origin stories discussed here: 'The rule of the sons then replaced the absolutism of the father some form of fraternity overthrew the reign of the king, and modernity was born'. See Joan Wallach Scott, *Sex and Secularism* (Princeton: Princeton University Press, 2018), 97.
21. Dods, 'The First Murder', 321.
22. Ibid., 323.
23. Jacques Lacan, 'Function and field of speech and language', *Écrits*, trans. Alan Sheridan (New York: Norton, 1977), 66.
24. Dods, 'The First Murder', 321.
25. Ibid., 321.
26. Jane Ward, *The Tragedy of Heterosexuality* (New York: New York University Press, 2020), 16.
27. Dods, 'The First Murder', 323.
28. Here my cadence mirrors Lacan's in 'The Mirror Stage'.
29. Sigmund Freud, *Totem and Taboo: Some Points of Agreement between the Mental Lives of Savages and Neurotics*, trans. James Strachey (New York: Norton, 1950), 142.
30. Geneviève Morel links masquerade, in the Lacanian sense, with not just comedy but with 'the phallus and its peekaboo games, which are a function of its nature as a signifier that appears and disappears'. Geneviève Morel, 'Feminine Jealousies', *Sexuation*, ed. Renata Salecl (Durham, NC: Duke University Press, 2000), 160.
31. Dods, 'The First Murder', 321.
32. Ibid., 323.
33. Ibid., 323–5.
34. Percy Bysshe Shelley, 'Ozymandias', in *Poems of Percy Bysshe Shelley* (New York: Thomas Y. Crowell Company, 1968), 21.
35. In 'What to the Slave Is the Fourth of July?', Frederick Douglass draws a comparison between the 'Pharoah and his hosts [who] were drowned in

the Red Sea' and the British government. See Frederick Douglass, 'What to the Slave Is the Fourth of July?', *The Oxford Frederick Douglass Reader*, ed. William L. Andrews (New York: Oxford University Press, 1996), 111. Mary Wollstonecraft uses the same device to argue for female equality and woman's right to an education. The last line of her *A Vindication of the Rights of Woman* from 1792 emphasises the parallel between patriarchy and the Pharaoh referenced in Exodus 5:6–19. In the Egyptian religious system, Pharaohs were thought to be divinely ordained. Mocking this belief and the Englishman's tyranny over his wife and daughter, Wollstonecraft concludes with this allusion to Exodus: 'Allow her the privileges of ignorance, to whom ye deny the rights of reason, or ye will be worse than Egyptian task-masters'. Mary Wollstonecraft, *A Vindication of the Rights of Woman*, ed. D. L. Macdonald and Kathleen Scherf (Peterborough: Broadview Press, 2001), 343.
36. Mary Diana Dods, 'The Mount of Olives', *Blackwood's Edinburgh Magazine* (1821), 655.
37. Mary Diana Dods, 'The Plague of Darkness', *Blackwood's Edinburgh Magazine* (1821), 555.
38. Freud, *Totem and Taboo*, 69.
39. Exodus 17:1.
40. Jacques Derrida, 'Literature in Secret', *The Gift of Death and Literature in Secret*, trans. David Willis (Chicago: University of Chicago Press, 1995), 141.
41. Ibid., 150.
42. Genesis 20:22.
43. Derrida, 149.
44. Dods, 'The Plague of Darkness', 557.
45. Ibid., 557.
46. Ibid., 561.
47. Ibid., 561.
48. Derrida, 149.
49. Dods, 'The First Murder', 323.

Chapter 9

George Sand, *Indiana* and the Transgressive Work of Idealism

Richard C. Sha

Critics have long read George Sand's *Indiana* (1832) as a transgressive novel whose target is marriage and traditional gender identities.[1] Yet, these same critics have not paid sufficient attention to Sand's coupling of transgression and idealism, understood here as a utopic promotion of a higher ideal and a heightening of certain characteristics like prettiness.[2] Transgression is a violation of duty or law, a moment of rule-breaking that potentially becomes the ability to entertain the possibility of other rules. Yet, for all of its rule-breaking, transgression violates only one set of norms, and it remains to be seen whether this violation amounts to meaningful change.[3] Even if the one set of rules is overturned, what prevents new rules from replacing the old and effectively a return to the status quo? What prevents a new version of the same normativity? I here turn to *Indiana* to consider why Sand couples transgression with the idealism of utopia.[4] My wager is that utopia provides a vantage point so that the consequences of transgression are not assumed and can be more readily evaluated.[5] Usually linked with material practice, transgression enables the work of social rules to become visible. Nonetheless, Sand recognises that this materialist view of transgression resists evaluation of its consequences since the concrete focus on rule-breaking along with its thrills neither addresses the resilience of the norm nor the gap between rule-breaking and meaningful change. In short, breaking the rules is hardly a guarantee of meaningful change, especially when it is by a single individual. Indeed, the emphasis on something broken can reduce the scale of the problem to the individual instead of the system, which can easily abject instances of the broken.[6] In this view, the concreteness of materialism requires abstraction to address whether the rule-breaking lives up to its hype and how far its meanings can be generalised. For that generalisation to be valid, abstraction has to be more than escapism or evasion, and it must provide a blueprint for transgression across scales. Indeed, Sand explicitly links abstraction and truth in *The Devil's Pool*

(1846) when she claims that 'art is not the study of positive reality; it is the search for an ideal truth'.⁷ Her insistence on truth as process implies that realism must be deferred until one has evaluated the features of the real, which are in keeping with one's ideal social order.

When coupled with transgression, utopia further enables us to see the idealism within transgression: the fact that transgression is typically better at calculating benefits over costs, the change versus the meaning of that change. For Sand, the anti-realism of utopia both invites contemplation about the scale of change needed and facilitates the evaluation of consequences – did any real change here actually happen, and are the changes enough? To press hard on these questions, Sand triples down on utopia, offering three versions of it: an imagined heaven, a return to a tropical island and a union with a kinder and gentler man. Utopia further helps us to see that while rule-breaking may be the start of something meaningful, it is never its end. In her journals, Sand praises the 'useful and vivifying' idealism of poets despite their inattention to reality. She concludes, 'one's spirit is uplifted with those of the inspired dreamers', and thus idealism for Sand offers something to aspire to as well as a source of inspiration.⁸ In short, Sand's bitter cocktail of transgression and idealism shows that transgression itself can be uncritically idealist and weighted towards self-congratulation, and therein she underscores the need to think about its consequences. She thus associates transgression with beginnings, not endings, so we pay more attention to what happens as a result of it and to what needs to happen.

Sand skews the temporality of transgression so that its consequences can be evaluated, explicitly distinguishing between unthoughtful and thoughtful versions of it. To Raymon's charge that Indiana has 'abandoned her duty', she tartly replies, 'I know what ... [duties] are and I didn't love you little enough to transgress them unthinkingly (*pour les violer sans réflexion*)' (I 188/224). Indiana distinguishes here between transgression for the sake of pleasure and a transgression that leads to a reassessment of what society defines as 'duty'. Here, transgression has value to the extent that it fosters reflection about duties and about the difference between selfish love for mere personal pleasure and a love that entails at least some selflessness as measured in a kind of personal cost. Crucial here is Indiana's idealism about duties – what they should entail – which facilitates the creation of a space between societal duty and her own sense of it. To wit, the subject 'I' is pitted against a plural 'they', and implicitly Sand questions whether the female subject can survive societal duties. Will there be any remainder if those duties are insisted upon?

The norm Sand challenges is heteronormativity, and thus stakes of her idealist transgression are high. So long as heteronormativity exists, Sand insists that women can be no more than an index of male superiority.⁹ Her heroine, Indiana, is trapped in a loveless and passionless marriage to Monsieur Delmare, courted by a selfish cad, Raymon, and eventually, after the death of her husband, betrothed if not married to someone who treats her more equitably, her cousin Ralph. Meanwhile, Raymon has impregnated his lover, Noun, Madame Delmare's maidservant, who carries Raymon's child and commits suicide because Raymon abandons her to pursue Indiana. With this range of men, Sand argues that under heterosexual normativity, there is no possible meaningful intimacy for women because even the most enlightened man of the bunch still understands sexual difference in terms of hierarchy. Indiana famously exclaims to her first husband,

> I know I am the slave and you're the lord. The law of the land has made you my master. You can tie up my body, bind my hands, control my actions ... But over my will, Monsieur, you have no power (*Je sais que je suis l'esclave et vous le seigneur. La loi de ce pays vous a fait mon maître. Vous pouvez lier mon corps, garrotter mes mains, gouverner mes actions ... mais sur ma volonté, Monsieur, vous ne pouvez rien*). (I 176/210).

Sand's attention to the scale of nation (*ce pays*) puts pressure on individual transgression. By highlighting Indiana's recognition of the law's power over her body, hands and actions, Sand makes the will seem hollow. In so doing, she offers a tempered utopianism that recognises the intractability of certain features of the social versus a celebratory one, which focuses on the triumph of the will at the expense of the imprisonment of her body. Even worse, despite being both neglected by her father and married to an awful man, Indiana dreams of being delivered by a future lover: she thinks to herself, 'a day will come when my life will be completely changed (*tout sera changé*) ... it will be a day when I shall be loved' (I 51/62). This example shows that Sand is not blind to the limits of idealism: one issue is learning when to use it and when to see its delusive potential.¹⁰ Note the passivity implied here, which strongly intimates delusion: this version of idealism demands that Indiana do nothing more than lie back and wait for all to be changed. When idealism is passive, it lends itself to feminisation, and not an empowering one.

There is more evidence of Sand's careful idealism. After Indiana learns that instead of pining away for her, Raymon has married Laure de Nangy, she retires to a drab hotel room, which Sand calls a 'prison cell of the mind and heart (*cachot de l'esprit et du Coeur*)' (I 234/278). This later symbolism effectively empties the earlier suggestion of any triumph of the will, for the will (*volonté*) has become a dungeon (*cachot*) for both Indiana's mind (*l'esprit*) and heart (*coeur*). That she is stuck there without money and hungry to boot sucks away any remaining redemptive possibility in the will, a point underscored by Sand's imagery of the room as a vast desert without water (*abandonné dans l'immensité d'un desert sans eau*) (I 235/279). Even the most iron will eventually succumbs to dehydration.

In a larger view, the range of male examples (Delmare, Raymon and Ralph) further suggests the resiliency of heteronormativity; for transgression to be meaningful, it needs to find ways to scale itself up so that a system, buttressed by national laws, can be thwarted. Pretty boy Raymon facilitates transgression against marriage, but this transgression is only skin deep and lasts only as long as a meaningless episode of pleasure. That the desire between Raymon and Indiana is never consummated underscores its hollowness. Indiana, to her credit, decides to spend a sexless night under his roof, risking her complete dishonour, so that she can test Raymon's commitment to her, but the thought of her dishonour renders her worthless to Raymon even though he is the one who has dishonoured her (I 165–6). In effect, then, Sand comments that this asymmetry behind honour means that it is only the man's honour that truly counts: Indiana's sacrifice of her honour, which is to say her entire self, has no value.

Having shown the curbs Sand places on idealism, allow me to elaborate upon how idealism grants transgression a higher standard to live up to. Naomi Schor has done the most to help us understand Sand's investments in idealism. She demonstrates that before the rise of the realist novel, there was an important tradition of the idealist novel, to which Sand belonged. Unlike the realist novel, which privileges empirical detail and historical specificity, the idealist novel has a utopian dimension, and Schor ties Sand's canonical marginality to a literary history in which realism triumphs over idealism. Indeed, the history of the novel is a history of the triumph of Realism. Realism frames idealism's utopic leanings as no more than a frivolous escapism or empty allegory. More recently, José Esteban Muñoz distinguishes between possibility and potentiality to highlight the fact that although utopia is most often associated with vague possibility so it can be dismissed, it is more invested in potentiality, and the difference is important because potentiality highlights the beginnings of a change that is already present, making utopia about more than mere escapism.[11] In this view, utopia can help form the basis of a meaningful politics. To the extent that Sand's idealism mutes her politics, it has made her work seem naïve. Like that of Muñoz, Sand's utopia measures potential against possibility, finding Indiana's vision of heaven, the Bourbon island and Cousin Ralph wanting. Finally, Muñoz's awareness of how utopia orients its audience towards a potential future and away from short-sighted pragmatism suggests that transgression is often too content to rest its laurels upon a rule-breaking that is already in the past tense. Sand's coupling of transgression and utopia thus insists that it must be more actively forward-looking even as it turns to perfection to help identify the main principles that can guide change. Imagining the kind of world one wants to live in can help one confront what must be changed in the world one does live in.

Schor is spot on when she reads Sand's idealism as the cause of her literary marginalisation. And her claim that Sand's idealism counters male fetishisation of women's bodies grants her idealism a feminist politics. Yet, when she understands idealism to be 'implying a norm, a stereotype', she downplays idealism's central 'as if' claim.[12] Kwame Anthony Appiah explains that idealism at its most powerful is a form of bracketing, a recognition that the claim is not yet or quite true, but when hazarded for specific purposes like moral improvement, might prove useful.[13] Schor construes Sand's utopia as a fixed standard, but I think that Sand is constantly moving the bar, the better to ask what really has changed? When morality is reduced to a fixed standard, it hypostatises rather than improves. It also loses any power to evaluate effectiveness. What Schor sees as Sand's failure to imagine a passionately sexual marriage along with a genuine feminine subjectivity does not give Sand's combination of transgression with idealism the credit it deserves.[14] Indiana does fall silent in the utopia of Bourbon Island, but Sand's larger point has to do with the scale of transgression, and the fact that the outside world has yet to be meaningfully changed alerts readers to the work necessary to make transgression have and sustain meaning.

By combining transgression with the suspension of the real within utopia, Sand demands that we evaluate the effectiveness of any changes that occur. In its insistent 'as if', idealism resists the substitution of one norm for another because whatever is substituted is bracketed. In describing Indiana's initial change upon arrival at Bourbon Island, for instance, Sand notes that 'her brow became serene again and it was as if (*et on eût dit*) a ray of the Divine had passed into her gentle, melancholy blue eyes' (*I* 242/288). Here, the conditional form of the verb advertises its not quite trueness, and Sand turns to a divine explanation because it paradoxically helps to phenomenalise the experience of utopia and thus lend it traction. Muñoz strategically defines queerness as a form of utopia that can never fully actualise itself, but this refusal of actualisation leaves open the vantage point so that both evaluation and reassessment are possible. Through her utopias, Sand argues that the mere desire for change is not enough: it must be shared and scaled up. That her conclusion is told from the very limited vantage of the outsider further suggests an ironised ending, one that reminds us of scale. Ralph and Indiana have achieved limited success within a small geographic area, and localised transgression needs to be globalised.

Sand's scepticism that transgression will lead to meaningful change can be seen in her decision to triple down on utopia. When Indiana's husband loses his fortune, and the two need to move to Bourbon Island out of financial duress, Indiana writes Raymon a letter in which she imagines a future heavenly redemption. Indiana tells Raymon to 'enjoy the liberty you have reclaimed at the expense of my whole life (*jouissez donc de cette liberté rachetée aux dépens de toute mon existence*)' (*I* 190/226). She accuses Raymon of worshipping 'the god of men, the King and founder and protector of your race' (i.e., men) in contrast to her belief in 'the God of the universe, the creator, the support, and hope of all creatures (*Le vôtre, c'est le dieu des hommes; le mien, c'est le Dieu de 'l'univer'*)' (*I* 190/227). Sand thereby contrasts a patriarchal, hierarchal god with a levelling God of the Universe, and if nothing else, this indicates the scope of change that would need to happen as well as the fecklessness of any single act of transgression. Tellingly, the god of man is uncapitalised, while the God of the universe is. Change is imagined here at a cosmological scale, but it is also in the details. Indiana admits 'yes, these are my dreams; they are all of another life, of another world (*ils sont tous d'une autre vie, d'un autre monde*), where the ruffian's law will not bear down on the head of the peace-lover' (*I* 191/228).

With this claimed utopia, Sand questions if the kinds of change Indiana envisions are even possible, even as she asks readers to choose between a God of hierarchy and violence and one of peace along with the social order that each of them underwrites. With her insistence on another life (*autre vie*), Indiana recognises she is merely a commodity, totally alienated from the rules of exchange because her whole existence is ransomed (*rachetée*) for Raymon's liberty. His liberty, moreover, is only very momentary, while the consequences she has to face will be permanent. What is framed as innocent economic exchange is thus, in reality, extortion, and for transgression to amount to actual change, Sand insists that the very political economy of heteronormativity will have to be rewritten. Sand's larger point here is that transgression against marriage will only work if the rules of political economy can be changed.[15] Because Indiana knows that she is articulating her dreams and not reality, utopia is hardly the naïve escapist plot device that it is too often accused of being.

Bourbon Island offers a second utopia, another chance to determine and evaluate the consequences of rule-breaking, especially since it represents at least for Ralph a nostalgic return to his and Indiana's childhood, which Ralph associates with perfect intimacy. That the Delmares must go there out of financial duress already begins to interject some realism. Even in paradise there are bills to pay, and Sand interjects realism into the natural description of the 'pure waters of turbulent rivers flow' (*I* 195). To underscore the limits of this utopia, Sand notes that Indiana often lowers 'her raffia window blind and retreats even from the daylight' (*I* 193). It is a less than satisfying utopia that demands withdrawal from it even as utopia's ability to blind is rendered literally both with the raffia and the retreat of daylight. The multiple levels of utopia suggest that transgression has a scalar problem. If transgression cannot effect transformation across scales, how can it compete with the resilience of heteronormativity? As a return to childhood, Bourbon Island threatens to be backward as opposed to forward-looking, and the problem to overcome is whether childhood intimacy can be combined with adult sexuality. Schor frames the question thusly: 'can ideal Eros deploy itself fully anywhere outside of utopia?'.[16] Sand refuses any answer in this novel.

Although the final union between Ralph and Indiana takes place on Bourbon Island, this happy ending is also undermined.[17] True enough, of all the men in the book, Ralph is the only one to have the capacity to consider Indiana's needs. After Delmare dies, Ralph treats the weak Indiana and lets her know that she is now free to marry her lover, Raymon, even though he is his rival (*I* 236). Ralph does not know that Raymon has already for reasons of money married Laure de Nangy, and here his ignorance makes his sacrifice genuine. And true enough, we are told that through Indiana's constant comparisons of the two men, Raymon and Ralph, she is able to extinguish 'every spark of her blind, disastrous love' for Raymon (*I* 243). Yet, how different are the two men in actuality? Indiana admits that Ralph considers women to be no more than domesticated animals (*I* 158) and that so long as she functions as his servant, 'he asks nothing more of me' (*I* 159). He also buys into the notion that 'all women are ... crazy' (*I* 26), and thus female unhappiness does not have to be taken seriously. True enough, Ralph imagines that Indiana has dishonoured herself with Raymon, and he admits 'I would have killed her first' (*I* 181). Here, Ralph has completely bought into the idea that women's monogamy is the key to their honour and self-worth. Ralph proclaims to Indiana, 'You came into my life as if you had been created for me' (*I* 249), transforming her from her own end into a mere means for his own happiness. At the very end of the novel, Ralph proclaims, 'I have Indiana' (*I* 271), as if she were merely a piece of chattel. From her first husband to Ralph, then, what has really changed? In this view, Ralph is no alternative to Delmare. He is his double.[18] That doubling is another means of asking what has really changed with the exchange of one master for another? Even though it is not certain whether Indiana and George are married or are even lovers,[19] this language of possession certainly hints at marriage, as does the fact that Indiana is referred to as Ralph's 'fiancée' (*I* 260) at the very moment they are about to plunge to their deaths. Moreover, the change of location without major change in the actors amounts to a superficial change. To make matters worse, while Delmare is still alive, Ralph functions as his censor, thus collapsing the differences between the two men. Sand comments,

> the unavoidable person of Ralph, who, at the least sound, would come and place himself between Delmare and his wife, forced him (Delmare) to control himself, for he had enough self-respect to master his temper before that strict though silent censor. (*I* 198)

His triangulating role further undermines his ability to stand in for a real difference.

A closer look at Sand's utopic ending enables us to track how idealism functions to sever transgression from consequence so that consequences can be evaluated. Sand candidly admits that the tropical setting of Bourbon Island potentially lulls readers into a false sense of security, and she calls attention to her own limited powers of representation to encourage readers to be more critical of this ending. Immediately before her chapter 'Conclusion', she writes,

> if the tale of Ralph's inner life had no effect on you, if you haven't come to love that good man, it's because I haven't been able to exert over you the power contained in the voice of a man whose passion is deep and genuine. And then I've not the moon's melancholy influence to help me; the song of waxbills, the scent of gilly-flowers, and all the lulling, intoxicating seductions of a tropical night don't invade your heart and head. (*I* 260)

Several features of this quotation demand explanation. With regard to her declared inability to get readers to love Ralph, Sand introduces doubt by denying herself the power of 'a man whose passion is deep and genuine' through the metonymy of 'a man' for either Ralph or the author (*'je n'ai pas pu exercer non plus sur vous la puissance que possède la voix d'un homme profondément vrai dans la passion'* [*I* 308]). The multiple potential substitutions, the double negative (*n'ai non plus*) and disembodied voice break any illusion, even as her description of this act as 'lulling' puts readers on their guard. The French feminine gender of both voice and passion, moreover, counter the grounding masculine authority being summoned. Furthermore, while Ralph's passions are often deep and genuine, they are not unalloyed with self-interest, thereby undermining their genuineness. In fact, no man in the text embodies wholly such genuine passion. Only by thinking about what is wrong with utopia can we begin to understand the principles at stake.

Sand furthermore opens her conclusion with the narrator's contemplation of volcanic rocks and fossils: 'the rock ... was warm and malleable, it received the imprint of the shells and creepers that stuck to it' (*I* 262). What seems like an ancillary detail is actually the setting up of the issue of scale. When compared to fossilised remains, which have lasted for centuries, will Indiana and Ralph's union amount to a meaningful change? Sand further evacuates her happy idealistic ending with a magical transition from Indiana's suicide pact to a tropical paradise where she endures and where she and Ralph together become hermits. We witness the pair about to jump to their deaths: 'then Ralph took his fiancée in his arms and carried her off to plunge with her into the torrent' (*I* 260). That the plunge into marriage is not unlike a plunge to their deaths allows Sand to ask whether marriage equals death.[20] Especially for women, marriage represents a death of subjectivity. Although we are left hanging, wondering what happens to the pair, a new narrator visits Bourbon Island and finds the home of Indiana and Ralph as he searches frantically for shelter in a grotto during a torrential storm. This suspension of the plot offers a further chance for deliberation about the degree to which the pair's commitment to each other changes anything, while the introduction of a new narrator reveals yet another point of view that must be factored into any interpretation. Is the relative silence of Indiana a given or merely a reflection of the narrator's friendship with Ralph?

Sand's insistent traffic between the real and ideal further hints that neither alone offers a solution.[21] Without the two poles, the real has nothing to aspire to, while the ideal never has a comeuppance. After Indiana and Delmare have moved to Bourbon Island, she receives a letter from Raymon that makes her think he is pining away for her when, in reality, he is trying to marry a rich woman (*I* 219). As a result, Indiana vows to return to him, and she covertly arranges to be taken by ship back to France. To get Raymon out of her system, she has to leave utopia and discover his cruelty. Her departure from Bourbon Island to reunite with Raymon is depicted as a dream, and thus utopia requires another utopia to sustain itself. In keeping with her dualistic imagery, Sand informs us through Ralph that Bourbon Island is where Ralph first considered suicide, connecting utopia with death. He urges them to return there, 'the place where suicide appeared to me at its most noble and solemn' (*I* 241). Indiana connects these waters of paradise with the drowning of Noun (*I* 241), yoking together baptismal imagery with death. She adds, 'to die as she did will be pleasing to me; it will be my atonement for her death, which I caused' (*I* 241). Utopia then is achieved through suicide, a kind of transcendence. But as an atonement, utopia is also realism: suicide. And without the unmet desires that utopia promises to cancel out, atonement is a kind of suicide, for the very drives that make the utopia appealing are snuffed out by their fulfilment. Sand's insistent traffic between utopia and realism, promise and consequence, demands a constant attention to actual outcomes, and not just to future prospects, even as future prospects begin to set a timeline of diminishing returns on transgression.

Ralph, the very best exemplar of masculinity, is still shot through with patriarchy, and thus Sand underscores the cruel optimism that heterosexuality can ever result in either equality or meaningful intimacy.[22] She shows the degree to which normativity, order and hierarchy go together, and the vantage point of utopia provides the ability to see systemic problems.[23] The appearance of equity between Indiana and Ralph is coupled with both an absence of any sexual passion between husband and wife and isolation from human community, raising the question of why eroticism and the lack of hierarchy seem incommensurate and further ironising this utopia. On the one hand, once the new couple arrive in Bourbon Island, 'the sacred, filial intimacy which brought them close to each other, cured his painful shyness and the other of her unfair prejudices' (*I* 242). On the other hand, this intimacy is 'filial' and emphatically not sexual or passionate. That Ralph and Indiana free their slaves reminds us that women's servitude is another kind of slavery: indeed Sand refers to Indiana as an 'oppressed slave' (*I* 216), and upon returning to Raymon from Bourbon Island, she declares 'it's your slave (*c'est moi, c'est ton Indiana, c'est ton esclave*)' (*I* 231/275). She is unable to sustain the pronoun 'I' while referring to herself. The economic impact of the freed slaves suggests that the erasure of women's 'slavery' is not going away anytime soon.[24]

Sand empties out this second utopia by making Ralph's love of Indiana somewhat incestuous. Although he claims his love is 'pure' (*I* 253), Ralph hopes that Indiana will 'belong ... to me forever' (*I* 254). When they were children, Ralph imagines Indiana as his daughter and wife, and these competing versions of intimacy suggest that Ralph's love is beyond societal norms, and not necessarily in a good way. Ralph also pledges to Delmare that he will look after Indiana as a brother, and he very much keeps this vow until the death of Indiana's husband. Sand concludes the novel not by emphasising Ralph and Indiana's accomplishments but rather the speculation of moralists who consider the couple's isolation from the rest of society. The narrator comments, 'some moralists blame your solitude. They claim every man belongs to society, which requires his presence. They add that you set men an example which is dangerous to follow' (*I* 270). By ending the novel with a focus on the moral judgment of a larger audience, the danger of the example, and with Indiana and Ralph's isolation from the rest of society, Sand demands that readers contemplate what the transgression of Indiana and Ralph actually achieves, and to see that the work of transgression is not yet finished.

Sand encourages continuously thoughtful transgression by never allowing pleasure to become a sufficient explanation for it. Her tactic here is to insist upon readerly discomfort. For this reason, Ralph and Indiana's transgressions always have an edge to them that troubles the normative lines between childhood and sexuality; filial love and sexual love.[25] Even worse, Ralph admits that when Indiana was 'still a child', he looked upon her as his fiancée (*I* 249). Having sexualised a child, Ralph attempts to dial back his desire:

> My kisses were a father's, and when your innocent playful lips met mine they did not find the burning flame of a man's desire. (*Mes baisers furent ceux d'un père, et quand vos lèvres innocents et folâtres rencontraient les miennes, elles n'y trouvaient pas le feu cuisant d'un désir viril.*) (*I* 250/297)

Here, the denial actively makes present the burning sexual desire that he is trying to contain. To the extent that eroticism demands penetration, can it survive without violence? Sand later wrote to her half-brother, Hippolyte, on the occasion of his daughter's wedding night, advising, 'make sure that your son-in-law does not brutalise your daughter on her wedding night … There is nothing as awful as the horror, pain, and disgust of a poor young girl, getting raped by a brute.'[26] The remainder of discomfort never allows transgression to be exhausted by pleasure, and in fact, while Indiana and Ralph can and do transgress, there is no evidence that they experience sexual pleasure together.

The absence of sexual passion even within utopia is no failure of imagination. This is a prod to readers to finish the work of transgression. It is also a plea to think about how feelings of intimacy and sexual intimacy can be brought together without or with less violence. That Sand never lets her readers escape fully feelings of discomfort cues us into part of her overall strategy. Sand simultaneously generates affective desire for a better future – where's the passion? – along with cruel optimism regarding the present. Ralph embodies this future in Bourbon Island, but at the same time, the lack of passionate mutual intensity between Indiana and Ralph highlights the cruelty of this optimism. Through the ambiguity of affect, therefore, Sand harnesses transgression and idealism to insist on second-guessing consequences. The remainder of affect undermines readerly satisfaction, making transgression not an end but a beginning.

The novel's conclusion furthers such affective discontent. Ralph and Indiana enjoin their visitor to 'return to the world. If some day it banishes you, remember our Indian cottage' (*I* 271). In this way, present utopia looks back at the world and offers itself as a metonymy of success but of potential banishment as well. By hinting that their visitor may someday be banished, Sand reminds us that the world has ways of responding to transgression and that rule-breaking has consequences. At the end, however, the Indian cottage becomes a small, remembered symbol of hope that some change is possible, but that overall victory is far from achieved. That Indiana has been transformed into a modifier for cottage, 'Indian', makes this symbol of hope simultaneously one of violence. 'Indian cottage', furthermore, alludes to Jacques-Henri Bernardin de Saint Pierre's novella of the same name. In that work, an English doctor collects truths in the form of books and manuscripts for the Royal Society, only to discover that the real truth lies in a secluded Indian cottage of a pariah and his wife, who, unlike the Brahmins – the supposed arbiters of Eastern wisdom – are passionately happy in their simple and non-materialistic lives. By comparing Ralph and Indiana to this couple of pariahs, Sand underscores the costs of transgression over its rewards. As the only two in the novella to give the English narrator shelter and hospitality, they embody both a precarious and reduced ideal, leaving the reader wanting more.

Sand's goal then is to get rid of not just one set of rules, like marriage, but of heteronormativity itself by showing its investments in hierarchy, its brutality and inability to treat difference as other than inferiority. So long as women are valued for their ability to suffer, misogyny is encouraged. One of the editors of *Indiana* shrewdly remarks that 'suffering renders [women] respectable to men'.[27] In the opening scenes of the novel, Delmare threatens to kill Ophelia, Indiana's pointer, and we are told he has already shot her spaniel because it ruined a hunt (*I* 18–19). Later, as Ophelia swims to Indiana, sailors gratuitously smash her skull, once again signalling the violence that props patriarchy up. Both hunting dogs simultaneously announce Indiana's gender transgression, tamped down by the name 'Ophelia' – whom Hamlet reduces to a 'country' while lying in her lap – and remind us of the violence surrounding men.[28] When Indiana responds to Delmare with cold obedience, the narrator comments, 'he would have then killed his wife if he had been in Smyrna or Cairo' (*I* 155). The transgression of marriage rules does what against this licensed violence against women, symbolically shown in the violence against Ophelia? (*I* 207). Later after Delmare reads Raymon's old letters, he 'grab[s] Indiana by the hair, thr[ows] her down, and kick[s] her on the forehead with the heel of his boot', prefiguring the later smashing of Ophelia's skull. Sand wryly comments that Indiana was 'wounded by the laws of society' (*I* 207, 209) because these laws permit such violence. Indiana's transgression of her marital duties is met with the societal laws, and as individual act meets systematic laws, the very scales of justice are called into question.

Sand leverages idealism against heteronormativity, and in the process, considers the degree to which idealism, far from evading the material, is necessary for any transgression that does not simply exchange one set of rules for another. She pits patriarchal utopia in which women are effectively erased against a higher utopia where intimacy for women may be realised, raising the stakes for transgression by abstracting its consequences. The most genuine glimmer of intimacy occurs between Indiana and her servant, Noun, and this genuineness is perhaps made possible by the fact that both Noun and Indiana are Creoles, mixed-race figures.[29] Noun and Indiana are sometimes mistaken for each other, indicating some interchangeability. Indiana kisses Noun 'with the warmth of a sister' (*I* 71), and when choosing whether to run away with Raymon or confess all to Indiana, Noun exclaims,

> I'll throw myself at Madame Delmare's feet, I will tell her everything as she'll forgive me, I know; for she's kind and she loves me. We've never separated, she won't want me to leave her. She'll weep with me, she'll take care of me, she'll love my child, my poor child. (*I* 70)

Muñoz argues that 'the interracial and the queer co-animate each other',[30] and perhaps this co-animation may provide a workable ground of intimacy because difference is shared and thus cannot become the basis for hierarchy. Sand thus uses idealism to test what has actually been changed, and her attention to how social class and racial formation impact gender invites readers to consider how meaningful transgressions are when intersectionality simply replaces one form of subordination with another.[31] Unfortunately, Noun's role as Indiana's servant also disrupts this intimacy. For our purposes, Sand contrasts what might be called subject positions with actual bodies, and even though mutuality should be possible between Noun and Indiana, hierarchy still frustrates it. Noun senses that she is losing Raymon and dresses like Indiana, only to realise that Raymon is actually in love with Indiana's trappings. He is intoxicated by the 'white, bejewelled figure' (*I* 62), so much so that he mistakes Noun for Indiana when Noun wears her clothes.

Heteronormativity is a system that entails women's subordination and violence against women, and it is not going away. Crucially, as a system, it eroticises transgression, and in this view, transgression is both the imprisonment of femininity and its potential liberation. Raymon 'thought ... Madame Delmare's love and forgiveness ... were unattainable, and the love of no other woman, no other happiness on earth, seemed worthwhile' (*I* 83). So long as married women can be reduced to an ultimate challenge to male powers of seduction, no sustainable relationship can ensue. Raymon 'loves society with its rules and shackles because it offers him opportunities (*des aliments*) for struggle and resistance, and if he hated disorder and violence, it was because they promised insipid, easy pleasures' (*I* 83/102). Here, rules eroticise rulebreaking, and this eroticisation of transgression culminates in Raymon's framing of the ultimate goal of seducing a married woman. Unlike the bland translation of 'opportunities', the French '*aliments*' imply that this seduction is like food for Raymon, and in a sense, his preying on Indiana is figured as a virtual cannibalism. Women who lose their honour lose everything, and thus they have every incentive to resist male seduction. Moreover, insofar as masculinity itself demands women's lapsed honour to prop up what is a fantasy of virility – the pleasure given must compensate for becoming a pariah – at bottom, Sand wonders who benefits from this rigged version of exchange. The spectre of cannibalism haunts Raymon's transgression, making its effects inescapably ambivalent.

Heteronormativity, of course, encompasses gender, suggesting again the limits of what transgression achieves. Indiana transgresses gender rules and does so most clearly during the hunt. Sand comments, 'this apparently frail, timid woman possessed a more than masculine courage, the kind of mad intrepidity that can sometimes be manifested as a nervous crisis in the weakest of creatures' (*I* 113). And yet, if 'masculine courage' defies gender, the nervous body reasserts it, and what in men might seem courage is here depicted as a kind of madness and a nervous crisis. Sand's larger point has to do with how gender transgression meets neurology and physiology, and the combined force of these sciences work to reassert and try to stabilise gender norms. Sand provides this explanation: 'her dreary life, filled with sorrows, needed this stimulus: she seemed then to be aroused from a lethargy and, in one day, expended all the unused energy that had been allowed to seethe in her blood for a year' (*I* 113). Sand lays the fault at the door of how women are socialised, and their lack of exposure to stimulation causes their blood to seethe, so much so that its excess energy will find an out. Physiology here explains Indiana's behaviour, and in tying femininity to an incipient behaviouralism, it is emptied of complexity even as it asserts the norm.[32]

As if the disciplines of physiology and neurology were not enough to meet transgression's challenges, Indiana's gender-bending practically provokes disgust in Raymon. Crucially, Raymon 'was frightened at seeing her gallop in this way (*Raymon fut effrayé de la voir courrir ainsi*)' (*I* 113/138). Moreover, 'he was frightened by such fierce determination and it almost turned him against Madame Delmare' (*I* 113). Indiana's courage frightens Raymon, which suggests that his own courage is vulnerable and that masculinity, too, is precarious. The narrator continues to describe her fearless riding. Indiana

> abandon[s] herself fearlessly to the fiery mettle of a horse she barely knew, urging it on boldly into the heart of the woods, avoiding with amazing skill the branches which, springing back sharply, struck her face, unhesitatingly crossing ditches, confidently taking risks on the slippery clay soil, not worrying about breaking her slender limbs, but anxious to be the first to reach the steaming trail of the boar. (*I* 113)

By equating Indiana to a horse's fury, Sand returns to the idea that the passions need to be restrained by the male rider. Indiana's transgression here is framed as a violation of natural hierarchy and as a perverse turn away from reason. That both genders can come undone highlights their construction as opposed to essence, and once the vocabulary of construction is in place, one can ask who benefits from this construction. To the extent that gender violation provokes a kind of disgust (*faillit le dégoûter* [*I* 139]), Sand highlights how deep-seated such expectations are. Sexual desire is not natural when gender violations can frustrate it or transform so easily desire into disgust.

The vantage point of utopia enables Sand to envision how self-interest fuels a system of misogyny. Her first husband only cares how Indiana makes him look to others. When Indiana refuses to go out and socialise, Delmare bristles and asks her, 'do you want others to think I keep you under lock and key?' (*I* 95). God forbid society sees patriarchy for what it is; the illusion of genteel protection must buffer his social honour. Although Raymon deludes himself into thinking he is beyond self-interest, Sand wryly comments, 'what man is so ungrateful to Providence as to reproach it with the misfortunes of others, if it has had only smiles and benefits for him?' (*I* 85). Although some claim that self-interest is good for society as a whole, Sand argues that it encourages selfishness because it relies on the prolonging of one's own pleasure at woman's total expense. In her letter to Raymon from Bourbon Island announcing that she has absolved and forgiven him, Indiana confesses that she initially thought Raymon was the worst kind of man: an egoist (*I* 188). Her instincts turn out to be correct. By connecting egoism to self-interest, Sand refutes the idea that if everyone pursues self-interest, society, as a whole, benefits. Sand also shows how marriage destroys the will for both men and women. Ralph is forced to marry his sister-in-law after his own brother's death, and Delmare is fittingly described as the man Indiana 'had been married to' as if she were a passive object (*I* 255). Sand shows how gender formation is synonymous with the formation of society itself. Raised by a violent father and a violent planter, Indiana marries Delmare. Sand comments, 'in marrying Delmare she had only changed masters' (*I* 51). At this rate, transgression will never scale up to break the rules of heteronormativity. Schor recognises the degree to which in Sand 'the opposition between idealism and realism in sexuality is the difference between altruistic and egoistic love'.[33] If we press this core insight, we recognise that until gender allows both men and women selves that can have ideals while living in reality so that they can strive for better, there can be no genuine intimacy. At the time of the novel, women bore the brunt of moral ideals too often reduced to either monogamy or chastity, placing them in an impossible bind.

Sand enumerates other reasons why transgression has limited effects. Though moral theorists place great hope upon reflection, she is more sceptical. For one thing, she recognises that 'vice does not see itself in its own ugliness, for it would frighten itself, and Shakespeare's Iago' (*I* 225). If vice cannot recognise itself, then reflection cannot even gain a foothold. Sand further argues that 'nothing confirms us in selfishness as much as reflection' (*I* 201). Far from an unambiguous cure, Sand paints reflection as the potential poison. As if these were not obstacles enough, a further challenge is that human beings have a tremendous capacity to massage our consciences (*I* 225). Sand argues,

> man rarely tramples his conscience underfoot in cold blood. He turns it over, squeezes it, pulls it this way and that, distorts it, and when he has perverted it, enfeebled it, and worn it out, he carries it about with him as an indulgent and easy-going guardian. (*I* 225)

The good news is that we do not simply cast aside our consciences. The bad news is that we all have our inner Iagos and excel at making them indulge us. These warnings return us to Sand's distinction between a thinking and unthinking transgression, and the reminder that reflection itself has blinders prompts consideration of how to get around these problems. Sand's combination of realism with idealism thus recognises that reflection cannot be a blanket solution and that any meaningful solution must grapple with reflection's affective residue: the cannibalism at the centre of the current political economy. For this reason, Sand's utopias are fundamentally unsatisfying; they flicker between real and ideal, and they create as many problems as they solve. Only when transgression is not a *fait accompli* can rule-breaking be evaluated for what it achieves. And only with careful evaluation can one consider the degree to which transgression actually challenges fundamental societal principles. Paradoxically through utopia, Sand is more thoughtful about transgression than she has been given credit for.

Notes

1. Sand's pseudonym continues to reinforce her transgressiveness. Sand was born Amantine-Aurore-Lucile Dupin on 1 July 1804. Sand's dropping of the final 's' in the French Georges 'signals a difference from the masculine as the same time as a rejection of the feminine'. Naomi Schor, 'Reading Double: Sand's Difference', in *The Poetics of Gender*, ed. Nancy K. Miller (New York: Columbia University Press, 1986), 249. For formatting help, I thank Janelle Grue. For their astute suggestions, I thank David Sigler and Kathryn Ready.
2. Naomi Schor, 'Introduction to *Indiana*', in *Indiana*, ed. Sylvia Raphael (Oxford: Oxford University Press, 2008), xiv.
3. Philosopher Mehdi Belhaj Kacem argues that the whole of anthropological experience today functions under the sign of transgression in part because nineteenth-century artists made transgressors into heroes. 'It is because the human animal is that which transcends the given by science that the appropriation of the laws of nature has an essentially transgressive structure' (183). He continues, 'the sexual life of the human animal is essentially a transgression of the Law of Nature' (183). My concern is that the totalising power of transgression undermines its power: as it explains everything, it explains nothing. In this view, Sand pits transgression against utopia so that we confront its limits. Retrospectively, we can recognise transgression as an earlier form of virtue signaling. Mehdi Belhaj Kacem, *Transgression and the Inexistent*, translated by Burcu Yalim (London: Bloomsbury, 2014).
4. All English references to *Indiana* are from the Oxford World Classics edition: George Sand, *Indiana*, translated by Sylvia Raphael (Oxford: Oxford University Press, 2008). Passages quoted in the original French come from Éditions de St Clair: George Sand, *Indiana* (Paris: Éditions de Saint Clair, 1969). Further citations to the English text will be given parenthetically, with *I*; citations to the French edition will be included in the same parenthetical citation as needed, as denoted after a slash (/).
5. For a study linking transgression with utopia, see Lucy Sargisson, *Utopian Bodies and the Politics of Transgression* (London: Taylor & Francis, 2000). Sargisson argues that utopia is too narrowly construed as a perfect 'blueprint of an ideal polity' (2). Her sense that utopias are transgressive in that they 'privilege social change in process' (11) and encourage 'paradigm shifts in consciousness' (13) is helpful. She also notes how the conventional use of the perspective of the visitor within utopias enables the expression of 'estranged perspectives' (8, 12). However, by linking transgression with

'internal subversive thinking' (2), she overestimates what transgression accomplishes. In keeping with much celebratory work on transgression, she mistakes the showing of porosity of borders as revolution accomplished: the 'stepping over of boundaries ... renders them meaningless' (10).

6. Leslie Rabine argues that Indiana only appears transgressive: 'the novel's rhetoric of rebellion conceals but is an integral part of a novelistic structure which encourages conformity to the feminine stereotypes then in force' (2). For all her horse riding, she is reduced to silence at the novel's end. Rabine emphasises that Indiana is only ever seen through male desire. Sandy Petrey submits that gender in *Indiana* has been eroticised, not sex, thereby enacting ideology. What turns Raymon on is not female anatomy, but rather female clothing (138–9). Sandy Petrey, 'George and Georgina Sand: Realist Gender in *Indiana*', in *Textuality and Sexuality: Reading Theories and Practices*, ed. Judith Still and Michael Worton (Manchester: Manchester University Press, 1993), 133–47. Leslie Rabine, 'George Sand and the Myth of Femininity', in *Women and Literature* 4, no. 2 (Fall 1976), 1–17.
7. Schor, 'Reading Double', 252.
8. George Sand, *Story of My Life: The Autobiography of George Sand*, ed. Thelma Jurgrau (Albany: SUNY Press, 1991), 72.
9. Joyal notes that Sand thought of marriage as a prison but nonetheless portrays Laure de Nangy, who has a marriage of convenience with Raymon, unflatteringly (135). Women in Sand who escape the oppressive force of marriage cannot seem sympathetic (136), and thus what have they actually escaped? Renée Joyal, 'Un feminisme particulier', in *George Sand toujours présente* (Montréal: Presses de l'Université du Québec), 131–51.
10. Sand makes clear that neither Delmare nor Raymon are immune to utopias, and she refers to their particular idealisations as 'sentimental stupidities'. Sand, *Indiana*, 119.
11. José Esteban Muñoz, *Cruising Utopia: The Then and There of Queer Futurity* (New York: New York University Press, 2009), 6–9.
12. Naomi Schor, *George Sand and Idealism* (New York: Columbia University Press, 1993), 91.
13. Kwame Appiah, *As If: Idealization and Ideals* (Cambridge, MA: Harvard University Press, 2017), 16.
14. Schor, 'Introduction', xv.
15. Harlan recounts how Aurore's own marriage was under the dotal system whereby she retained her property but relinquished all income from it during the marriage. Sand writes that she urged her future husband, Casimir, to 'resist with all his might this conservative property measure which almost always results in the sacrifice of an individual's peace of mind to the tyrannical immobility of real estate' (104). Elizabeth Harlan, *George Sand* (New Haven: Yale University Press, 2004).
16. Schor, *Idealism*, 106.
17. James Vest argues that the romance tradition helps explain Sand's strange ending, allowing some relief from social pressures. In his view, Ralph and Indiana are 'transfigured' in having become 'socially acceptable' (38). Ralph claims to 'pity this society which despises me' (Sand, *Indiana*, 271). Vest turns to romance to make coherent the novel, but Sand's romance is

considerably more ironic than he acknowledges. James Vest, 'Dreams and the Romance Tradition in George Sand's *Indiana*', in *French Forum* 3, no. 1 (January 1978), 35–47.
18. For a powerful reading of Sand's strategy of doubling, see Naomi Schor's 'Reading Double'. For Schor in this text, doubling takes on the need to establish difference within sameness (258).
19. Schor, *Idealism*, 106.
20. Schor reads this doubleness as the difficulty of negotiating the imaginary and the symbolic, the personal and the political. Schor, *Idealism*, 106.
21. Schor questions the faith in the ability of 'sordid details of reality' to counteract the 'ideological pollution' of the abstract. Schor, *Idealism*, 110.
22. I refer here to the late Lauren Berlant's especially canny term, which refers to how the very things we think will help us flourish can often prevent that very flourishing. See Berlant, *Cruel Optimism* (Durham, NC: Duke University Press, 2011).
23. See Daston on norms and normativity: Lorraine Daston, *Against Nature* (Cambridge, MA: MIT Press, 2019). Daston argues that the drive to ground claims in nature reveals a desire for order, but the difference in the kinds of order nature offers necessarily frustrates the use of examples of nature to authorise versions of order. On political ideals and idealism, see Appiah, *As If*, chapter 4.
24. Schor argues that in her later novels, Sand tries to preserve marriage from systematic critique because she thought it was one of the few ways in which the gulf between rich and poor could be ameliorated. Schor, *Idealism*, 89.
25. Schor argues that Indiana's chastity represents to Sand 'the most significant form of resistance to the implacable determinations of the marriage plot'. Schor, *Idealism*, 88. I think this overestimates chastity as transgression.
26. Harlan, *George Sand*, 104.
27. George Sand, *Indiana*, ed. Eric Bordas (Paris: Editions Gallimard, 2004), 78.
28. William Shakespeare, *The Tragedy of Hamlet, Prince of Denmark* 3.2.105. *The Norton Shakespeare: Based on the Oxford Edition*, ed. Stephen Greenblatt et al. (New York: Norton, 1997).
29. Schor submits that Creole in French has a double meaning: '(1) of mixed or black race (multiracial); (2) a white person born in the colonies (monoracial)' (Schor, 'Introduction', xvii).
30. Muñoz, *Cruising Utopia*, 93.
31. Although Rabine argues that white purity is maintained by Noun's racial and class identity along with her sexual transgression, Indiana herself is ambiguously racialised. Rabine, 'Myth of Femininity', 13–14.
32. On how French physiology shapes norms simultaneously as an average and an ideal, see Ian Hacking, *The Taming of Chance* (Cambridge: Cambridge University Press, 1990), 168.
33. Schor, *Idealism*, 98.

Chapter 10

Emily Brontë's Shelleyan Poetics of Sexual Ambivalence

Amanda Blake Davis

In scrutinising Emily Brontë's 'defiant post-Romantic individualism', Michael O'Neill identifies a persisting attraction to 'strategies of ambiguity, ambivalence, redefinition' as key to her poetic identity.[1] Brontë's lyrical power draws upon these three strategies, allowing her to stave off the strictures of certainty in favour of amorphous modes of self-expression. Brontë redefines the traditionally masculine Romantic lyric through her uses of ambiguity and ambivalence, owing in no small part to the formative influence of Percy Bysshe Shelley, a Romantic whose poetry is hallmarked by ambivalence.[2] This chapter draws together two extant but unconnected crucial elements of Emily Brontë's poetry, sexual ambivalence and the influence of Percy Shelley, to foreground Brontë's identity as a Romantic poet writing beyond the gender binary. Emily Brontë's strategies of ambivalence and ambiguity eschew the boundaries of a strictly masculine or feminine self-identity, transgressing the binaries of sex and gender through lyric poetry.

While shaping her sister's posthumous reputation as a poet, Charlotte Brontë foregrounds her sister's individuality and gendered difference as central to Emily's authorial identity. For Charlotte, Emily's poems are 'not common effusions, nor at all like the poetry women generally write'.[3] Charlotte's emphasis upon Emily's resistance to gender norms distinguishes the latter from her sisters, despite their collective sharing of what John Hewish describes as 'curious asexual pen-names'.[4] However, the Brontë sisters' pen-names, 'Ellis Bell', 'Currer Bell' and 'Acton Bell', are sexually ambiguous rather than asexual. Instead of adopting conspicuously masculine monikers, the ambiguity of the sisters' pen-names allows them to subtly evade the divisiveness of the male/female binary. Contrary to Anne K. Mellor's assertion that Emily 'Brontë's works conform to a specifically masculine Romanticism', which she had 'absorbed from her enthusiastic reading of Percy Shelley',[5] the sexual ambiguity and ambivalence in Brontë's poetry can be differently understood within the context of Romantic perversion explored by Richard C. Sha, where literary depictions of transgressive sexuality become loci of liberation, and where Romantic sexual difference 'resists the neat binary opposition between male and female'.[6] Rather than 'conform[ing] to a specifically masculine', or feminine, Romanticism, Brontë forges a resistance to binary expressions of gender and sexuality, sharing Shelley's affinity for non-binary pronouns and gender-fluid characters. Critical studies of gender and sexuality in Brontë's writings gravitate towards the binary of male and female and heterosexual or homosexual desire, excepting Angela Leighton's profitable reading of Brontë's poetry beyond the male/ female and heterosexual/homosexual binaries.[7] This chapter explores Brontë's lyrical expressions of selfhood and sexuality that transgress and transcend the male/female binary with attention to two poems of crucial importance to Brontë: Shelley's *Epipsychidion* (1821) and the 'Ode to the West Wind' (1820).

Shelley's subversion of heteronormative desire and identity in *Epipsychidion* and the 'Ode to the West Wind' point up their fundamental importance to Brontë. Her lyrical expressions of selfhood and sexuality transcend the male/female binary and mark her as a distinctively Romantic poet whose lyrics aspire beyond a recognisably masculine or feminine mode. Brontë's poetic identity is empowered by sexual ambivalence. *Epipsychidion* is 'clearly a poem of importance for Brontë', Michael O'Neill affirms.[8] Edward Chitham agrees: 'It is clear that Emily had read it and was very strongly attracted to it'.[9] However, critical studies of *Epipsychidion*'s influence on Brontë gravitate around *Wuthering Heights* (1847). Patsy Stoneman claims that the novel is 'Emily Brontë's experiment in reversing the genders of Shelley's free love' in *Epipsychidion*; John Hewish views that, in *Wuthering Heights*, 'Emily Brontë's hypothesis may be of the same order as that of *Epipsychidion*'; and Camille Paglia asserts that '*Wuthering Heights* is *Epipsychidion* with nature written in'.[10] The influence of *Epipsychidion* upon *Wuthering Heights* is undeniable. Both share the formal pattern of a nested tale communicated to the reader by an intermediary figure who gives voice to the dead; unconsummated love; a tangled web of romantic relationships; and sexual transgressions. Shelley's poem complicates past and future, lyrical speaker and subject, binary demarcations of gender and divisions of literary form through its combination of poetry and prose. Like *Epipsychidion*, *Wuthering Heights* enfolds a narrative of the dead within the living present, being a 'Romantic prose-poem' composed by 'a woman who pressed at the limits of gender'.[11] But the influence of *Epipsychidion* extends well beyond Brontë's 'great, mad poem in prose',[12] drawing in particular upon Shelley's poetics of sexual ambivalence.

In *Epipsychidion*, the poem's 'Emily', a textual figuration of its dedicatee, Teresa Emilia Viviani, is doubly imprisoned within the spatial construct of a convent and the temporal construct of heteronormative marriage:

> Poor captive bird! who, from thy narrow cage,
> Pourest such music, that it might assuage,
> The rugged hearts of those who prisoned thee,
> Were they not deaf to all sweet melody.[13]

Deprived of her own agency, Emily is initially represented as a feminine object in terms familiar from a longstanding tradition of male-authored lyric poetry. She appears traditionally feminised as passive, weak and subject to masculine will and desire. But the fourth stanza of the poem disrupts its courtly artifice by declaring Emily

> Seraph of Heaven! too gentle to be human,
> Veiling beneath that radiant form of Woman[.][14]

A series of metaphorical shifts transport Emily from 'Woman' to a veiled form that transcends the heteronormative binary. Heteronormativity is a construct that confines women through the spatial and temporal institutions of marriage, childbirth and death, a figurative prison that is as oppressive as the convent walls that surround the real Teresa Emilia Viviani. Anticipating Jack Halberstam's definitions of 'queer time' and 'queer space' as temporal and spatial occurrences that develop 'at least in part, in opposition to the institutions of family, heterosexuality, and reproduction',[15] Shelley creates a queer time and space in poetry where heteronormative conventions no longer bind Emily.

Shelley's description of Emily as 'Seraph of Heaven' recalls John Milton's angels who 'Can either sex assume, or both', fluidly shifting between and beyond the gender binary.[16] Through thirteen lines of metaphorical transference, Emily shifts away from the designation of 'Woman' and towards intermediate states:

> Thou Moon beyond the clouds! Thou living Form
> Among the Dead! Thou Star above the Storm![17]

The moon, androgynous in Shelley's translation of Plato's *Symposium* as *The Banquet*,[18] is distinguished by its mutability, and in becoming a 'living Form / Among the Dead', Emily embodies Halberstam's 'queer time', refusing the binaries of life and death, male and female. Shelley 'turned to sexuality as a site for thinking about liberation', Sha writes, noting that in the Romantic period, 'biological sex was more elastic and thus could become a ground for liberation'.[19] Emily's sexually ambiguous identity in *Epipsychidion* promotes 'sexuality as a site for thinking about liberation', and, responsive to *Epipsychidion*, Brontë carries Shelley's thoughts across into her own poems of liberation, struggle and identity.

Epipsychidion's elimination of the gender binary is one facet of the poem's ambiguity. The anonymous Author of the Advertisement foregrounds the poem as a posthumous fragment, thereby acknowledging its unrealised future state. In its fragmentary form, and its blending of poetry and prose forms alongside demarcations of gender, *Epipsychidion* embodies Shelley's early meditation upon gendered difference. In a letter of 1812, Shelley writes to Elizabeth Hitchener:

> I understand you, when you say we are free. Liberty is the very soul of friendship, and from the very soul of Liberty art thou my friend – aye, & such a sense as this can never fade. 'Earthly those passions of the Earth which perish where they had their birth, but Love is indestructible' – I almost wish that Southey had not made the glendoveer a male – these detestable distinctions will surely be abolished in a future state of being.[20]

Shelley's Emily approaches this 'future state of being' and its erasure of the 'detestable distinctions' of male and female with degrees of ambiguity in the published poem. However, Shelley is far more explicit in fragments associated with *Epipsychidion*. For example, in the single-volume edition of the *Poetical Works of Percy Bysshe Shelley* owned by the Brontës,[21] Mary Shelley includes the following fragmentary passage:

> Here, my dear friend, is a new book for you;
> I have already dedicated two
> To other friends, one female and one male,
> What you are, is a thing that I must veil.[22]

This fragment's implication of gender identity beyond the male/female binary is expanded upon in later editions, where the passage is extended into 'Fragments connected with *Epipsychidion*'. Therein, the subject's sexual ambiguity is considered further:

> And as to friend or mistress, 'tis a form;
> Perhaps I wish you were one. Some declare
> You a familiar spirit, as you are;
> Others with a more inhuman
> Hint that, though not my wife, you are a woman;
> ...
> And others swear you're a Hermaphrodite;
> Like that sweet marble monster of both sexes,
> Which looks so sweet and gentle that it vexes
> The very soul that the soul is gone
> Which lifted from her limbs the veil of stone.[23]

Brontë's poetry of sexual ambivalence draws upon Shelley's liminal states between male and female and between life and death as they are explicated in these fragments and within the published poem. Shelley's lyrical address to the sexually ambiguous Emily opens a space of potentiality beyond the boundaries of male and female, rejecting heteronormativity and its temporal patterning of birth, marriage, childrearing and death. In Algernon Charles Swinburne's ekphrastic poem *Hermaphroditus* (1866), Natalie Prizel identifies 'an intersex aesthetic' where 'transgenre mediation[s]' promote intersex identities, and this identification can be usefully transported into the transgressions of sex, time and space that permeate Brontë's poetry. Like Swinburne, Brontë finds an influential source of intersex identity in *Epipsychidion* and its associated fragments.[24] A potential inspiration for Shelley's intersex figuration of Emily is his viewing of the sculpted, sleeping form of the Borghese Hermaphrodite in Rome,[25] a clear influence upon Swinburne's *Hermaphroditus*, and one that more subtly informs Brontë's sexually transgressive lyricism. The 'intersex aesthetic' of *ekphrasis* that enlivens *Epipsychidion* and its connected fragments carries across into Brontë's own artistry, where her identity as a poet is veiled and unveiled in her ambiguously gendered transformations between Ellis Bell and Emily Brontë. Charlotte Brontë's posthumous shaping of Emily's poetic identity is infused with Shelleyan allusion. In likening *Wuthering Heights* to a sculpted 'crag' amidst the moorland in her 'Editor's Preface' to *Wuthering Heights*, Charlotte invokes Shelley's 'Ozymandias', as Amber K. Regis has perceptively noted.[26] Charlotte writes: 'With time and labour, the crag took human shape: and there it stands colossal, dark, and frowning, half statue, half rock in the former sense' recalling the 'Half-sunk' and 'shattered visage' of Shelley's colossal wreck, interposing its 'frown / And wrinkled lip' upon the Heathcliff-like shape described by Charlotte.[27] But the ekphrastic figure of Emily's labour is also described as a sexually ambiguous sculpture, being at once masculine: 'terrible and goblin-like', but also 'almost beautiful', and femininely clothed in 'blooming bells and balmy fragrance'.[28] In intermingling the masculine and the feminine and the monstrous and the beautiful in this sculpted shape, Charlotte incorporates Shelley's hermaphroditical form – 'the sweet marble monster of both sexes' – into Emily's poetic identity emphasising his importance to Emily as a poet of sexual ambiguity.

Tatsuo Tokoo has revealed that lines 1 to 96 of the 'Fragments connected with *Epipsychidion*' in actuality predate the poem's composition and instead assigns them to the autumn or winter of 1819 alongside Shelley's fair copy of the 'Ode to the West Wind' and Act 4 of *Prometheus Unbound* (1820).[29] The sexually ambiguous addressee of Shelley's 'Fragments connected with *Epipsychidion*' is conceived in near contemporaneity to the composition of the 'Ode to the West Wind'. Both poems' connected formations of queer times and spaces are taken up and propelled forward by Brontë; as Eve Kosofsky Sedgwick writes, 'Queer is a continuing moment, movement, motive', 'recurrent, eddying, *troublant*'.[30] Brontë's Romantic lyrics propel the queer futurity of Shelley's 'West Wind' forward with impassioned momentum. A stream of sexual ambivalence flows from the 'Ode to the West Wind' to *Epipsychidion* by way of these fragments, where Brontë's amorphous gendering of the wind in her poetry reveals a deeper connection between these formative works: Shelley's *Epipsychidion*, its connected fragments, and the 'Ode to the West Wind'.

In the 'Ode to the West Wind', Shelley 'feminises the gentle west wind of spring (Zephyrus), the bringer of clear skies, traditionally personified as a young man',[31] recalling the ode's origin as a powerful female voice: Shelley's proto-feminist hero, Cythna. Cythna's speech in Canto 9 of *Laon and Cythna; or, the Revolution of the Golden City* (1817), later *The Revolt of Islam* (1818), is 'the long first draft of the *Ode to the West Wind*', Stuart Curran notes.[32] Therein, 'the winds of Autumn fade' and 'Spring comes', ushering forth 'The future, a broad sunrise; thus arrayed'.[33] The 'Ode to the West Wind' carries forth Cythna's prophesied future by intimating a 'future state' beyond the male/female binary. Shelley subverts the traditionally active and passive sexual positions of male and female in the fourth sonnet of the *terza rima* sequence by erotically imaging himself as 'A wave to pant beneath thy power, and share / The impulse of thy strength'.[34] Shelley's ode mingles male and female binary positions in ecstatic lyricism until these 'detestable distinctions' are undone through an erotic union. The speaker's self-association with a wave resembles the masculine 'blue Mediterranean' of the third sonnet,[35] but any certainties of sex give way to fluidity in the masculine speaker's traditionally feminine position, panting beneath the feminised Zephyrus's sexualised 'power'. The ode's sexual 'perversion', to employ Sha's use of the term, becomes more prominent still as the speaker yearns to share in Zephyrus's 'strength' by becoming 'as in my boyhood':[36] a reversal of male puberty into a fluid, feminised state.[37]

Inhaling the oracular breath of Shelley's ode, Brontë versifies sexual ambivalence in pursuit of a freer 'future state of being' unlimited by divisions between male and female. Shelley's penultimate cry to

>Be thou, Spirit fierce,
>My spirit! Be thou me, impetuous one![38]

is interwoven into Catherine's intimations of an intersubjective existence within Heathcliff: 'Nelly, I am Heathcliff – he's always, always in my mind – not as a pleasure, any more than I am always a pleasure to myself – but, as my own being.'[39] Brontë's poetic prose gusts forth through the use of repeated dashes that visually connect Heathcliff to Catherine, infusing the lyrical power of Shelley's ode with the poet's address to Emily in *Epipsychidion*:

> How beyond refuge I am thine. Ah me!
> I am not thine: I am a part of *thee*.[40]

More than a soul, the Romantic-period usage of 'spirit' 'obliquely refers to the animal spirits, the agents of nervous action', Sha writes, where 'eighteenth-century physicians increasingly understood sex and its relation to the nerves and the nervous system', making it 'impossible to conceive of sex as being exhausted by anatomy, because sexuality now encompassed the entire essentially nervous body'.[41] Sharing in the sexual fluidity of Shelley's ode as much as *Epipsychidion* and its connected fragments, Brontë imagines in poetic prose the shared states of being that are possible beyond the male/female binary. Through imaginative identification with and artistic allusion to Shelley, Brontë forms a distinctly Romantic poetic identity that nostalgically draws upon the sexual ambiguity of the Romantic period as a locus of liberation, in stark contrast with the increasingly divided gendered spheres of Victorian Britain.

Brontë's responsiveness to the sexual ambivalence of Shelley's feminine Zephyrus extends beyond her poetry and prose into the visual arts. In a watercolour painting known as *The North Wind* (1842), Brontë enacts a reversal of ekphrasis from the literary to the visual arts, following James Heffernan's definition of ekphrasis as '"the verbal representation of visual representation"'.[42] The verbal is given new life through a transformation into the visual by way of Brontë's watercolour: a 'copy', Christine Alexander and Margaret Smith note, of 'William Finden's engraving of Westall's *Ianthe*' (1839) that 'appeared in numerous editions of Byron published by John Murray'.[43] 'Finden's engraving of the painting by Westall of Lady Charlotte Harley' is of 'the "Ianthe" to whom Byron dedicated the opening Canto of *Childe Harold* in 1813', Winifred Gérin writes.[44] However, a reader of Shelley as keen as Brontë would have also been reminded of the Ianthe of Shelley's *Queen Mab* (1813) in viewing this engraving. Affirming *Queen Mab*'s influence on Brontë, Edward Chitham pursues the painting's Shelleyan connection further by 'wonder[ing] whether originally it [*The North Wind*] was "The West Wind", as the wind occurs in Shelley's "Ode to the West Wind"'.[45] But Brontë transforms and redefines rather than imitates, ambiguously renaming *Ianthe* as *The North Wind* and carrying across Shelley's feminised Zephyrus of the 'Ode to the West Wind' from the literary to the visual. Christine Alexander and Jane Sellars observe that Brontë's 'portrait of the young woman fleeing has a more mature, challenging expression compared to the wide-eyed innocence of Westall's original'.⁴⁶ Brontë's rendition of *Ianthe* is not simply more mature than the child of Finden's engraving; it is transformed into an androgynous figure whose sexual ambivalence is heightened by Brontë's retitling of her portrait as *The North Wind*. The North Wind, Boreas, is like its Classical counterpart, Zephyrus, the West Wind, traditionally personified as male.⁴⁷ Brontë's renaming of her painting's feminine figure as *The North Wind* points up her recognition of Shelley's own ambivalent gendering of Zephyrus in his 'West Wind' and emphasises the engagement of her art with the sexually ambiguous in both text and image.

The many editions of Byron containing Finden's engraving include, Edward Chitham notes, 'Moore's *Life of Byron*, published in 1833', where Brontë would have encountered details of Shelley's death along with 'Finden's engraving of his portrait "from an original in the possession of Mrs. Shelley"': the portrait of Shelley painted by Amelia Curran in 1819.⁴⁸ Strikingly, the strong nose, determined gaze, flushed cheek and dark hair of Brontë's watercolour visually echo Curran's portrait of Shelley, transforming *The North Wind* into a sexually ambiguous, androgynous figure. *The North Wind*, much more than an imitation or copy of Finden's engraving, demonstrates Brontë's proclivity for redefinition and Romantic self-identity, carrying across her poetic skill into the visual arts. Spanning the visual and the literary, Brontë's artistry draws out the sexual ambivalence of Shelley's poetry, foregrounding Romantic sexual fluidity as a locus of liberatory potential. Visually echoing Shelley's 'Ode to the West Wind', Brontë's painting reveals her awareness of how gender, form and identity are amorphised in Shelley's ode.

In 'The Night-Wind' (1846), a lyric frequently associated with *The North Wind*, the eroticised wind, despite its seemingly masculine sexual advances upon the speaker, is markedly ungendered, being referred to with Shelley's neuter pronoun of choice of 'it':⁴⁹

> The soft wind waved my hair
> …
> I needed not its breathing
> …
> Its kiss grew warmer still – ('The Night-Wind', 6; 9; 26)⁵⁰

For Margaret Homans, the 'night-wind' is a masculine seducer of the feminine speaker; however, Angela Leighton pointedly notes that

Figure 10.1. 'The North Wind', Emily Brontë, Watercolour, 1842, once in possession of the Heger family; present location unknown. Reproduced as a frontispiece to *Brontë Society Transactions* 11 (1949). Reproduced in this volume by courtesy of the Brontë Society.

Figure 10.2. 'Percy Bysshe Shelley', Amelia Curran, Oil on canvas, 1819, © National Portrait Gallery, London.

'Emily's wind is neutral'.[51] By incorporating Shelley's neuter pronoun, 'it', Brontë creates a space wherein the lyric is unbound from its traditional male and female positions of speaker and subject. In 'The Night-Wind', Brontë's sexually charged poetry refuses to conform to masculine or feminine pronouns, eliminating the bounds of binary gender. By adapting Shelley's hallmark ambivalence, Brontë's poetic power rises to the fore in her ability to shape lyric selves that shift and slip between recognisably male and female identities. In 'The Night-Wind' and its evocation of *The North Wind*, the poet's artistry is sensually erotic, where both lyricist and apostrophised addressee refuse singularly masculine or feminine expressions of sexual desire. The light of the androgynous moon mingles masculine penetration with feminine receptivity, where it

> shone through
> Our open parlour window
> And rosetrees wet with dew ('The Night-Wind', 3–4)

The consensual eroticism of 'The Night-Wind' contrasts with the violent penetration enacted by the markedly masculine sun of 'Stars':

> Blood-red, he rose, and, arrow-straight,
> His fierce beams struck my brow ('Stars', 21–2)

The sun, approximated to the masculine in Shelley's translation of Plato's *Symposium*, is 'the source of all tyrannies' in Shelley's poetry.[52] For Brontë, too, the sun often seems a harbinger of masculine oppression. The sun is distinguished from the stars and speaker of the poem through the use of gendered and ungendered pronouns, where the solar body's masculine designation of 'he' contrasts with the ambiguously ungendered speaker and stars and their amorous union that 'proved us one' (16):

> All through the night, your glorious eyes
>   Were gazing down in mine
> ...
> I was at peace, and drank your beams
>   As if they were life to me:
> And revelled in my changeful dreams ('Stars', 5–6; 9–11)

Brontë draws upon Shelley's ambiguous, eroticised intermingling in *Epipsychidion*, wherein the Moon is described as a 'Queen', but is notably ungendered by the neuter pronoun 'its'. In a dream sequence that is adapted within 'Stars', Shelley's feminine Other

> sate beside me, with her downward face
> Illumining my slumbers, like the Moon
> ...
> I stood, and felt the dawn of my long night
> Was penetrating me with living light:
> I knew it was the Vision veiled from me
> So many years – that it was Emily.[53]

Shelley's Emily is a feminine figure who 'penetrat[es]' the poem's male speaker 'with living light', complicating and combining binary sexuality. In 'Stars', Brontë moves beyond Shelley's hermaphroditical Emily by making both her poem's speaker and subject sexually ambiguous.

Determined to locate a 'heterosexual romance' in 'Stars' (1846), Margaret Homans is troubled by Brontë's sexual ambiguity in this poem, where 'The difficulty with assimilating the night and stars to other masculine figures ... is that nowhere is it indicated that they are masculine'. 'Addressing the stars', Homans continues, 'the speaker has no recourse to a pronoun, and those attributes of the stars that might indicate gender are feminine and maternal as often as they are masculine'.[54] But it is Brontë's rebellion against conformity that empowers her poetry, where her lyrics create queer spaces of liberation unbound by temporal, spatial and binary constraints. 'Queer subcultures produce alternative temporalities by allowing their participants to believe that their futures can be imagined according to logics that lie outside of those paradigmatic markers of life experience', Halberstam writes.[55] *Epipsychidion* similarly rejects the trajectory of heteronormative 'life experience', espousing polyamory alongside non-binary expressions of identity and desire. Shelley's repeated apostrophe to the poem's Emily is internalised by Brontë and is recast through the queer eroticism and non-binary identities of her distinctively Romantic lyrics and the prose-poetry of *Wuthering Heights*.

In another 1846 poem beginning 'Loud without the wind was roaring', Brontë invokes Shelley amidst 'the slopes where the north-wind is raving' (33), extending her watercolour painting's visual mingling of Shelley into verse. Brontë mixes the autumnal leaves of Shelley's 'Ode to the West Wind' with the springtime song of his 'To a Skylark', where a tune is heard 'Through the waned Autumnal sky' (2):

> 'It was spring, for the skylark was singing'.
> Those words they awakened a spell –
> They unlocked a deep fountain whose springing
> Nor Absence nor Distance can quell.
>
> In the gloom of a cloudy November
> They uttered the music of May –
> They kindled the perishing ember
> Into fervour that could not decay ('Loud without the wind was roaring', 11–18)

Shelley's influence appears in these lines within Brontë's use of inverted commas, which, although not quoting directly from Shelley's 'To a Skylark', establishes a presence that is at once implied and recreated through her own poetic voice. Brontë continues to invoke Shelley's skylark, conjuring an autumnal landscape

> Where the lark – the wild skylark was filling
> Every breast with delight like its own. ('Loud without the wind was roaring', 49–50)

In echoing the 'shrill delight' of Shelley's ethereal bird,[56] Brontë invokes Shelley as an inspiring Other. In the 'Ode to the West Wind', Shelley's 'incantation of this verse' is summoned by Brontë as the words that 'awakened a spell'. Brontë blends Shelley's 'Skylark' with his West Wind and her own *North Wind*, pairing the Zephyrus of May with the Boreas of November and forging a combined poetic power. Shelley's 'dead thoughts', 'Ashes and sparks, my words among mankind!' are given new, eternal life in the 'perishing ember' of Brontë's lyrical utterance 'that could not decay'.[57]

Wild winds blow through Brontë's verse,[58] where Shelley's ashes and sparks are rekindled through Brontë's distinctively Romantic mode of lyrical address. *Epipsychidion*, the 'Ode to the West Wind' and the fragments that bridge these two influential works are connected by their coupled uses of apostrophe and ambiguity, strategies adopted and deployed by Brontë with renewed power. When used in a sexually ambivalent way, apostrophe disrupts heteronormative, binary patterns of identity and time in Shelley's and Brontë's lyrics. Apostrophe enables a temporal disturbance, similar to Halberstam's concept of queer time. In its movement from 'linear time' to 'discursive time', Jonathan Culler writes, 'The temporal movement from A to B, restructured by apostrophe, becomes a reversible alternation between A' and B': a play of presence and absence governed not by time but by poetic ingenuity or power'.[59] Apostrophe and queer time function in tandem in Brontë's poetry, forging a range of lyrical identities that transgress the male/female binary and a distinctly masculine or feminine Romanticism.

In 'Song', Brontë allusively addresses Shelley's 'West Wind' while upsetting the boundaries of life and death. An ambiguously ungendered speaker meditates upon their 'lady's' moorland grave and ensures her existence in 'future years' through the perpetually revitalised poetic utterance assured by the blowing of a Shelleyan 'west-wind':

> Blow, west-wind, by the lonely mound,
>   And murmur, summer-streams –
> There is no need of other sound
>   To soothe my lady's dreams. ('Song', 25–8)

Brontë's sexual ambivalence accompanies a bright uncertainty that denies death's finitude, where the rhyming of 'mound' with 'sound' raises the dead from their graves through the promise of poetic incantation. Shelley's 'ashes and sparks' are reignited by Brontë in 'A Day Dream (On a sunny brae, alone I lay)' (1846), where self and Other are blended in ecstatic poetic union:

> We thought, 'When winter comes again,
>   Where will these bright things be? ('A Day Dream', 25–6)

Brontë conjures an imaginative affinity with Shelley in these lines by using the plural pronoun 'we', and allusion to his ode's final, questioning line: 'If Winter comes, can Spring be far behind?'.[60] The power of Brontë's artistry arises from her indomitable individuality. In the closing lines of 'A Day Dream', Shelley's influence shifts from allusion to inspired re-creation, where Brontë breathes new life into Shelley's 'Ashes and sparks, my words among mankind':[61]

> Methought, the very breath I breathed
>   Was full of sparks divine ('A Day Dream', 45–6)

Brontë's textual and visual engagements with Shelley reveal neither conformity to a specifically masculine or feminine Romanticism nor a strictly heterosexual or homosexual identity. Instead, Brontë gleans from Shelley's poetry of sexual ambivalence a recognition of the Romantic lyric as a site of liberation and ambiguity. Ultimately, Brontë redefines herself as a Romantic poet through her distinctively and sexually ambiguous lyrical self-expression, shaping in verse the liberated, non-binary 'future state' imagined by Shelley.

Notes

1. Michael O'Neill, 'What Thou Art: Emily Brontë's Visionary Religion', *Brontë Studies* 37, no. 4 (2012): 366.
2. Madeleine Callaghan identifies 'ambivalence, rather than confusion' as 'the hallmark of Shelley's art'. 'Shelley and the Ambivalence of Idealism', *Keats-Shelley Journal* 64 (2015): 95.
3. Charlotte Brontë, 'Biographical Notice of Ellis and Acton Bell, by Currer Bell', in *Wuthering Heights and Agnes Grey. By Ellis and Acton Bell* (London: Smith, Elder and Co., 1850), quoted in Emily Brontë, *Wuthering Heights*, ed. Alexandra Lewis (New York: Norton, 1991; repr. 2019), 301.
4. John Hewish, *Emily Brontë: A Critical and Biographical Study* (London: Macmillan, 1969), 164. Emily, Charlotte and Anne first published their verse in the *Poems* of 1846 under the pen names of 'Ellis Bell', 'Currer Bell' and 'Acton Bell', respectively.
5. Anne K. Mellor, *Romanticism and Gender* (New York: Routledge, 1993), 186 and 190.
6. Richard C. Sha, *Perverse Romanticism: Aesthetics and Sexuality in Britain, 1750–1832* (Baltimore: Johns Hopkins University Press, 2009), 82. 'Biological sex was a much more mobile set of categories than it is now', Sha explains. 'That the Romantic period worked through competing models of sex – from one sex to two – meant that sexual difference had not yet hardened into stone' (212).
7. Margaret Homans locates narratives of 'heterosexual romance' and 'heterosexual love' in Brontë's poetry and in *Wuthering Heights* in *Women Writers and Poetic Identity: Dorothy Wordsworth, Emily Brontë, and Emily Dickinson* (Princeton, NJ: Princeton University Press, 1980), 158 and 161. Situating Brontë within a similarly heteronormative sphere and suggesting sexual 'inversion', C. Day Lewis claims that Brontë's poetry is marked by 'her sex; the limitation of not being a man', and of possessing 'a masculine cast of mind in a woman's body', 'The Poetry of Emily Brontë', *Brontë Society*

Transactions 13, no. 2 (1957): 95. Janet Gezari meanwhile rejects 'tired interpretations' of Brontë's writings that assume 'that sexual experience is heterosexual experience' in *Last Things: Emily Brontë's Poems* (Oxford: Oxford University Press, 2007), 16. See also Jean E. Kennard's 'Lesbianism and the Censoring of *Wuthering Heights*', *NWSA Journal* 8, no. 2 (Summer 1996): 17–36 and Deborah Denenholz Morse's 'Brontë Violations: Liminality, Transgression, and Lesbian Erotics in Charlotte Brontë's *Jane Eyre*', *Literature Compass* 14, no. 12 (2017): 1–14. Angela Leighton, in considering '[c]laims, like Margaret Homans' and Irene Tayler's, that Emily's muse figures are male' on the assumption 'that the speaker is female', conjectures instead that 'gendered readings of Emily's work are often difficult to sustain', offering an openness beyond the male/female binary, 'The poetry', in *The Cambridge Companion to the Brontës*, ed. Heather Glen (Cambridge: Cambridge University Press, 2002), 66.
8. Michael O'Neill, '"Visions Rise, and Change": Emily Brontë's Poetry and Male Romantic Poetry', *Brontë Studies* 36, no. 1 (2011): 58.
9. Edward Chitham, 'Emily Brontë and Aspects of Platonic Attitudes', *Brontë Studies* 44, no. 3 (2019): 261.
10. Patsy Stoneman, '"Addresses from the land of the dead": Emily Brontë and Shelley', *Brontë Studies* 31, no. 2 (2006): 130; Hewish, 147; Camille Paglia, *Sexual Personae: Art and Decadence from Nefertiti to Emily Dickinson* (London: Yale University Press), 449.
11. Paglia, *Sexual Personae*, 439.
12. Lewis, 'The Poetry', 85.
13. Percy Bysshe Shelley, *Epipsychidion*, 5–8. Shelley's poetry is quoted from Percy Bysshe Shelley, *The Major Works*, ed. Zachary Leader and Michael O'Neill (Oxford: Oxford University Press, 2003; repr. 2009), unless stated otherwise.
14. Shelley, *Epipsychidion*, 21–2.
15. Jack Halberstam, *In a Queer Time and Place: Transgender Bodies, Subcultural Lives* (New York: New York University Press, 2005), 12.
16. John Milton, *Paradise Lost*, ed. Stephen Orgel and Jonathan Goldberg (Oxford: Oxford University Press, 2004), 17, Book I, lines 423–4.
17. Shelley, *Epipsychidion*, 27–8.
18. '[T]hat sex which participated in both sexes, from the Moon, by reason of the androgynous nature of the Moon', Percy Bysshe Shelley, *The Banquet*, quoted in James A. Notopoulos, *The Platonism of Shelley: A Study of Platonism and the Poetic Mind* (Durham, NC: Duke University Press, 1949), 430.
19. Sha, *Perverse Romanticism*, 77 and 80.
20. Percy Bysshe Shelley, *The Letters of Percy Bysshe Shelley*, ed. Frederick L. Jones, 2 vols. (Oxford: Oxford University Press, 1964), i, 195.
21. 'The Brontës had a copy of Mary Shelley's 1839 edition of her husband's *Poems*', wherein Emily would have read *Epipsychidion* and Mary's collected 'Fragments', 'Shelley, Percy Bysshe' in *The Oxford Companion to the Brontës*, ed. Christine Alexander and Margaret Smith (Oxford: Oxford University Press, 2003), 460.
22. 'To — ', in *The Poetical Works of Percy Bysshe Shelley*, ed. Mary Shelley (London: Edward Moxon, 1839 [1840]), 319, lines 1–4.

23. 'Fragments connected with *Epipsychidion*' quoted in Percy Bysshe Shelley, *The Complete Works of Percy Bysshe Shelley*, ed. Roger Ingpen and Walter E. Peck, 10 vols. (London: Ernest Benn Limited and Gordian Press, 1965), ii, 1–4; 38–49; 57–61, 377–8. For a comprehensive editorial history of these 'Fragments', see volume 4 of *The Poems of Shelley*, ed. Michael Rossington, Jack Donovan and Kelvin Everest (Abingdon: Routledge, 2014), 173–4.
24. Natalie Prizel, 'Intersex Aestheticism and Transgenre Mediation: Swinburne's Ekphrastic Androgynes', *Victorian Poetry* 57, no. 4 (2019): 491, author's emphasis.
25. 'At Rome he had seen a statue of the hermaphrodite, which was kept at that time in the Palazzo Borghese. There had been in fact two hermaphrodite statues in Rome, but one of them, the original Greek work of fifth century BC, had been sold to Napoleon and shipped to the Louvre, where it remains', Richard Holmes writes, continuing, 'Shelley's hermaphrodite was a much restored but nevertheless magnificent Hellenistic copy, exquisitely reworked by Andrea Bergondi', *Shelley: The Pursuit* (London: Harper Perennial, 2005, first published by Weidenfeld and Nicolson, 1974), 605.
26. Writing of Charlotte Brontë's posthumous shaping of Emily, Amber K. Regis observes that 'in transforming Emily's art, Brontë transforms Ellis Bell: she inscribes a different legacy for her sister, reimagining the dead novelist as a poet yet to find her audience'. Amber K. Regis, 'Interpreting Emily: Ekphrasis and Allusion in Charlotte Brontë's "Editor's Preface" to *Wuthering Heights*', *Brontë Studies* 45, no. 2 (2020): 170.
27. Shelley, 'Ozymandias', 4–5.
28. Charlotte Brontë, 'Editor's Preface to the New Edition of *Wuthering Heights*', quoted in Emily Brontë, *Wuthering Heights*, ed. Alexandra Lewis, 310.
29. Tatsuo Tokoo, 'The Composition of *Epipsychidion*: Some Manuscript Evidence', *Keats-Shelley Journal* 42 (1993): 98.
30. Eve Kosofsky Sedgwick, *Tendencies* (Durham, NC: Duke University Press, 1993). Sedgwick's definition continues with the observation, 'The word "queer" itself means across – it comes from the Indo-European root – *twerkw*, which also yields the German *quer* (transverse), Latin *torquere* (to twist), English *athwart*', xii.
31. Percy Bysshe Shelley, *The Poems of Shelley*, ed. Geoffrey Matthews, et al., four vols to date (London: Routledge, 1989–), iii, 205n.
32. Stuart Curran, *Shelley's Annus Mirabilis: The Maturing of an Epic Vision* (San Marino: Huntington Library, 1975), 27.
33. Shelley, *Laon and Cythna*, IX 2686; 2688; 2691.
34. Shelley, *Ode to the West Wind*, 4.45–6.
35. Ibid., 3.30.
36. Ibid., 4.48.
37. In the Romantic period, 'the fact that there was only one feminized sex before puberty and two complementary sexes afterward means that biological sex was fluid, developmental, and that anatomy itself was not a destiny but a process'. Sha, *Perverse Romanticism*, 81.
38. Shelley, *Ode to the West Wind*, 5.61–2.
39. Brontë, *Wuthering Heights*, 64–5.
40. Shelley, *Epipsychidion*, 51–2. The emphasis is Shelley's.

41. Sha, *Perverse Romanticism*, 90 and 81.
42. Quoted in Regis, 'Interpreting Emily', 169, emphasis removed.
43. 'Finden, Edward and William', in *The Oxford Companion to the Brontës*, 197.
44. Winifred Gérin, *Emily Brontë: A Biography* (Oxford: Clarendon Press, 1971), 44.
45. Edward Chitham, *Western Winds: The Brontës' Irish Heritage* (Cheltenham: The History Press, 2015), 162.
46. Christine Alexander and Jane Sellars, *The Art of the Brontës* (Cambridge: Cambridge University Press, 1995), 116.
47. Brontë would have been familiar with the four winds of Classical tradition and their genders and pairings in her readings of Homer's *Odyssey* and *Iliad*, likely two of the '4 Books of Homer' listed in the catalogue of sale at Haworth Parsonage, published by Joanna Hutton in 'The Sale at Haworth Parsonage: on October 1st and 2nd, 1861', *Brontë Society Transactions* 14, no. 5 (1965): 48.
48. Edward Chitham, 'Emily Brontë and Shelley', *Brontë Society Transactions* 17, no. 3 (1978): 193.
49. On Shelley's uses of gendered and ungendered pronouns, see Amanda Blake Davis, 'Androgyny as Mental Revolution in Act 4 of *Prometheus Unbound*', *Keats-Shelley Review* 34, no. 2 (2020): 160–77.
50. Brontë's poetry is quoted from Emily Brontë, *The Complete Poems*, ed. Janet Gezari (London: Penguin Books, 1992), with line numbers to appear parenthetically within the body of the text.
51. Homans, *Women Writers*, 124. Leighton, 'The poetry', 67.
52. '[T]he male was produced from the Sun', Notopoulos, 430. W. B. Yeats, 'The Philosophy of Shelley's Poetry', in *Essays and Introductions* (New York: Macmillan, 1961), 93–4.
53. Shelley, *Epipsychidion*, 292–3; 341–4.
54. Homans, *Women Writers*, 158. For Gezari, 'Brontë's sun is monstrously masculine', but 'her stars are not just feminine but maternal and nurturing', 30.
55. Halberstam, *In a Queer Time and Place*, 14.
56. Shelley, 'To a Skylark', 20.
57. Shelley, *Ode to the West Wind*, 63; 67.
58. On the prevalence of winds in Brontë's poetry, see Homans, *Women Writers*, 104–61 and Chitham, *Western Winds*, 162–3.
59. Jonathan Culler, *Theory of the Lyric* (Cambridge, MA: Harvard University Press, 2015), 227.
60. Shelley, *Ode to the West Wind*, 5.70.
61. Ibid., 5.67.

Chapter 11

Primroses in the Porridge: Hareton Earnshaw's Transgression against his Homosocial Family in *Wuthering Heights*

Chantel Lavoie

Wuthering Heights (1847) is a novel both weighed down and driven by transgression. Embodying transgression is Heathcliff, rescued as a foundling from the streets of Liverpool by Mr Earnshaw and favoured above Earnshaw's son, Hindley. Catherine Earnshaw transgresses against respectability with the notion that she can love two men and, through marriage, raise one to the same status as the other. Both Heathcliff and Catherine transgress against the very edicts of heaven by refusing to go there if it means they cannot be together. Even where their bones rest in the earth is transgressive, side by side and outside the churchyard. However, the transgression I address in this chapter is about the family of males consisting of Heathcliff, the old servant Joseph, and Hareton Earnshaw – a trio that the younger Cathy tears asunder as a result of her living at the Heights as Linton Heathcliff's widow.[1] These three men form a family in which there is undoubtedly hatred, as is the case in many families. There is also love. Indeed, the paradox of co-existing hatred and love powers the novel. One way of thinking about how this paradox manifests in the homosocial household of males is to consider J. Hillis Miller's contention that *Wuthering Heights* demands readings 'which best account for the heterogeneity of the text, its presentation of a definite group of possible meanings which are systematically interconnected, determined by the text but logically incompatible'.[2] Emily Brontë's novel transgresses the ideal of the nuclear family specifically by reproducing it in the triad of Heathcliff, Joseph and Hareton. At the same time, the text transgresses one of its own transgressions by including love and nurturing in the household made up of a hard-hearted usurping master, an aged servant and an ignorant boy, and by turning that trio into a real family as much as a nightmarish perversion of one.[3]

As we learn along with the frame narrator Lockwood in the autumn of 1801, the original heterosexual family at the Heights has collapsed, with women leaving or dying. This happens at Thrushcross Grange, too, most notably with the death of Catherine Earnshaw Linton, who belongs to both houses. However, the Grange is never without female inhabitants. Catherine dies, leaving her daughter, Cathy, in the care of her husband and Nelly Dean. In the nearly nineteen years Nelly lives away from the Heights, it is a homosocial home. The consistent inhabitants Heathcliff, Joseph and Hareton live in a house that others find inhospitable. Indeed, Sandra Gilbert posits that a reader of Brontë's novel will soon decide that 'hell is a household very like Wuthering Heights', a state Gilbert attributes largely to the text being 'motherless'.[4] Even so, apart from Heathcliff's deep grief over Catherine's death, the tripartite family of working males does not seem especially unhappy as a unit. Although largely lacking feminine comforts, they appear curiously satisfied with the household dynamic – Heathcliff, because life without Catherine is as he vengefully wills it to be; Joseph (who does miss having an Earnshaw head the household), because he has been there for decades and gets satisfaction from ranting against the wickedness of others; and the boy, Hareton, because he knows no better. It is others who enter there who feel miserable, particularly women and unmanly males, such as the girlishly pretty, sickly Linton, Heathcliff's son.

The Heights is also a celibate household apart from the three months in which Heathcliff's wife Isabella lives there, a period that results in her pregnancy from sex that has nothing to do with love, and may be rape: a sexual transgression, if not at the time a crime.[5] The obsessed Heathcliff desires only a dead woman, engaging in some measure of necrophilia – another example of transgression – when he embraces Catherine in her grave more than six years after her death; Joseph's religion together with his work leave no room in his mind or heart for romance, and certainly not for sex; and Hareton, again, is a child. Emily Datskou argues that Brontë 'produces a queer temporality' in the text. Since 'the characters and the plot structure largely repeat the events of the past, the novel's plot cannot be said to progress but essentially turns back on itself'.[6] While I do not interpret the repetition in this regressive way, Datskou's point is suggestive considering the length of time that homosocial relationships dominate characters' lives. For all his love and languishing for Catherine, before and after her death, Heathcliff's relationship with Joseph is the longest domestic relationship of his life, as the two live together before and after Heathcliff's unexplained absence of three years for a total of eighteen years. This is twice as long as the nine years Heathcliff spent living in the household with Nelly before her rejoining it in the weeks before his death. Moreover, lack of sex in the relationship between Joseph and Heathcliff does not negate its resemblance to a marriage, in which respect it is no different from many marriages between women and men, certainly in the Victorian period.

There are in fact different ways that the gendered stereotypes of the nuclear family might be charted onto the three males: Hareton is always the child, while either Heathcliff or Joseph can be seen as the father of the household. Heathcliff is the owner of the property, a dominant male and Joseph's 'maister', while Joseph is a servant, as well as being devoutly religious (a characteristic more associated with women than with men). James Quinnell points out that Joseph is also 'the custodian of the hearth', tending to the fire and often cooking the porridge.[7] Carolyn Steedman remarks, drawing on William Blackstone's 1765 *Commentaries on the Laws of England*, 'it was an important legal fiction – or fantasy – of the second half of the eighteenth century [when Brontë's novel is set] that the service relationship might stand as the model and pattern for relationships between husband and wife, parent and child'.[8] However, Joseph, being a generation older than Heathcliff, has also disciplined and, to some extent, raised Heathcliff, and so those fatherly (or grandfatherly) characteristics are in his favour when it comes to Hareton. Joseph's fondness for the Old Testament also aligns him with patriarchal religion. What is indisputable is that by the age of five, Hareton Earnshaw is being raised by two men, neither of whom is an Earnshaw.

Responsibility for Hareton does not translate into Heathcliff being a model father, of course. In addition to his other transgressions, Heathcliff rejects attitudes towards paternity that Joanne Bailey identifies as already established in the early modern era, paternity being 'one of the badges of mature manhood, a sign of fertility and a conveyer of authority so powerful that childless men acted as surrogate fathers to children or assumed symbolic versions of fatherhood as philanthropists and godfathers'.[9] Heathcliff's role as a biological father is a failure in every way except legally, his son Linton living apart from him most of his life, coming home sickly, and dying soon after, with no love lost between father and son.[10] Heathcliff, therefore, takes no delight in biological or surrogate fathering, although he revels in his power over both boys. Not content with Hindley Earnshaw's death at twenty-seven, Heathcliff makes the orphaned Hareton even more like himself as a child – destitute, dependent and uneducated. This is revenge against the dead man, but in making that man's son like himself as a boy, it is interpretable as an act of (transgressive) fatherhood.

Without a doubt, Joseph, who was hard on Heathcliff as a boy, hates Heathcliff as a man. He rejoices when Heathcliff dies, happy that 'the lawful master and the ancient stock were restored to their rights', prior to which Joseph strove to make Hareton proud and arrogant as an Earnshaw (*WH* 295). As his deep loyalty has ever been with the Earnshaws and the Heights, it is often argued that Joseph's obedience to Heathcliff is only a manifestation of loyalty to the place, and in order to keep his place.[11] Judith Stuchiner reminds us that Joseph is

> a live-in servant, he wakes with the family, eats with the family, and, for all intents and purposes, sleeps with the family; after he has done his chores, read his Bible, and said his prayers, Joseph retires to a garret above the kitchen that has served as his sleeping quarters for the last sixty years.[12]

Still, the hatred Joseph feels for Heathcliff is different from that which Hindley Earnshaw felt for the man; Joseph and Heathcliff work together to keep the Heights producing and earning – the inverse, essentially, of how the dissolute Hindley lost the land to his enemy. On top of making the land pay, the other project in which Heathcliff and Joseph are inextricably linked is raising Hareton Earnshaw – something else at which Hindley ultimately failed.

Losing his mother following childbirth, Hareton benefits from Nelly Dean's love and instruction until he is 'nearly five years old' – that is, before the age of breeching. Nelly misses the boy terribly when she leaves to look after Catherine (and then little Cathy) at the Grange. Such early nurturing for Hareton is important, strikingly contrasted with the cursing Nelly encounters when she meets with the boy ten months after she leaves the Heights. Not only does he no longer recognise her, he throws a stone at her (*WH* 100). The boy's incivility here speaks to what Judith E. Pike notes about boys entering the male sphere when they were breeched: 'This casting off of petticoats sometimes led to the rejection of female authority, derisively called "petticoat government"'.[13] Indeed, notes Anthony Fletcher, for centuries, 'extracting their boys from maternal influence was a long-established issue upon which fathers were united and determined'.[14] Nelly's departure is thus the beginning of the household of men. The time Isabella Linton (Heathcliff's wife) spends around Hareton is short and without sympathy. No housekeeper who comes into the home is maternal, and only one is named – the uncharitable Zillah.[15] Nelly acknowledges some comfort is restored to the Heights 'under female management' by housekeepers, but that management is not familial as it was when she was there herself (*WH* 177).

Nelly explains to Lockwood that the transgression committed against Hareton results in the fact that 'he lives in his own house as a servant deprived of the advantages of wages, and quite unable to right himself, because of his friendlessness and his ignorance that he has been wronged'

(*WH* 169). Judy Giles notes that domestic service relations in this period 'produced structures of feeling that involved deeply felt ideas about obligation, privacy, authority and "place" and that these might manifest themselves in contempt and deception, as well as condescension and deference'.[16] While we see some of this mixture in Joseph, there is no contempt or deception in Hareton with respect to Heathcliff. Hareton's ignorance regarding his own position is evidence of arrested development, as it is not only wages of which the boy has been deprived. Nelly was forced to abandon Hareton when she had 'just begun to teach him his letters' (*WH* 82).[17] Such early literacy was understood to be a mother's purview, what Donelle Ruwe identifies as the 'Enlightenment emphasis on the importance of the mother as the first inculcator of a child's foundational sense impressions and thus, the child's life-long habitus'.[18] The motherless (and subsequently Nelly-less) Hareton is then taught to read by the curate until his father dies, and Heathcliff stops the lessons (just as Hindley had done to Heathcliff as a boy). Thus, between landlessness and ignorance, Hareton Earnshaw, who 'should now be the first gentleman in the neighbourhood', is reduced to a farmhand working for bed and board (*WH* 168). The deprivation of literacy is hence part of the 'degradation' linking Hareton and Heathcliff, as the latter was already degraded when Mr Earnshaw brought the foundling into his home and became more so once Hindley stopped his lessons.[19] All of this suggests non-familial sentiment, yet it connects Heathcliff and Hareton on a deep level: Mrs Earnshaw had shown no love to the child when he was brought into her home; her son Hindley had exploited Heathcliff as a worker once the former took control of the house and land.

In his early weeks at Wuthering Heights, Heathcliff was treated more like an animal than a child, 'houseless, and as good as dumb', wont to remain silent even when pinched and beaten by Hindley (*WH* 34). Later, the impression that Hareton makes on the women who encounter him at the Heights is also bestial – Isabella and Zillah compare him to a growling dog whose incomprehensibility is peppered with curses. As Ruwe notes, 'for … classical humanists of the eighteenth century, the power of language distinguishes humans from animals'.[20] Well aware of such power and in keeping with his larger scheme of marrying Cathy Linton to his own son, Heathcliff ensures he has 'tied [Hareton's] tongue' when the latter first meets Cathy because Heathcliff knows the well-built youth is physically appealing and might otherwise prove welcome company to the girl (*WH* 194).

The evolution of Hareton's speech is a concern for several scholars. In addition to taking on Joseph's Yorkshire accent as he works alongside the servant on the farm, the boy is encouraged by Heathcliff to speak coarsely and to curse. Emily M. Baldys emphasises that Hareton's 'contact with the warped domestic sphere has been the most prolonged of all the characters; he has been born and raised in an atmosphere that debilitates even those who briefly encounter it'.[21] As such, Baldys identifies tropes of disability – specifically, nineteenth-century ideas about 'idiocy' in Hareton, in the animalistic vocabulary used to describe him as 'unnatural cub' (*WH* 67), 'bear' (13) and 'infernal calf' (186) – terminology that evaporates as he develops intimacy with Cathy. Thereupon, 'freed from the influence of Heathcliff and united to Cathy near the end of the novel, the implications of disability gradually disappear until … the erasure of disability facilitates the restoration of patrilineal succession and heteronormative romance'.[22] This restoration is made possible by a gun accident in which Hareton injures his arm. The wound incapacitates him so that he cannot conduct his usual chores or hunt (both masculine pursuits) and keeps him indoors. As Irene Wiltshire observes, 'by the time Cathy has rescued Hareton from this degradation as a servant at the Heights', the young man 'casts off his regional speech almost entirely … he is ready for marriage to Cathy, and a life of gentility at the Grange'.[23] Hence, although Hareton has been raised to be brutish and uneducated for posthumous revenge against his father Hindley and to make Edgar Linton (his uncle) suffer, the boy nonetheless has inborn qualities of strength, bravery, intelligence and kindness. These require cultivation, and Catherine Earnshaw, junior, is the woman for the job.

The word 'brute' and derivatives thereof are applied to Hareton prior to this cultivation both within the novel and by critics. As Steedman summarises, the boy 'is reduced to the level of a beast (or a feral child, or brutish country lout)'.[24] However, 'brutalising' conveys a range of treatments. Hareton was mistreated in that he was deprived of his birthright and not provided with much comfort, and certainly not luxury, and his early lessons in reading were cut short by Heathcliff; yet, the child was not beaten or starved as he might have been, and as the children of many biological and foster-parents have been. Nelly states Heathcliff 'had not treated him physically ill', but rather

> appeared to have bent his malevolence on making him a brute: he was never taught to read or write, never rebuked for any bad habit which did not annoy his keeper; never led a single step towards virtue, or guarded by a single precept against vice. (*WH* 176)

Even so, and rough as Hareton is, the vices that undid his father and lost the boy his inheritance are never at issue for Hareton. Moreover, Hindley Earnshaw's having dropped his son over the banister and his dissolution through alcohol and gambling prior to death indicates that his son's upbringing would not have been exemplary even had his 'Devil Daddy' lived (*WH* 100). When Nelly is still at the Heights, she too is brutally treated by Hindley as she tries to protect Hareton from both his father's 'wild-beast's fondness [and] his madman's rage' (*WH* 67). Therefore, both Heathcliff and Joseph actually contrast with the boy's biological father in ways that reflect relatively well on them.

Hindley Earnshaw's actions, like his emotions, are obviously extreme. Still, he can be read as representative of a group rather than a singular alcoholic and gambler. Pike points out that the novels of Anne Brontë, for instance, advance 'a trenchant critique of how fathers in the upper and middle classes [were] instilling in their young sons corrupted models of manliness' through gaming and drinking clubs and sociability with other men.[25] In contrast to common practices among fathers, therefore, the roughness and insensitivity with which Heathcliff inculcates Hareton might not be as corrupting or damaging as those practices common with boys being raised in the (all too) usual way of fathers in the upper and middle classes. Further, much debate surrounded the benefits and dangers of boarding schools, a standard for the class to which Hareton nominally belongs. Marianne Thormählen even observes that 'it is tempting to regard Hareton as an implicit illustration of Rousseau's contention that the formal education of a boy should be deferred until adolescence'.[26] Hareton knows no better, but his life could be worse. Indeed, Linton Heathcliff, the privileged boy lovingly raised by his mother before his traumatic move to the Heights, is the one convinced to act like a tyrant to Cathy, whereas Hareton comes to risk Heathcliff's wrath by defending her.

This is not to understate the harm that Heathcliff does to Hareton. Thomas Vargish points out that

> revenge for [Heathcliff] becomes an obsessive attempt to create patterns which reflect the conditions of his own degraded youth and which provide direction and form when all other impulses toward direction and form have been blocked by the loss of everything valued.[27]

Aiming to pervert Hareton's education and potential as his own was thwarted, Heathcliff might also not be capable of doing otherwise in this story so freighted with repetition. Miller argues that the 'representatives' of his 'old enemies', as Heathcliff refers to Hareton and Cathy, 'have stood for the infinite distance between Heathcliff and Catherine'.[28] But Hareton also stands for 'infinite distance' between Heathcliff's boyhood and his manhood. Alison Booth notes that Heathcliff is 'more than the erotic center of the novel. Cruel as he is, he is also a victim[,] … abused and exploited'.²⁹ Heathcliff might otherwise have reproduced the pattern of care that the old Mr Earnshaw, who rescued and took him in, showed him. He does not do that, but he does choose to retain Joseph – who had beaten and terrified him and Catherine – in his household. The familiar (familial), however miserable, holds great power.

Certainly, *Wuthering Heights* is as much about power as it is about love, and perhaps more so. As Jeff Hearn argues 'Debates about fathers and fatherhood need to be more explicitly gendered and more explicitly about power'.³⁰ The power of the fatherhood at the Heights for most of the novel is shared. For his part, Joseph inherits the primary care of Hareton from Nelly and treats the boy better than he ever treated Heathcliff or Catherine as children. James Quinnell believes Joseph

> has an interest in Hareton. This is hinted at by the personal interest with which 'Joseph came up with Hareton, to put him to bed'. There is a surprising sense of care presented here: Hareton was not abandoned to his own devices to put himself to bed.³¹

Arguing that Nelly Dean's unreliable narrative misleads us about her fellow servant, Quinnell contends that Joseph's 'place in the novel is elegiac rather than ironic'.³² Such sympathetic interpretation of Joseph belongs to a wide range of readings of this character – from laughable servant to religious fanatic, to loyal retainer, to symbol of the working class, figure of tragedy, serious representative of important dissenting tenets and recently back to a humorous and even witty man. Returning recently to Joseph's comedic possibilities, Graeme Tytler points out the old man is 'capable of considerable wit, usually resorting to it most virulently when voicing his disapproval of, say, Isabella, Cathy and Linton Heathcliff'.³³ Tytler notes other instances of critical humour, including against Heathcliff and Nelly, but it is significant that those with whom Joseph is 'most virulent' come to live at the Heights once it is the domain of the tripartite family of men. True, Isabella, Cathy and Linton are all hostages, and Joseph's mockery smacks of his pettiness about what he can get away with against people his master dislikes, but that is not all there is to it. The laziness demonstrated by Isabella, Linton and Cathy draws his ire – a reminder that he, Hareton and Heathcliff contribute to the farm and earn their keep with their labour.

The ascendance of Cathy Linton near the end of Brontë's novel confirms George E. Haggerty's suggestion that an 'understanding of what happens in Gothic fiction is to say that order is restored and normativity – especially heteronormativity – is re-established at the close, and readers can return to their lives with a sense that marriage has contained all transgression'.³⁴ In *Wuthering Heights*, this final containment comes with the nuptials impending for Hareton and Cathy. What is contained with this conclusion is multifaceted since, as Emily Baldys notes, by reaching this point with Cathy, 'Hareton acquires romantic love literacy, the land and household of his ancestors, and the capacity for intellectual and emotional maturation'.³⁵ That there have been lacunae where each of these should be in Hareton's life is certain, but there have been other kinds of love.

Not long before his death, Heathcliff admits to Nelly, 'five minutes ago, Hareton seemed a personification of my youth, not a human being – I felt to him in such a variety of ways, that it would have been impossible to have accosted him rationally' (*WH* 285). He begins to enumerate these ways with the statement that 'in the first place, his startling likeness to Catherine connected him fearfully with her' and then moves on to say that every face he encounters, including his own, 'mock me with a resemblance' because the world 'is a dreadful collection of memoranda that she did exist, and that I have lost her!' (*WH* 285). To my mind, he does not adequately explain the 'variety of ways' that the sight of Hareton assaults him. As this presence encompasses Heathcliff's gender and youth, Catherine Earnshaw's eyes and therefore the two of them together, Hareton seems at that moment to be the son that he and Catherine did not have. The 'variety of ways' indeed includes the paternal. When they first meet Lockwood, Heathcliff scoffs that Hareton is 'Not my son, assuredly!' (*WH* 13), but that assurance is now crumbling as he calls the boy 'a personification of [his] youth' in the weeks leading up to his own death. Long before this, Heathcliff admitted to Nelly he would have 'loved the lad had he been some one else' (*WH* 193). The hatred Heathcliff feels for 'the lad's' father seems watered down by time and by that lad's character, in which Heathcliff sees himself.

There is never any doubt that Hareton loves Heathcliff, and from early on. When Hindley dies, and Heathcliff lifts the boy onto the table with the words 'Now, my bonny lad, you are mine!', the man threatens to 'see if one tree won't grow as crooked as another' (*WH* 168). He refers to Hareton as his 'property', but he also later does the same with his own son, who loathes him, and the feeling is mutual. Nor does Heathcliff push Hareton away when the little boy, standing on the table, 'played with Heathcliff's whiskers, and stroked his cheek' (*WH* 168). Evidence of his paternal role is Hareton's perception of Heathcliff as 'his one friend in the world' as the boy grows, in Heathcliff's words, 'damnably fond' of the man others despise (*WH* 195). In the final weeks when Hareton must stand up for Cathy against his foster-father, we see real unhappiness in Hareton: he defends his cousin but tells her 'he'd rather she would abuse himself, as she used to, than begin on Mr. Heathcliff' (*WH* 283). Faced with Heathcliff's death and 'the only one who suffered much' from it, Hareton,

> sat by the corpse all night, weeping in bitter earnest. He pressed his hand, and kissed the sarcastic, savage face that every one else shrank from contemplating; and bemoaned him with that strong grief which springs naturally from a generous heart, though it be tough as tempered steel. (*WH* 295)

Hareton's response cannot merely be attributed to his good heart. So many people hate Heathcliff in his lifetime, and he earns this hatred. Hareton stands as proof that Heathcliff, warped as he is (and seemingly inhuman at times), is not altogether unworthy of love or mercy.

Heathcliff's grim end as the grinning corpse in the rain-soaked bed, followed by the rumour of his and Catherine's ghosts on the moor, invite the kind of reading Peter D. Grudin posits – that, despite the years that pass after the latter's death, Nelly's trustworthy 'emphases, her focus, remain with her grander characters, Heathcliff and Catherine' in contrast to 'the banal romance of Hareton and Cathy'.[36] However, more recent studies of domesticity, along with the importance of the education of males in the novels of all the Brontë sisters, trouble this dismissive notion of 'banal romance' that pales alongside the Byronic appeal of brooding Heathcliff and the haunting memory of Catherine. For instance, looking beyond interpretations of Hareton as an uninteresting brute or mere victim, Sara Martin has a hopeful reading of the young man 'as a possible alternative to Heathcliff's doomed Romantic-Gothic patriarchal power', by functioning as a 'blurred mirror image' of the latter's masculinity.[37] Indeed, Martin calls the second half of the novel a justification of 'Heathcliff's dismissal in order to help women readers overcome their idealisation of inhumane men like him as Romantic heroes'.[38] Instead, Hareton – handsome, land-owning Hareton – is on the verge of a good marriage and already enjoying Cathy's love.

Such resolution is the kind to which D. Michael Jones takes exception. Jones praises Brontë's novel as exemplifying how transgression 'is necessary for authenticity and genius', and argues that *Wuthering Heights* points out flaws in the triumph of domesticity. He states that its conclusion illustrates the extent to which 'Victorian domesticity became the centre of human life. It is through the great "not", through excluding or repressing all difference as deviance, that Victorian middle-class domesticity became the only natural form of human life'.[39] Given that the hellishness in *Wuthering Heights* relates primarily to it being 'a motherless book', the lovingly scolding femininity with which Cathy illuminates Hareton's life provides a remedy to this absence alongside romance.⁴⁰ That having been said, the fact that so many mothers died early in the period – including, as we see in the novel, during or shortly after childbirth – implies that consolation must be possible outside the maternal, even if only in bowls of porridge and a gruff old man putting a child to bed. Deprivation of mental stimulation and creature comforts notwithstanding, Hareton's childhood was most likely better than Heathcliff's had been as a street-orphan in Liverpool. In the second half of the book, Heathcliff, Joseph and Hareton, although spending time outdoors, still spend time inside, eating, sleeping, Joseph reading his Bible and Hareton polishing his gun in the evenings. The Byronic and the semi-domestic co-exist until Cathy tips the scale. Within the three- to four-month period of her arrival, Linton dies, Nelly returns, a new heterosexual alliance forms for Hareton and the homosocial family collapses. The robust, big-hearted young man of twenty-three choosing Cathy's love commits a transgressive act against the topsy-turvy, anti-romance world of Heathcliff's household at the Heights.

This transgression has not yet occurred at the start of the novel when a storm forces the unwelcome Lockwood to spend the night at the Heights. Jones interprets Lockwood's nightmare about the unknown Catherine when her 'ghost bleeds' as a material representation of all the blood ties in Brontë's novel.⁴¹ I see the visual horror of the blood-soaked bedclothes being reconfigured in a scene that marks the transition from Gothic to domestic near the end: Cathy 'had sidled up to [Hareton], and was sticking primroses in his plate of porridge' (*WH* 279). Although the entire novel has come between these scenes of blood and flowers, temporally less than six months have passed – this in a story whose events cover about thirty-two years. Both edible and colourful, a joke and a treat, the primroses make Hareton laugh and Heathcliff lose his temper. Cathy's act is a lovely, dangerous moment when the edible petals add colour and flavour to the gruel they eat every day, seemingly for most meals. The young woman has transgressed the daily porridge – a meal that Isabella threw on the floor on her first night at the Heights, moving Joseph to call her 'Miss Cathy' and condemn her 'flinging t'precious gifts uh God under Fooit' (*WH* 131). The spots of colour that are the primroses on the oatmeal contrast with the blood-soaked sheets of Lockwood's dream – they are small, lovely, healthy and a sign of the romance that is wrestling with the Gothic, hope that wrestles with despair. Richard C. Sha is not talking about Emily Brontë when he argues, 'Where aesthetics gains from sexuality the possibility of a concrete mode of engagement in the world, sexuality can profit from the aesthetic distrust of purpose, as well as by the legitimating pedigree of this aesthetic distrust of purpose'.⁴² Yet, Sha's observation suits this moment when the flowers touch the gruel – a symbol of the beauty Cathy adds to Hareton's life and their future within the legitimate pedigree of joining these Earnshaws in matrimony.⁴³ While the act of adorning the bowl of porridge with primroses represents the romance growing between Hareton and Cathy, my point here is that the quotidian porridge that has sustained Hareton to this point is also representative of the love felt for Hareton by Joseph, and even by the tortured Heathcliff.

Since Catherine's ghost is somehow kept out of the Heights, the blood-soaked sheets in Lockwood's dream might suggest that the family now in the house, which has a woman in the form of Cathy, but not a wife or daughter, is nightmarishly perverse. In contrast, the innocent primroses Cathy introduces to the bowl of porridge near the end of the narrative are healthy and loving. However, I return to Miller's contention that *Wuthering Heights* invites 'possible meanings which are systematically interconnected … but logically incompatible'.⁴⁴ Cathy has also convinced Hareton to plant flowers, first digging up Joseph's currant and gooseberry bushes to make room for them. The act seems to Joseph a desecration.⁴⁵ Upon the old man's revelation that 'shoo's taan my garden frough me, un by th'heart! Maister, Aw cannot stand it!' an already tense scene caused by Hareton laughing at the primroses sees Cathy defy Heathcliff, as well as threaten to tell Hareton 'all about' Heathcliff, and assert that 'If you strike me, Hareton will strike you!' (*WH* 281, 282). It pains Hareton to have to choose between Cathy and Heathcliff, and he cajoles rather than coerces his foster-father: 'He had his hand in her hair; Hareton attempted to release the locks, entreating him not to hurt her that once' (*WH* 82). In defending Cathy and essentially taking her side (for he does not contradict her threat), Hareton transgresses the celibate misanthropy and misogyny at the Heights. Flowers seeded in the garden and inserted into a bowl of porridge signify a future heterosexual love for Hareton in the house with his ancestor's name carved above the door.⁴⁶ Hitherto a labourer, foul-mouthed and unkempt – like Heathcliff was as a boy, and as Joseph (substituting predicting damnation for cursing) has been all his life – Hareton's disloyalty to both older men, although necessary and indeed good according to Brontë's conclusion, is not that of a servant, but filial disloyalty. So, both of Hareton's parents, Heathcliff and Joseph, are defied in favour of romantic love and heterosexual normativity, similar to heterosexual parents being defied by their child in favour of romantic love. Heathcliff and Joseph are losing their boy.

The conflict in this scene is cast as a family-destroying one. Heathcliff believes at first that Joseph's complaint about flowers replacing his bushes is a complaint against Nelly; Joseph counters the assumption:

't's noan Nelly! ... Thank God! *Shoo* cannot stael t'sowl uh nob'dy!' (*WH* 281). While it is worth noting that Nelly has been back at the Heights for a few weeks by this time, and her first-person account is important here, she has not lived there for almost nineteen years, and Cathy has been there for a little less than nine months.[47] Nelly's reappearance signals the beginning of the end of the tripartite family of men, and of Heathcliff. Joseph's lament that Cathy 'steals' Hareton's soul is curious, given Nelly's earlier assertion that Joseph was confident Heathcliff had ruined Hareton, whose 'soul was abandoned to perdition' (*WH* 176).[48] The soul-stealing of which he here accuses Cathy seems a theft of Hareton's soul from himself and his family, Joseph in particular.

Joseph's grief and loneliness when Hareton is won over by Cathy leave some critical readers conflicted. Given the servant's treatment of the girl, I am not entirely convinced by Judith Stuchiner's defence of Joseph in the claim that Cathy's 'meanness to Joseph is undeniable'.[49] Stuchiner has a point about the loyal servant's genuine grief at losing his 'favourite', as does Quinnell in saying that Joseph 'feels that Cathy has taken Hareton away from him'.[50] Naturally, the battle for Hareton Earnshaw is a battle for harmony and love. Still, we cannot say there is no love in the household apart from the bewitching that Joseph accuses Cathy of committing once she influences her cousin. To be sure, Heathcliff, Joseph and Hareton interact in ways that are not particularly nurturing, or even healthy. But they are family ways. So, it is little surprise that Hareton's laughter over his porridge, Joseph's lament and Cathy's new defiance precipitate Heathcliff's transgression of the boundary between life and death, for it is after this that Heathcliff at least in part starves himself to death. Strictly speaking, Heathcliff is the first to abandon the homosocial family, but he does so only when Hareton is evidently on his way out of it.

When Lockwood finds himself snow-bound at the Heights on the fateful night he spends in confused and haunted dreams, he first requests a guide through the storm back to the Grange. Rebuffed, he asks, 'Are there no boys at the farm?' (*WH* 15). The simple answer, no, reflects the smallness of the household at this point, along with Heathcliff's tight control over it. After Heathcliff's death, Nelly Dean apprises Lockwood that Joseph will remain at the Heights once Hareton and Cathy marry, and she accompanies the newlyweds to the Grange. They will leave 'perhaps a lad to keep [Joseph] company' (*WH* 296). As much as Joseph rejoices at the death of the usurper Heathcliff and welcomes the restoration of the Earnshaws to their rightful place, he has, even so, lost the last of his family.

Notes

1. In keeping with convention, the name Catherine here refers to the first Catherine Earnshaw (Linton), Cathy refers to her daughter. I especially wish to thank Sarah Winters and Steve Lukits for insightful suggestions during the writing of this chapter.
2. J. Hillis Miller, *Fiction and Repetition: Seven English Novels* (Cambridge, MA: Harvard University Press, 1982), 51.
3. All in-text references to *Wuthering Heights* are to the following edition: Emily Brontë, *Wuthering Heights*, ed. Alison Booth (London: Penguin, 2012). Citations to this text will be given parenthetically, with *WH*.
4. Sandra M. Gilbert and Susan Gubar, *The Madwoman in the Attic: The Woman Writer and the Nineteenth-Century Literary Imagination*, 2nd ed. (New Haven: Yale University Press, 2000), 260.
5. In addition to the piety that characterises Joseph, the lack of attraction between Nelly and Joseph leaves no room for thinking of Joseph as a sexual being; this is underscored near the end of the text when the old man scoffs that Nelly 'wer niver soa handsome' (*WH* 281).
6. Emily Datskou, 'Queer Temporalities: Resisting Family, Reproduction and Lineage in Emily Brontë's *Wuthering Heights*', *Brontë Studies* 45 (2020): 132–43, 138.
7. James Quinnell, '"It is well that he does remain there": The Importance of Joseph in *Wuthering Heights*', *Brontë Studies* 43 (2018): 198–208, 205.
8. Carolyn Steedman, *Master and Servant: Love and Labour in the English Industrial Age* (Cambridge: Cambridge University Press, 2007), 201.
9. Joanne Bailey, 'Family Relationships', in *A Cultural History of Childhood and the Family in the Age of Enlightenment*, ed. Elizabeth Foyster and James Marten (New York: Bloomsbury Publishing, 2014), 15–31, 25. Other important scholarship in the study of family during the period include, most famously, Lawrence Stone, *The Family, Sex and Marriage in England, 1500–1800* (New York: Harper and Row, 1977), as well as Eileen Spring, *Law, Land and Family: Aristocratic Inheritance in England, 1300–1800* (Chapel Hill: University of North Carolina Press, 1993) and Katie Barclay, *Love, Intimacy and Power: Marriage and Patriarchy in Scotland, 1680–1850* (Manchester: Manchester University Press, 2011).
10. Hindley is still alive for a year and a half of this time, but virtually useless as a father. For more expansive studies of fatherhood in the novel, see Fuli Lui and Yulong Miao, 'The Absence of Fatherhood: Interpreting the Orphan Image in *Wuthering Heights* from the Perspective of Family Complexes', *Forum for World Literature Studies* 10, no. 1 (March 2018): 124–36, and Linda Ray Pratt, '"I Shall Be Your Father": Heathcliff's Narrative of Paternity', *VIJ: Victorians Institute Journal* 20 (1992): 13–38. For a fascinating reading of Heathcliff as the usurping 'cuckoo' in the novel, see J. Carroll, 'The Cuckoo's History: Human Nature in *Wuthering Heights*', *Philosophy and Literature* 32 (April 2008): 241–57.
11. See Quinnell, 'Importance of Joseph', 199.
12. Judith Stuchiner, '*Wuthering Heights*: Brontë's Parable of the Unforgiving Servant', *Religion and the Arts* 24, no. 1–2 (April 2020): 65–83, 66.

13. Judith E. Pike, 'Breeching Boys: Milksops, Men's Clubs and the Modelling of Masculinity in Anne Brontë's *Agnes Grey and The Tenant of Wildfell Hall*', *Brontë Studies* 37, no. 2 (2012): 112–24, 113.
14. Anthony Fletcher, *Growing up in England: The Experience of Childhood, 1600–1914* (New Haven: Yale University Press, 2010), 149.
15. Histories of parenting confirm Nancy Chodorow's observation that 'When biological mothers do not parent, other women, rather than men, virtually always take their place'. Nancy Chodorow, *The Reproduction of Mothering: Psychoanalysis and the Sociology of Gender* (Berkeley: Berkeley University Press, 1999), 3.
16. Judy Giles, 'The Politics of Domestic Authority', in *The Politics of Domestic Authority in Britain since 1800*, ed. L. Delap, Ben Griffin and Abigail Wills (London: Palgrave Macmillan, 2009), 204–20, 212.
17. Not only did Catherine want Nelly at the Grange, Hindley also 'wanted no women in the house, he said, now that there was no mistress' (*WH* 82).
18. Donelle Ruwe, *Mothers in Children's and Young Adult Literature from the Eighteenth Century to Postfeminism* (Jackson: University Press of Mississippi, 2016), 40.
19. One of the most quoted lines of *Wuthering Heights* is Catherine's exclamation to Nelly, 'It would degrade me to marry Heathcliff' (*WH* 73).
20. Ruwe, *Mothers*, 33.
21. Emily M. Baldys, 'Hareton Earnshaw and the Shadow of Idiocy: Disability and Domestic Disorder in *Wuthering Heights*', *Philological Quarterly* 91 (2012): 49–74, 61.
22. Ibid., 51.
23. Irene Wiltshire, 'Speech in *Wuthering Heights*: Joseph's Dialect and Charlotte's Emendations', *Brontë Studies* 30 (2005): 19–29, 22–3.
24. Steedman, *Master and Servant*, 195. Thormählen suggests that Hareton's having been born of a loving union, even though he never knew his mother, together with Nelly's care in early childhood, 'seem to have inoculated Hareton against the brutalizing effects of the Heathcliff regime' in 'Bringing up Boys', 65.
25. Pike, 'Breeching boys', 113.
26. Thormählen, 'Bringing up Boys', 65–6. Nevertheless, 'It is hardly accidental that those motherless women writers should have represented maternal love as a boy's best hope for success in this world and salvation in the next' (68).
27. Thomas Vargish, 'Revenge and *Wuthering Heights*', *Studies in the Novel* 3 (1971): 7–17.
28. Miller, *Fiction and Repetition*, 63.
29. Introduction to *WH*, xx.
30. Jeff Hearn, "Men, Fathers and the State: National and Global Relations", in *Making Men into Fathers: Men, Masculinities, and the Social Politics of Fatherhood*, ed. B. Hobson (Cambridge: Cambridge University Press, 2002): 245–72, 245.
31. Quinnell, 'Importance of Joseph', 203.
32. Ibid., 199.
33. Graeme Tytler, 'Comedy in *Wuthering Heights*', *Brontë Studies* 46, no. 1 (2021): 18–29, 20.

34. George E. Haggerty, 'The Failure of Heteronormativity in the Gothic Novel', in *Heteronormativity in Eighteenth-Century Literature and Culture*, ed. Ana de Freitas Boe and Abby Coykendall (London: Routledge, 2016), 131–50, 131.
35. Baldys, 'Shadow of Idiocy', 63.
36. Peter D. Grudin, '*Wuthering Heights*: The Question of Unquiet Slumbers', *Studies in the Novel* 6 (Spring 1974): 389–407, 407 and abstract.
37. Sara Martin, *Representations of Masculinity in Literature and Film: Focus on Men* (Cambridge: Cambridge University Press, 2020), 22–3.
38. Martin, *Representation*, 23.
39. D. Michael Jones, *The Byronic Hero and the Rhetoric of Masculinity in the 19th Century British Novel* (Jefferson, NC: McFarland, 2017), 37 and 35.
40. Gilbert and Gubar, *Madwoman*, 260.
41. Jones, *Byronic Hero*, 39.
42. Richard C. Sha, *Perverse Romanticism: Aesthetics and Sexuality in Britain, 1750–1832* (Baltimore: Johns Hopkins University Press, 2009), 2–3.
43. Worth noting is another red and white moment when Heathcliff calls Edgar Linton a 'milk-blooded coward' (*WH* 105). On the relationship between women and plants in this era, see Samantha George, *Botany, Sexuality and Women's Writing, 1760–1830: From Modest Shoot to Forward Plant* (Manchester: Manchester University Press, 2017), esp. 22–42.
44. Miller, *Fiction and Repetition*, 51.
45. Concerning the digging up of Joseph's bushes, see Terry Eagleton, *Myths of Power: A Marxist Study of the Brontës* (London: Macmillan, 1975), 117. See, too, James L. Hill, who writes 'while Hareton's flower garden might well symbolize the triumph of culture, it is difficult to see quite how the replacement of edible by decorative plants points towards a renewal of vitality' in 'Joseph's Currants: The Hermeneutic Challenge of *Wuthering Heights*', *Victorian Culture and Literature* 22 (1994): 267–85, 267. Further, in terms of the land at the end of the novel, Beth Torgeson argues, 'Hareton's change in status foretells trouble because Hareton will become a landed esquire who will collect rent from others' in *Reading the Brontë Body: Disease, Desire and the Constraints of Culture* (New York: Springer, 2005), 124.
46. F. A. C. Wilson interprets these combined flower incidents as part of the 'sexualized flexibility' he reads in the novel. See 'The Primrose Wreath: The Heroes of the Brontë Novels', *Nineteenth Century Fiction* 29, no. 1 (June 1974): 40–57.
47. Nelly moves back at the end of January 1802 when Lockwood leaves the Grange; Heathcliff dies in April.
48. Quinnell notes the echoes of 'heart' in 'hearth' are not to be ignored in Joseph's rant, as Carolyn Steedman points out the proximity of 'soul' to 'soil' and the significance of both to the servant's role in the family and relationship to the land. Quinnell, 'Importance of Joseph', 206; Steedman, *Master and Servant*, 215. See, too, Stuchiner, 'Servant Speaks', 195. Related to what the novel says about land and, inevitably, masculinity, Helen Broadhead notes how 'the traditional, fixed, feudal hierarchy, based on land ownership, was breaking down, and was being challenged, and replaced by a new social order, based on individualistic commercial

enterprise'. Broadhead, '"Crumbling Griffins and Shameless Little Boys": The Social and Moral Background of *Wuthering Heights*', *The Brontë Society Transactions* 25, pt. 1 (April 2000): 53–65, 53.
49. Stuchiner, 'Servant Speaks', 194.
50. Quinnell, 'Importance of Joseph', 204.

Index

Note: page numbers in italics refer to illustrations

abolitionism, 134, 137n35
Addison, Joseph, *Spectator* No. 37, 90, 91, 92, 102n40, 102n42, 102nn44–5, 104n78
Agamben, Giorgio, 49n10
Ahmed, Sara, 32, 33, 35
Aikin, John, *Essays on Song-Writing* (1772), 96–7, 101n28
Alberg, Jeremiah L., 5
Alexander, Christine, 164, *165*
Alexander, Meena, 16–17
Allen, Graham, 106
Appiah, Kwame Anthony, 143
Astell, Mary, 19, 23
Austen, Jane, 20, 24, 25, 98–9
　Mansfield Park (1814), 20
　Sense and Sensibility (1811), 98–9

Backscheider, Paula, 37
Baillie, Joanna
　Rayner (1804), 20, 24
Baldys, Emily M., 179, 182
Ballaster, Ros, 103n51
Bannerman, Anne, 'The Dark Ladie' (1802), 20, 24
Barad, Karen, 42–3
Barbauld, Anna Letitia, 19, 21, 86–105
　'Allegory on Sleep', 86, *87*, 97–8, 99n2, 99n4
　'On Romances' (1773), 95
　'On the Origin and Progress of Novel-Writing', *The British Novelists* (1810), 89–91, 95–6, 101n25
　The British Novelists (1810), 89–90, 93, 101n35
　Correspondence of Richardson (1804), 101n25
　A Legacy for Young Ladies (1826), 86

Barker-Benfield, G. J., 103n56
Baron, Dennis, 127
Barrin, Jean, *Venus in the Cloister* (1683), 15
Bataille, Georges, 5–6, 55, 57, 59, 60, 66
Beckford, William, 18, 25
Beddoes, Thomas, 19, 90, 94, 95, 102n44
　Hygeia, or Essays Moral and Medical (1802–3), 89, 100n21, 101nn23–4
Behn, Aphra, 18, 34, 93, 103n51
Behrendt, Stephen C., 18, 20
Bekker, Balthasar, 99n6
Bell, Charles, 121n9
Bennett, Betty, 127
Bennett, Jane, 32, 38
Béres Rogers, Kathleen, 110, 123n43, 125n60
Berlant, Lauren, 157n22
Blackstone, William, *Commentaries on the Laws of England* (1765), 176
Blackwood, William, 126, 128
Blackwood's Edinburgh Magazine, 126, 127, 130
Blake, William, 16, 23, 25
bodymind, concept of, 106, 120n5
Booth, Alison, 180–1
Braunstein, Néstor A., 3, 4
Brison, Susan, 73, 78, 79, 80, 82, 83
Broadhead, Helen, 189n48
Brontë, Anne, 158, 170n4, 180
Brontë, Charlotte, 158, 162, 170n4, 172n26
Brontë, Emily, 158–73
　'A Day Dream (On a sunny brae, alone I lay)' (1846), 169–70
　'Song', 169
　'The Night-Wind' (1846), 165–7
　The North Wind (1842), 164–5, *166*, 173n47

Brontë, Emily (*cont.*)
  Wuthering Heights (1847), 159, 162, 163–4, 168, 174–90
Brooks, Marilyn, 73, 78
Bunnell, Charlene E., 106
Burney, Frances (Fanny), 24, 110, 122n21
Burwick, Frederick, 29n45, 106
Butler, Eleanor *see* Ladies of Llangollen
Butler, Judith, 46
Byron, Lord, 14, 18, 21, 23, 25, 110, 123n34, 127, 136, 164, 165
  Bride of Abydos (1813), 26
  Childe Harold (1813), 164
  Manfred: A Dramatic Poem (1817), 26, 110
Byronic hero, 18, 20, 24, 183, 184

Callaghan, Madeleine, 170n2
Cannon, Walter Bradford, 124n48
Carlson, Julie A., 55–6
Catherine (character, *Wuthering Heights*), 188n17, 188n19
Cavendish, Margaret, *Convent of Pleasure* (1668), 32
Charke, Charlotte, 31
Chitham, Edward, 159, 164, 165
Chodorow, Nancy, 188n15
Clemit, Pamela, 124n49
Coleridge, Samuel Taylor, 19, 58, 86, 109
Collings, David, 59–60, 67
Colman, George, the Elder, *Polly Honeycombe: A Dramatick Novel of One Act* (1761), 90
consumption, Romantic depictions of, 118–19, 125nn61–2
Corsivart, Jean-Nicolas, 121n9
Couvray, Jean-Baptiste Louvet de, *Les Amours du Chevalier de Faublas* (1786–91), 92
Cox, Philip, 28n16
Craciun, Adriana, 17–18, 19, 20, 29n29
Crébillon, Claude Prosper Jolyot de, *Le Sopha conte moral* (1742), 92
Culler, Jonathan, 169
Curran, Amelia, 165, *166*
Curran, Stuart, 163

d'Arblay, Frances (Fanny) *see* Burney, Frances (Fanny)
Dacre, Charlotte, 29n29
  Confessions of the Nun of St Omer (1805), 20, 24
  The Libertine (1807), 20
  Zofloya; or, the Moor (1806), 20
Damer, Anne Seymour, 21, 24

Darwin, Erasmus, *The Botanic Garden* (1791), 6–9, 121n9
Daston, Lorraine, 157n23
Datskou, Emily, 175
Davidson, Angus (cut), 14
de Staël, Germaine, 94
death, eroticisation of, 52–7, 59–61, 63–7, 112
Derrida, Jacques, 32, 61, 134–5, 136
Dods, Mary Diana, 21, 126–38
  'The First Murder: The Rejection of the Offering' (1821), 127, 130–3, 135–6
  'The Mount of Olives', 134
  'The Plague of Darkness' (1821), 130, 132–4, 135
  friendship with Mary Shelley, 127–9
Donoghue, Emma, 37–8
Douglass, Frederick, 137n35
Downing, Lisa, 60, 62
Dunne, Linda, 37

Eberle, Roxanne, 2, 4
Edelman-Young, Diana, 106
Edgeworth, Maria, *Tales of Fashionable Life* (1809), 18, 28n20
Elfenbein, Andrew, 24, 46, 47
euporia, 32, 40, 49n10; *see also* masturbation

Fanon, Frantz, 48n1?
Farr, Jason S., 107, 113, 121n6
femme fatale, 15, 18, 20, 24
Ferguson, Frances, 77
Fielding, Henry, 18, 90, 93, 94
  Joseph Andrews (1742), 104n66
  Tom Jones (1749), 18, 93
Finch, Anne, 34
Fletcher, Anthony, 177
Fordyce, James, *Sermons to Young Women* (1766), 88–9
Foucault, Michel, 3, 4, 10, 14, 15–16, 22, 27n9, 32, 87, 98
  on medical perception, 121n8
Freeman, Elizabeth, 44
Freud, Sigmund, 5, 7, 34, 48n1, 131, 134
  Totem and Taboo, 132, 135, 137n20
Friedman, Geraldine, 126
Fuseli, Henri, 69n1

Gallop, Jane, 124n50
Garofalo, Daniela, 4
George, Sam, 9–10
Gérin, Winifred, 164
Gessert, Astrid, 4
Gezari, Janet, 170n7, 173n54

Gilbert, Sandra, 175
Giles, Judy, 178
Gillingham, Lauren, 106
Godwin, William, 21, 52, 69, 70n2, 100n21, 106, 109, 112, 123n38
   Memoirs of the Author of A Vindication of the Rights of Woman (1798), 21, 101n21, 112, 123n38
Gordon, Charlotte, 128
Gordon, George *see* Byron, Lord
Gothic, the, 25-6, 29n43, 33, 50n31, 57-8, 135, 181-2, 183, 184
Graffigny, Françoise de, 94
Gray, Thomas
   'A Progress of Poesy: A Pindaric Ode' (1757), 95
   'Elegy in a Country Church-yard' (1751), 62, 63, 95
Grudin, Peter D., 183

Haggerty, George, 25-6, 29n43, 37, 181-2
Halberstam, Jack, 160, 168, 169
Halperin, David, 27n9
Hands, Elizabeth, *The Death of Amnon. A Poem* (1789), 20-1
Haraway, Donna, 76
Harding, Sandra, 76
Hareton (character, *Wuthering Heights*), 188n24, 189n45
Harlan, Elizabeth, 156n15
Harpold, Terence, 106
Hartley, David, *Observations on Man, His Frame, His Duty, His Expectations* (1749), 121n10
Hawkins, Anne Hunsaker, 109, 117, 125n57
Hays, Mary, 21
   An Appeal to the Men of Great Britain in Behalf of Women (1798), 72
   The Victim of Prejudice (1799), 20, 72-85
Haywood, Eliza (née Fowler), 25, 93
Hearn, Jeff, 181
Heathcliff (character, *Wuthering Heights*), 188n19, 189n43, 189n47
Heffernan, James, 164
Hegele, Arden A., 121n16
Heliodorus, *Theagenes and Chariclea*, 95
Henderson, Andrea K., 10, 24, 25
Hewish, John, 158, 159
Heydt-Stevenson, Jillian, 3
Hill, James L., 189n45
Hindley (character), 187n10, 188n17
Hitchcock, Tim, 14, 16, 21
Hogarth, William, *A Harlot's Progress* (1731), 93
Holmes, Richard, 172n25

Homans, Margaret, 16, 17, 165, 167, 170n7
homme fatal, 15, 18
homosexuality, 53, 131, 159
   as identity category, 16, 21, 25-6, 27n9, 170
   see also Sapphic sexuality
Hufeland, Christoph Wilhelm, 88, 104n82
Hunter, John, 22
Hunter, William, 22

incest, 20-1, 25-6, 130-2, 135, 148-9
   in Mary Shelley, *Mathilda*, 106, 107-11, 113-20, 122n25, 124n44, 124n50
Inchbald, Elizabeth121n10
   Lovers' Vows (1798), 20
   Nature and Art (1796), 20
intersex, 161-2, 172n25
Irigaray, Luce, 116, 125n53

Johnson, Claudia L., 93
Johnson, Samuel, 14, 18, 93
   The History of Rasselas, Prince of Abissinia (1759), 67
Jones, D. Michael, 183-4
Jones, Vivien, 19
jouissance, 4, 7-11, 131, 134-5
   in Mary Wollstonecraft, 'The Cave of Fancy', 52-3, 55, 58-61, 66-8
   in Sarah Scott, *Millenium Hall*, 40, 44-8
Joyal, Renée, 156n9

Kacem, Mehdi Belhaj, 155n3
Kant, Immanuel, 53, 59, 63, 64
Kearn, Jean B., 37
Keats, John, 17, 25, 28n16
Kelly, Gary, 32
King, Helen, 111-12
Kitchiner, William, 127, 128
Knox, Vicesimus
   Elegant Extracts ... for the Improvement of Young Persons (1796), 89
   Essays, Moral and Literary (1778), 89
Komisaruk, Adam, 2
Kraft, Elizabeth, 101n25
Kristeva, Julia, 35, 37, 46, 48n1

La Calprenède, Gauthier de Costes, seigneur de, 90, 93-4, 103n61
La Vergne, Marie-Madeleine Pioche de, 93-4
Lacan, Jacques, 3-4, 10, 32, 35, 45, 48n9, 67, 132-3, 137n28, 137n30
   'Kant with Sade', 53-4, 63, 64
Ladies of Llangollen (Eleanor Butler and Sarah Ponsonby), 21
Lamb, Caroline, 20

Lamb, Mary, 29n29
Landon, Letitia Elizabeth, 19, 21, 24
  'The Fairy of the Fountain' (1835), 20
Lanser, Susan, 38
Laqueur, Thomas, 14, 22, 25, 90, 91, 98
  on masturbation, 25, 87–8, 99n6, 102n38, 102n40
  on the two-sex model, 16, 18, 31
law, 5, 20, 31–2, 72–4, 76–8, 83–5, 139, 141, 151, 176
Lawlor, Clark, 118, 125nn61–2
Le Sage, Alain-René, 89, 94
Lee, Sophia, 26
Leigh, Augusta Maria, 26
Leighton, Angela, 159, 165–6, 170n7
Lennox, Charlotte, *The Female Quixote* (1752), 101n35
Lewis, C. Day, 170n7
Lewis, Matthew, *The Monk* (1796), 18, 26, 57–8
Lifton, Robert J., 125n57
Liggins, Emma, 121n7, 123n35
Linnaeus, Carl, 8
Lister, Anne, 21
Locke, John, 23
  Essay Concerning Human Understanding (1690), 92
Lokke, Kari, 58, 67
Lubey, Kathleen, 25
Lyndsay, David *see* Dods, Mary Diana

McAllister, David, 63
Macaulay, Catharine, 19
McCarthy, William, 86, 99n2, 99n4, 101n25
McGonegal, Julie, 39–40
McGrath, Roberta, 111–12
MacKinnon, Catharine, 76, 77
Marivaux, Pierre de, 89, 94
Marten, John, *Onania*, 99n6, 102n40
Martin, Sara, 183
masochism, 18, 24, 25–6, 53
masturbation
  novel-reading and, 8, 88–98, 99n2, 99n4, 100n20, 101n28, 101n35, 102n38, 102nn42–4, 103n56, 104n78, 105n88
  pathologisation of, 19, 22, 25, 31–2, 38, 86–8, 98–9, 99n6, 100n15, 100n21, 101n23, 102n40, 104n80
May, Rebecca E., 61
Mellor, Anne K., 17, 106, 158
Melville, Herman, *Billy Budd* (1891/1924), 69
Mesch, Rachel, 136n4
Milesian Tales, Barbauld's comments on, 95, 96

Miller, D. A., 4
Miller, J. Hillis, 174, 180, 185
Montolieu, Isabelle de, 94
Moody, Elizabeth, 'To Dr. Darwin, On Reading His Loves of the Plants' (1798), 6–9
More, Hannah, 18, 103n58
Morel, Geneviève, 137n30
Moscucci, Ornella, 111–12
motherhood, 23, 112, 119, 184, 188n15
Mudge, Bradford K., 91, 102n42
Muñoz, José Esteban, 44, 142–3, 151

Nagle, Chris, 24
necrophilia
  in art, 69n1
  condemnation of, 53
  Georges Bataille and, 5–6, 55, 57, 59, 60, 66
  in Mary Wollstonecraft, 'The Cave of Fancy', 52–69
Nesvet, Rebecca, 106, 112, 122n25, 123n34
Nitchie, Elizabeth, 106
Nussbaum, Felicity, 116, 125n55

O'Driscoll, Sally, 37
O'Neill, Michael, 158, 159
O'Quinn, Andrew, 14, 25
Opie, Amelia, *The Father and Daughter* (1801), 20

Paglia, Camille, 159
pathography, 109–10, 116–17, 120, 121n16
Payne, John Howard, 129
Peakman, Julie, 2–3, 4, 10, 53
Penney, James, 1
perversion as a concept, 10–11
Petrey, Sandy, 156n6
phallocentric model of sex, 16, 21
Phillips, Katherine, 34, 41–2, 45
Pike, Judith E., 177, 180
Plato
  parable of the cave, 55
  The Symposium, 160, 167
Polwhele, Richard, 6, 19
Ponsonby, Sarah *see* Ladies of Llangollen
Poovey, Mary, 28n20, 123n32
Pope, Alexander, 14
pornography, 15, 52, 61, 69n1, 102n42
Porter, Roy, 124n47
Poulain de la Barre, François, 23
Praz, Mario, *La carne, la morte e il diavolo nella letteratura romantica* (The Romantic Agony), 1, 2, 10, 11, 14–15, 18, 27n4, 112, 123n34
Preciado, Paul B., 31

Price, Margaret, 120n5
Prizel, Natalie, 162
psychoanalysis *see* Freud, Sigmund; Lacan, Jacques; Winnicott, Donald

queer readings, 25–6, 29nn42–3, 33–4, 35, 43–4, 47–8, 48n9, 126, 167–8
queer theory, 3, 24, 132, 160, 163; *see also* Ahmed, Sara; Halberstam, Jack; Sedgwick, Eve Kosofsky
Quinnell, James, 176, 181, 186, 189n48

Rabine, Leslie, 156n6, 157n31
Radcliffe, Ann, 2, 25, 26
rape *see* sexual violence
Reeve, Clara, 26, 101n28
Regis, Amber K., 162, 172n26
Rennie, Eliza, 128
resistive embodiment, definition, 106–7
Reynolds, Stephen, 109
Richardson, Alan, 26, 108, 121n10
Richardson, Samuel, 89, 90
  Clarissa: or the History of a Young Lady (1747), 77, 79, 82
  Pamela; or, Virtue Rewarded (1740), 77
Richman, Jared S., 107, 121n6
Richter, Johann Paul Friedrich, 89
Robinson, Isabella, 21, 126, 129
Robinson, Mary, 19, 21, 24, 29n29, 105n88
Roche, Regina Maria, 26
Rogers, Katharine M., 103n60
Rohrbach, Emily, 44
romances *de longue haleine*, 90–1
romantic friendship, 21
Ross, Marlon B., 17
Roudinesco, Élisabeth, 53
Rousseau, Jean-Jacques, 95, 180
  Confessions (1782–9), 91
  Émile, ou De l'éducation (1762), 102n38
  Julie, ou la Nouvelle Heloise (1761), 94
Rowe, Elizabeth Singer, 34
Rowlandson, Thomas, 15
Ruston, Sharon, 111, 115, 124n46
Ruwe, Donelle, 178

Sade, Donatien Alphonse François de, 15, 18, 58, 64, 67, 112, 123n34
  Philosophy in the Bedroom (1795), 52, 60
sadism, 16, 18, 26–6, 135; *see also* Sade, Donatien Alphonse François de
Saint-Pierre, Jacques-Henri Bernardin de, 94, 150
Salzman, Christian Gotthilf, 100n21
same-sex desire, 21, 23–4, 34, 105n88; *see also* homosexuality; Sapphic sexuality
Sand, George, 155n1

The Devil's Pool (1846), 139–40
Indiana (1832), 139–57
Santner, Eric L., 55
Sapphic sexuality, 21, 31–2, 34, 37–8, 46–7; *see also* homosexuality; same-sex desire
Sargisson, Lucy, 155n5
Schiebinger, Londa, 107, 111–12, 123n32
Schor, Naomi, 155n1, 157n29
  on George Sand and idealism, 142, 143, 145, 154, 157nn20–1, 157nn24–5
  on George Sand's strategy of doubling, 157n18
Schuller, Kyla, 38
Scott, Joan Wallach, 137n20
Scott, Sarah
  The History of Sir George Ellison, 43
  Millenium Hall (1762), 30–51
Scott, Sir Walter, 93
Scudéry, Madeleine de, 90, 93–4, 101n35, 103n61
  Artamène, ou le Grand Cyrus (1649–53), 91, 104n66
  Clélie (1654–6), 91, 104n66
Sedgwick, Eve Kosofsky, 25, 40, 50n31, 98–9, 100n20, 163, 172n30
Sellars, Jane, 165
separate spheres, doctrine of, 2, 23
Seward, Anna, 9, 23
sex work, 31, 72, 74–5, 76–7
sexology, 3, 6, 7, 14
sexual violence, 16, 20–1, 23, 72–4, 77–84, 110, 114, 122n25, 149, 175
Sha, Richard C.
  on masturbation, 98, 124n45
  on the Romantic era, 14, 22–3, 164, 184–5
  on perversion, 1, 3, 112, 159, 160–1, 163
  on 'sex' and 'sexuality', 22, 114, 170n6, 172n37
Shaffer, Julia, 124n50
Shelley, Mary Wollstonecraft, 2, 14, 21
  Frankenstein (1818), 121n6, 121n16, 128
  friendship with Mary Diana Dods and Isabella Robinson, 127–9
  Mathilda (c.1819–20; 1959), 20, 26, 106–20, 122n25, 124n44, 124nn49–50
  Poetical Works of Percy Bysshe Shelley, 161, 171n21
Shelley, Percy Bysshe, 14, 18, 21, 123n34, 127, 134, 158–9, 166, 171n21, 172n25
  'Ode to the West Wind' (1820), 159, 162–3, 164–5, 168–9
  'Ozymandias', 134, 162
  'Stars' (1846), 166–7
  'To a Skylark', 168

Shelley, Percy Bysshe (*cont.*)
  The Banquet, 160, 171n18
  The Cenci (1819), 110–11
  Epipsychidion (1821), 159–63, 164, 167, 168, 169
  Laon and Cythna (1817), 26, 108, 110, 122n26, 163
  Prometheus Unbound (1820), 42, 133, 162–3
  Queen Mab (1813), 164
  Rosalind and Helen (1819), 26
  on the sun, 166–7, 173n52
Sidney, Sir Philip, *Arcadia* (1593), 92, 102n45
Smith, Charlotte, 24, 26
  Beachy Head (1807), 58
Smith, Margaret, 164
Smollett, Tobias, 90
sodomy, laws against, 15, 16, 31, 53, 131
Southcott, Joanna, 24
Southey, Robert, 19, 161
Spenser, Edmund, *The Faerie Queene* (1590–6), 97
stalking, 74; *see also* sexual violence
Stanback, Emily B., 109, 113, 121n16
Steedman, Carolyn, 176, 179, 189n48
Sterne, Laurence, 89, 93
Stoneman, Patsy, 159
Stuchiner, Judith, 177, 186
Sunstein, Emily, 129
Swinburne, Algernon Charles, *Hermaphroditus* (1866), 162

Tarr, Clayton Carlyle, 81
Tayler, Irene, 170n7
Taylor, Jeremy, 91
Thormählen, Marianne, 180, 188n24, 188n26
Tierney-Hynes, Rebecca, 102n43
Tissot, Samuel-Auguste, 100n21, 104n80
  De la santé des gens de lettres (1768), 88
  L'Onanisme. Dissertation sur les maladies produites par la masturbation (1760), 88, 102n38
  Three Essays (1773), 124n45
Todd, Janet, 37
Tokoo, Tatsuo, 162–3
Torgeson, Beth, 189n45
transgender identity *see* Dods, Mary Diana 'Doddy'
Traub, Valerie, 38
Turner, Kate, 50n31
two-sex model, 16, 18, 23–4, 31, 170n6, 172n37

Ty, Eleanor, 72, 73, 74, 79
Tytler, Graeme, 181

utopias, 25–6, 83, 155n5
  in George Sand, *Indiana*, 139–55, 155n3, 156n10
  in Sarah Scott, *Millenium Hall*, 32–3, 35, 37–43

Vargish, Thomas, 180
Vest, James, 156n17
Victorians
  and the dead, 63
  and sexuality and gender, 3, 14, 18, 112, 119, 136, 164, 176, 183
Viviani, Teresa Emilia, 160

Ward, Ian, 73, 76
Ward, Jane, 132
Weeks, Jeffrey, 27n1
Wenger, Alexandre, 88, 100n15
Westall, Richard, *Ianthe*, William Finden's engraving of (1839), 164–5
Whytt, Robert, *On the Vital and Other Involuntary Motions of Animals* (1751), 115, 124n47
Williams, Helen Maria, 21, 24
Williams, Jane, 128, 129
Wilson, F. A. C., 189n46
Wiltshire, Irene, 179
Winnicott, Donald, 30, 48n1
Wolfson, Susan, 17
Wollstonecraft, Mary, 19–20, 21, 23, 24, 29n29, 47, 100n21, 112, 123n38
  'The Cave of Fancy', 52–69, 109
  Maria, 44
  Mary: A Fiction (1788), 59, 60, 67
  Posthumous Works (1798), 52, 69
  Thoughts on the Education of Daughters (1787), 52
  A Vindication of the Rights of Woman (1792), 103n56, 111, 115, 103n56, 124n46, 137n35
  Wrongs of Woman (1798), 20
women and medicine, 121n7, 123n32, 125n55
Wordsworth, Dorothy, 26
Wordsworth, William, 18, 21, 26, 58

yonic things, 32, 34–5, 37–43, 48n9, 102n42

Zigarovich, Jolene, 55
Zupančič, Alenka, 38